e-Shock

Second Edition

e-Shock

The New Rules—Internet Strategies for Retailers and Manufacturers

Second Edition

Michael de Kare-Silver

American Management Association

New York • Atlanta • Boston • Chicago • Kansas City • San Francisco • Washington, D.C.
Brussels • Mexico City • Tokyo • Toronto

Special discounts on bulk quantities of AMACOM books are available to corporations, professional associations, and other organizations. For details, contact Special Sales Department, AMACOM, a division of American Management Association, 1601 Broadway, New York, NY 10019.
Tel.: 212-903-8316.   Fax: 212-903-8083
Web site: www.amacombooks.org

This publication is designed to provide accurate and authoritative information in regard to the subject matter covered. It is sold with the understanding that the publisher is not engaged in rendering legal, accounting, or other professional service. If legal advice or other expert assistance is required, the services of a competent professional person should be sought.

Library of Congress Control Number: 00-135341
ISBN 0-8144-7116-1

Printing number

10   9   8   7   6   5   4   3   2   1

Contents

Acknowledgements

The stimulus for writing this book came when I read announcements by Wal-Mart, Home Depot, Tesco and others that they were opening new stores, yet at the same time relaunching their websites. Was this not a contradiction in terms? Could retailers operate both physically and electronically without one cannibalising the other? Would not electronic sales (presumably mostly over the internet) significantly reduce numbers visiting the stores and so the profitability of the physical space? Could retailers just carry on as before investing heavily in land and buildings while the virtual world beckoned ever more eagerly? Would that new route to market eventually dominate? How many consumers were already willing and interested in shopping electronically? When would it all reach critical mass?

The purpose of this book is to answer those questions. The aim is to provide a practical guide to the future consumer retailing scene, how electronic commerce will develop, what impacts it will have, pin down when it will happen and suggest a framework to help retailers and manufacturer suppliers determine their optimum response. I have drawn on many years of consulting experience with companies in different sectors, observing and advising on market, customer and channel challenges. Other research and interviews have been carried out, tests and trials observed and evaluated and ideas checked with client companies whose confidentiality I must respect but whose ambitions and intentions are clear.

Forecasting future market developments can never be an exact science but I have also been enormously encouraged in my conclusions and convictions by a number of people. First, thanks to partners at the Kalchas Consulting Group, former colleagues at Computer Sciences Corporation and colleagues at Great Universal Stores. They helped create the experiences and opportunities to write this book and have been stimulating in their own thinking and perspectives. Others have acted as important sounding-boards, reinforcing some basic premises but steering me clear of unwarranted prejudices. Among this group I would like to thank David Stoddart especially, retail analyst at Henderson Crosthwaite, and intellectual soulmate, Simon Wright of Virgin, Mike Nevin of Dixons, Chris Warmoth of Procter & Gamble, a friend and deep thinker, and Svea Kordt and Ragnar Nilsson of Karstadt. A few other people have been more generally inspirational in encouraging me to put pen to paper. I am grateful to Robert Heller, whose own writings and teachings constantly challenge the status quo; Lord Peter Walker, whose own achievements continue to set a benchmark; and Walter Goldsmith, a constant fount of energy and ideas.

As for the composition of the book, it could not have happened without the vision and support of Stephen Rutt, my publishing editor, and also Elaine Howells and Louise Crawford, whose marketing enthusiasm has been infectious. David Oates, author and writer in his own right, provided a critical role early on helping to organise initial musings and ideas, writing up some early drafts and providing additional context. As for the typescript, especial thanks to Jo Mountford and Lorraine Oliver who in their personal time painstakingly transcribed my physical labours into ordered electronic prose. Finally, but most importantly, a special thanks to my wife, Deborah, whose sound commercial instincts and critical appraisal have helped keep the ideas here firmly rooted in what is practical and achievable.

Michael de Kare-Silver

Note: The author and publishers are grateful to Netscape Communications Corporation for permission to use material on the jacket of the book. However, Netscape Communications Corporation has not authorised, sponsored, endorsed or approved this publication, and is not responsible for its content. Netscape and the Netscape Communications Corporate Logos are trademarks and trade names of Netscape Communications Corporation. All other product names and/or logos are trademarks of their respective owners.

Preface to *e-shock: the new rules*

Let's cast our minds back. When did e-commerce get going? Around 1995 in the USA and Scandinavia, perhaps 1997 in the UK, Germany and Singapore and probably only in 1999/2000 in Southern Europe. In all just a very few short years. Yet the impact has been truly astonishing.

We are living through a fundamental shift in the way business gets done, goods get bought and people communicate. It *is* a revolution and it's coming at us on all sides. Consumer demand for things more convenient, easier, quicker and preferably cheaper knows no bounds. Plus the love for the latest gadgets and gizmos (witness the Japanese craze for latest internet/e-mail mobile phones). The new net literate, 12- to 18-year-old generation is just growing up comfortable, confident and expecting to interact in this way. Why bother with paper and mail and faxes and engaged tones on the phone? Why worry about getting to the bank branch or shop closing hours? That's old generation stuff.

And business is not just keen to respond. It's looking at any way it can to exploit this new technology to find advantage versus competitors. It's prepared to invest billions. (Drucker's estimate is c. $1trillion per annum). Dell, Compaq, Hewlett Packard, lined-up with Intel and Microsoft, are still determined to make the PC the main communication and commerce medium for the future. Sony, Phillips, Nintendo, Canal+, Sky and others are fighting for TV to be the gateway in the home. BT, AT&T, NTL, Kingston, Nortel, Cable & Wireless and many others are building infrastructure via cable, satellite or telephone lines to improve dramatically bandwidth and make things work faster, more efficiently. And what about the Nokia, Ericsson WAP/3G global ambition?

Have no doubt, e-commerce is here and it's going to become an ever-growing part of our everyday lives. But revolutions of this magnitude don't happen overnight. It's still true that Rome wasn't built in one day. It takes time to build new global businesses spanning many countries, languages and cultures. It takes time and huge investment to establish new brands that people recognise, are clearly differentiated and have a strong value set. As Jeff Bezos of Amazon has said: *'today is just day 1 of the internet and it's still just 1.00am of day 1!'*

ix

Facing up to this environment, though, is requiring a significant shift in the way people think about doing business. Some of the old models are just no longer applicable. Developments are taking place at lightning speed. Businesses are rolling out across Europe, for example, in around 12 months. Previously the time frame might have been 5 to 10 years! First-mover advantage is becoming more important; joint ventures and alliances ever more critical. There's no place to hide! It's like the gold rush. You have to put your stakes in the ground now. And there's only a certain amount of open territory left!

As a result there is a new game in town and new rules that go with it. Winners in the future will inevitably be those who recognise these new rules early and learn to play by them. There are new tricks, new advantages to be discovered, more ways to add shareholder value. The media, the analysts and the investment community generally have now turned the spotlights full on and despite the glare and the dazzle business has to make the right moves.

In this new 2001 edition of *e-shock*, the focus is on these new rules and they are discussed in more detail in Chapter 1. There is a set of 10 rules that are generic and affect almost every company. There are then 10 rules for retailers followed by 10 rules for manufacturer suppliers. It is going to be a question of live by them or die!

Preface to *e-shock*

In the course of just twelve months we have seen almost daily new technology innovation, pioneers changing the rules of the game and a rush of companies trying to take advantage.

- 'Internet access can now be obtained for free! Dixons Freeserve has turned the internet world on its head and rivals are rushing to put out free services of their own.'

  (*Wall Street Journal*)

- 'PCs for free! FreePC.com was first to market and others are following.'

  (*Computer Weekly*)

- '$1 trillion is the forecast for e-commerce in year 2000.'
  (*John Chambers, CEO, CISCO*)

- 'By 2002, almost every mobile phone will be web capable.'
  (*New York Times/Yankee Group*)

- 'The internet population will reach nearly 100 million adults in the USA alone in 2000.'

  (*IntelliQuest*)

No one now dares to suggest e-commerce will just be a minority interest. Indeed as CBS Market Watch and others have pointed out, there are as many women as men now shopping on line: 'women dominated the 1998/99 holiday period accounting for almost 60% of on-line shoppers'. It's no longer a question of if or when it will happen. It's now a case of 'how quickly can we get on board, how can we take advantage and how come we let others get ahead of us?'

But the real issue is whether sales over the internet are beginning to affect bricks 'n' mortar stores. Will e-commerce reach a point sometime soon where 'traditional' retailers find their consumers *preferring* to buy electronically and so visiting stores less?

If this begins to happen in a material way then the whole retail community faces agonising decisions. Can they keep the physical stores still profitable? Do they sell both physically and electronically? Should they even abandon traditional ways of selling and rush full-scale into the virtual arena? After all, as the analysis on page 171 shows, it will only take a 15% drop in numbers of consumers visiting stores for many shops to fall below breakeven and become unprofitable?

What is the evidence so far?

- 'One of Britain's largest travel firms the AA [the Automobile Association] has announced the closure of all 140 of its high street stores: "It seems our customers prefer to deal with us by phone or fax or over the internet. Our high street stores were becoming economically unviable."'

  (*Evening Standard*)

- '39% of people with access to the internet say they are going to the store or mall *less* often now they can buy products on line. This is significant to retailers as Americans who use the internet hold 60% of the buying power of the total US population.'

  (*Greenfield On-Line Research*)

- 'Traditional retailers are being left behind. A list of the top 50 most popular web shopping sites contains few bricks 'n' mortar stores. Internet upstarts dominate.'

  (*New York Times*)

- 'As for WH Smith [one of Britain's leading retailers], these new routes to market [internet and interactive digital TV] will only serve to cannibalize their existing High Street business. Will Smith the retailer exist in five years? We recommend taking profits and selling the shares.'

  (*analysts at Teather & Greenwood*)

It looks as though retailers are going to have to face up to a fundamental reappraisal of their ways of doing business. At minimum they are going to have to become 'multi-channel operators', expert at reaching and interacting with their customers in a variety of ways, not just through their physical stores. It will be a question of being available wherever and whenever their customers want to shop, rather than the more traditional approach.

Manufacturer suppliers are also now being forced to confront their traditional routes to market. They have been slow to respond. They have been fearful of upsetting their retail distributors. But consumer demand is strong and becoming impatient.

A few have begun to experiment. Procter & Gamble is selling perfumes and colognes like Hugo Boss on its website, Unilever is making sure its products are available and promoted on others' websites like Net Grocer, Compaq is starting to abandon its legions of traditional branch distributors and aims for 30% of its sales direct by 2000, following on Dell's lead and success. Hewlett Packard, Merrill Lynch, Chrysler-Daimler Benz are also beginning to move away from their traditional intermediary base. But if they do not act faster and more aggressively their market space is going to be taken away by the thousands of new internet ventures coming to market all over the world.

The issues, challenges and opportunities appear clear but can we say the shape of e-commerce is now established? Can we begin to define what the new success factors will be? Can we begin to predict the outcomes with a little more certainty?

The answer is: not yet! There's yet another wave of development and innovation coming. Its impact could be even more far-reaching than anything we have seen so far. It's home-shopping via the TV.

There is no dependency on PCs – free or otherwise. There is no need for any technical computer expertise at all. It is simply about exploiting the box that sits in every living room – and increasingly in the bedroom and the kitchen and the kids' playroom – in almost every household throughout the developed world.

Communication and content companies are coming together working with manufacturers and retailers to produce home-shopping channels that broadcast digitally straight on to the TV. Today's TVs can pick up the signals with a simple decoder box. The new generation of digital TVs will all have the decoding boxes built in. By 2005, more than 50% of the population in UK and USA will have a digital TV or decoder in their home. A simple revised remote control will provide click-and-connect access back up the telephone line or cable for shopping – at last from the easy comfort of your home.

It is this next wave of interactive home-shopping – this new phenomenon – that I wanted to explore in this revised edition. As a result there is a new chapter (pp. 275 ff.) which explores the mass reach of TV home shopping, its appeal and the impact we can expect. There are interviews with four people who are experts in their field: Curtis Kopf of Amazon.com, Bruce Lynn of Microsoft's Web TV, Mike Nevin of

Dixons and Freeserve, and James Ackerman of BiB, the joint venture in TV home shopping between British Telecom, HSBC, Matsushita and News International.

The e-commerce revolution goes on, changing our everyday lives and the shape of business in the future. We are fortunate enough to be alive and witnessing for ourselves a revolution as profound as any that mankind has experienced to date. As the Chairman of the Bank of Montreal, Matthew Barrett, has said: 'We are standing at the threshold of a New World. It is as if we had just invented printing or the steam engine.'

"This 'digital revolution'—can we muscle in on that?"

Introduction

There's a new milestone being reached in business and commerce. The beginning of the twenty-first century is going to see a radical transformation in the retailing of goods and services. There's a revolution taking shape in how people shop. In just a few years it's going to reach a significant point in its evolution. Happening with remarkable speed, it's forecast to reach critical mass and start having a serious impact by around 2005. It's the advent of mass electronic shopping.

New technologies such as the internet, web and digital TV, interactive kiosks and videophones are making visits to the shops increasingly unnecessary. As they develop they will enable more and more people to order from their home or their office or any place they can make an electronic connection. By just the year 2002 the internet is predicted to reach into some 60% of households across the USA and into 40% or more homes in the UK and Germany, with other developed nations racing to catch up.

Electronic access is becoming more widespread, the equipment more user-friendly, quicker and cheaper to buy. It offers to save time and promises lower prices. It provides the convenience of 24-hour shopping to any place across the globe whenever the consumer wants it. There's no restriction on physical location, drive times, catchment areas and planning restrictions. It operates in the freedom of cyberspace.

It's new and it's exciting. It's going to be the next wave of electrical gadgetry to reach into the home. It will be volume merchandised for mass consumption. It will have the marketing push of the likes of Sony, Dell and Microsoft. Word of mouth will communicate the advantages. The media will avidly report on progress.

The latest innovations will be widely reviewed, heightening awareness, expectations and desire. Computer, telecommunication and media companies will continue to pour in massive investment. They will be looking to constantly improve and accelerate the commercialisation of electronic interactions. There's an unstoppable momentum that's gathering pace, with a new advance to report almost every week. The electronic age is drawing ever nearer and consumer shopping will never be the same again.

Gone will be the days of pushing heavy shopping carts up and down the aisles, loading up with the weekly groceries, dragging tired and reluctant children behind, waiting in line at the check-out, unloading into the trunk of the car, driving home amid heavy traffic, unloading from the car again and reloading into kitchen cupboards or the fridge freezer. The shopping chores will all be done electronically. The standard weekly food and household order will be set up with a local home delivery company. An e-mail, a phone call or fax quoting a reference number will automatically trigger a reorder to be delivered at a pre-agreed time. Specials for the week will be added by ticking off the electronic order form. Payment will automatically be deducted from the bank account through a secure encrypted payment network. The frustrations of shopping for staple and basic items will be a thing of the past.

The convenience of electronic shopping will not just be confined to food and household products. It will impact many other sectors. On the internet today computers, books, music CDs, flowers and wine are already significant sellers. QVC has demonstrated the possibilities of selling jewellery, hardware, DIY, electricals and health and beauty products through its TV home shopping network. Catalog companies like Great Universal, Next, Spiegel and Eddie Bauer have shown that where it's well merchandised and marketed consumers will confidently buy clothes by mail order, phone and fax – even before trying them on. In the financial services arena companies like Direct Line in insurance and Citibank and First Direct in consumer banking have pioneered the selling of their services electronically. ATMs have proven consumer comfort with simple easy-to-use electronic technology. No need to visit the bank branch any more when all basic banking can be done through a hole in the wall and increasingly now by phone or via the PC.

With chores out of the way, basic shopping done and delivered, financial affairs taken care of, a whole new world of consumer opportunity opens up. Suddenly there's more time for family and friends. There's the opportunity to relax, pursue hobbies and have more quality leisure time. When people do go out shopping, expectations of a more enjoyable experience will be high. Their emphasis will be on seeing new things, trying new products. Shopping will develop as more of an integrated social and leisure experience. Consumers will treat it as more of a day out. Visits to large shopping centres will grow in popularity. It will present the opportunity to see a complete range of products with all the leading suppliers and distributors represented. There will be special areas and crèches for leaving young children with highly trained staff in superb facilities. There will be a wide choice of places to eat, meet friends and socialise. In the bigger centres and malls there will be additional social and entertainment facilities – for example, with sports and fitness clubs and movie theatres.

This type of large-scale shopping environment is already seen in locations across the USA and in a few massive centres in Europe such as the Metro Centre in England and CentrO in Germany. In these places often a theme park atmosphere is deliberately created to encourage people to visit, spend an extended amount of time in the one location and explore the vast array of shops. At CentrO, for example, there is everything from the Gap, Coca-Cola, Original Levi's Store, jazz clubs, a Warner movieplex, Planet Hollywood, an Irish pub through to clothing department stores, designer fashion shops and food supermarkets. At new shopping centres being established in the USA some of the sites are being described as 'Centre Parcs meet Ikea' or 'Disneyworld meets Wal-Mart'. These sites can be so vast that they can incorporate ski slopes and canoe runs. Not surprisingly where they are established they are seeing sales booming as they attract the greater share of consumer spending in a wider and wider catchment area.

More centres are being planned in Europe. The UK alone, despite tight planning controls, will see a significant increase in major shopping developments over the next five years. There will be four new sites opening in Manchester, Dartford, Glasgow and Bristol. There will be substantial extensions to existing centres in Birmingham and Newcastle. Planning permission has already been given for two greenfield sites in Paddington and White City in west London. These will all create opportunities for retailers to start developing their 'stores of the future'.

The shopping scene is changing and retailers will need to develop. Standing still carries a high risk of being disintermediated, cut out of the supply chain as electronic ordering grows. But the changing environment is one of opportunity as well as challenge. There's a potential to forge new sources of advantage and competitive differentiation and in principle retailers remain best placed to pursue that. After all, they are closest to the end consumer, they have that relationship right now. They have built strong consumer franchises reinforced by their own brands and reward and loyalty bonuses. They have the best database of who their customers are, what are their habits and preferences.

As they move into the next century retailers will have a range of options. At one extreme they could transition their business to become a full electronic home-delivery operation gradually moving out of their physical retail estate. As an alternative they could look to revitalise their physical presence and evolve the store proposition to meet some of the changing consumer demand. Many have already begun down this path. UK grocers like Tesco and Sainsbury have expanded their service range to include banking, dry-cleaning, flowers, newspaper and magazines, coffee shops and gas stations. Others like Levi's, Doc Martens shoes and clothing and Nike have filled their stores with video walls, museum artefacts and related merchandise to give more reasons to visit and enhance the total shopping experience.

The days of extensive shelving, racks of products, shopping carts, aisles and check-out counters will soon be over. To remain attractive retailers will have to go back to the drawing board and rethink how to use and exploit the total physical space at their disposal. They can start to experiment with totally new ways of shopping – make the experience, for example, part electronic part physical, partner with others to provide integrated social, leisure and entertainment facilities and excite consumers so they still want to visit despite the temptations of electronic shopping.

Yet as we enter the new millennium the retailing community at large is still ambivalent about electronic commerce, its potential and how it will develop. They naturally fear their sizeable investments in their physical retail estates being undermined. They are reluctant to encourage their consumers to think and act electronically, not wanting to see cannibalisation of store sales and drop in store traffic.

While they hesitate in their response they are leaving themselves vulnerable in their market places. Dedicated electronic sellers like Amazon.com, Webvan, Dell, 1-800-FLOWERS, Direct Line and others have established themselves. They are unencumbered by existing infrastructures. They have no distribution channel conflicts. They can take advantage of the internet's immediate global reach and with effective marketing quickly exploit that growing group of consumers who unequivocally prefer to shop electronically. If existing retailers don't watch their markets carefully they might find a whole segment of their customer base moving away from them, determined to avail themselves of a rival's service which is better suited to their needs. In some sectors like books in the USA, personal insurance in the UK, music CDs, flowers and computers the entry barriers are already being erected, making it more costly and difficult for an existing physical retailer to move into electronic selling – there's already entrenched electronic competition!

And as retailers experiment and remain uncertain about their strategy for electronic shopping so there is a threat from another quarter. Manufacturer suppliers, long squeezed by their consolidating and sophisticated retailer customers, now find themselves with a chance to fight back and establish their own direct links with the end consumers of their products. They can simply bypass the retail chains. And for sure they are evaluating their options. Unilever, Heinz, Procter & Gamble, Campbell and Nestlé – five of the world's biggest consumer goods companies – are all exploring the electronic world. To date their own initiatives have been cautious, not wanting to disturb their existing retail customer base until they are more certain of the size of the electronic shopping opportunity. But, for example, the day may be not far off when we see Procter & Gamble, Unilever, L'Oréal, Kimberley Clark and Rubbermaid combine with a joint venture to provide 'The Household Goods Shop.com'. This could be an internet site offering a full range of all a consumer's household goods needs, regular orders with home delivery at lower prices direct from the manufacturer.

Electronic Shock? Every part of the retail scene is going to go through a significant transformation in the coming years. Those who stand still will surely decline and risk becoming some of the early dinosaurs of the twenty-first century. Those who win will be companies who develop a close understanding of what their customers will want, what will be their needs, whether they want electronic facilities for the sort of goods and services the company offers, how quickly they'll want to change and whether they'll all move that way or just a proportion. By developing this understanding of the electronic marketplace retailers *and* manufacturers will be able to develop clear long-term plans for responding to the new challenges and keeping their customers. It's all about to take place so rapidly – and reach critical mass within the next ten years – that there's certainly no room for complacency and little time left for continued ambivalence. Only by facing up to the electronic shopping revolution can future business be secured.

1 The New Rules of the Game

Introduction

The internet revolution continues at a pace. Many companies are now scrambling to catch up, working out how best to embrace the new internet and wireless technologies, looking to adapt to the different opportunities for communication and interaction, adjusting to the new ways of doing business.

But it is not proving easy to master the new environment. Competition is moving fast, alliances are being formed, joint ventures negotiated and new market forces are being unleashed faster than was ever thought possible. It is proving such a demanding and even frenetic situation that old ways of doing business are having to be thrown out of the door.

There is a fundamental shift taking place and there's no going back. Fifty years of teaching at Harvard Business School are being turned on their head as companies wake up to the new disciplines. There is a new game in town and it is now about learning and embracing the new factors for success.

Not quite the law of the jungle, but certainly survival of the fittest! The changes are coming from all sides. The impact is wide ranging. What is needed for sure is a checklist, a consolidated list of what are the key things to think about, explore and react to. We need to be utterly clear about what the new rules of the game are.

In this chapter we set out ten new rules to live – or die – by. If you like, the Ten Commandments. There's ten new rules that affect every company and organisation. There's ten specifically designed for (r)etailers and then ten for manufacturers and suppliers. Working to each new rule will help set the agenda and framework for change: a survival guide for the new generation of wannabe business successes!

Before examining each of the rules in detail let's just consider their broad impact and application. The fundamental shift that is taking place in the way businesses need to operate just cannot be ignored. Symptomatic of the new rules is the growing dominance of e-commerce companies in the league table of top firms. In the UK FTSE 100, for example, new entrants include leading technology players as well as established companies, like Cable & Wireless (ranked 18), which are being proactive in the e-commerce telecommunications environment. But there are also new entrants such as Dixons' Freeserve. These aggressive e-commerce chart-toppers are pushing out the old-guard firms such as Associated British Foods (104), Allied Domecq (105) and Hanson (108). This shake-up in the old order is also illustrated by looking at 'upstarts' like leading e-tailer Amazon.com. In 1999 Amazon, which had only been in existence for five years, took a stake in Sotheby's, which had been around for 200 years. But there was a vast discrepancy in each company's market value. Amazon was valued then at around $20 billion. Sotheby's, on the other hand, had a just £200 million valuation. The new guard replacing the old!

The new rules of the game also mean there has to be a different approach to the way businesses are valued in the market place. A new set of metrics has entered the picture. Instead of focusing on price–earnings (PE) ratios, it is important to think about revenue multiples as well as the number of customers the New Economy companies are able to attract and the loyalty they can generate from those customers. The new focus is on 'lifetime value'. Essentially, this is the number of customers multiplied by the expected spend of those customers on an annualised basis. Profits are no longer the overriding measure. Investors have had to find new ways to appreciate the long term potential of a company and to evaluate growth and profits in the future, rather than market share and profits today.

Such reappraisal is enormously healthy. For many years companies were often unable to invest for the long term because they were saddled with short-term attitudes, earnings-per-share (EPS) dilution models and intransigent investment banking attitudes. Now the e-commerce revolution has breathed new life into companies' growth ambitions and it is enabling the more forward-thinking to relaunch and re-invigorate their long term investment intentions. In that way, companies that want to can start moving, instead of stagnating.

The changing rules of the game are also forcing the business world to move increasingly to electronic-only communication. General Electric (GE) was one of the pioneers of this trend when several years ago it informed its suppliers that it would in future only deal with them via the internet, dispensing with paper documents, reducing the cost of transactions and achieving greater efficiency all round. GE's radical move generated considerable interest in business-to-business (B2B) trading. Many other companies are looking to follow GE's example.

Anything that lowers costs, speeds up transactions and generally increases efficiency has to be taken very seriously.

What's more, under these new rules of the game, employees are expecting to be rewarded differently. They want a share in the benefits that are being generated by the e-commerce market and its rapidly escalating values. Their demands tend to be translated into substantial bonuses or stock options. They believe – and why not? – that they are entitled to a share of the cake. If they are creating substantial amounts of shareholder value, of course they should be rewarded. Established companies of the old economy are now struggling to find the right financial formulae to keep happy these often young and dynamic employees involved in the e-commerce side of the business.

Many 'old guard' companies are not taking the e-commerce onslaught lying down. Far from it. Some of them are fighting back with a vengeance. In many cases, industry leaders are forming consortia to attack new upstarts on a united front. *The Sunday Times* reported (summer 2000) in an article menacingly entitled *The Empire Strikes Back* that airlines, hotels and other old economy businesses were moving on line in a huge counter-attack against 'New Economy' companies. Garth Alexander, the article's author, suggested that hundreds of on-line travel agents 'could be forced out of business by two new master sites being set up by the airlines. Some 27 airlines, including American, Continental, Delta, Northwest and United, have joined forces to form a $100 million site, codenamed T2. Several carriers, led by Continental, are planning another site that will offer deeply discounted fares and challenge businesses such as Priceline.com and Lastminute.com.'

The Sunday Times article goes on to mention that on-line estate agents are coming under attack from a consortium of America's top home builders, which are banding together to create a centralised on-line listing and sales site. Adds Alexander: 'An even bigger crisis faces on-line wholesalers and B2B sites. In the last month old economy companies have announced half a dozen new private on-line exchanges. Each threatens the existence of dozens of internet fledglings.'

In addition, points out Alexander, General Motors, Ford and DaimlerChrysler are setting up a huge on-line bazaar, tapping into a $240 billion a year market. A consortium of 14 energy and petrochemical companies, including BP Amoco and Royal Dutch/Shell, is targeting the flourishing business of on-line energy exchanges and setting up its own global procurement exchange. It expects to handle $100 billion of goods in its first year. Another on-line exchange has been set up for metal trading. America's three leading aerospace manufacturers are also clubbing together with Britain's BAe Systems. Five of the largest American meat and poultry producers have joined Farmland Industries, a big farmer co-operative, to create an on-line wholesale marketplace. And 50 of the world's largest consumer products groups, including Procter & Gamble, Nestlé and Unilever, are forming their private B2B exchange.

Some well-established companies, such as Tesco, with its world-leading electronic shopping business, and Prudential with its Egg on-line financial services operation, are also in the forefront of e-commerce. Research studies leave Morgan Stanley Dean Witter in no doubt that the 'balance of power lies with the traditional strong retail brands' in terms of success on the internet. 'After all, their purchasing power, experience, brand reputation and infrastructure are not easily emulated. While many commentators may feel their historical base could easily be rivalled by the dotcoms, we think there is no substitute for experience and brand strength, which few e-tailers have at present.'

Both the New Economy dotcoms and the established bricks-and-mortar companies face a challenge that will test their resolve and ingenuity. So what precisely are the new rules of the game that they will have to tackle to be successful? Let's consider the detail.

The Ten Basic Rules

1	E-commerce investments *can* be earnings diluting
2	Forget PE ratios when evaluating an e-business
3	Consider internet flotations as part of the formula for delivering shareholder value
4	Alliances are key
5	Networking is key
6	Customer knowledge really is power now
7	Data must move real-time
8	Implementation must be in weeks, not years
9	Take a portfolio approach to risk
10	Share the rewards with employees

*Rule 1 – E-commerce investments **can** be earnings diluting.* In the world of e-commerce, throw away all those earnings per share dilution models! The old corporate finance models no longer need apply. E-commerce activities are predicted to grow so fast that investors want to encourage companies to invest now to build up the foundations. For the right e-commerce propositions the City not only accepts dilution, it positively encourages it. There is a growing acceptance that rewards can come later – and maybe not for five or even ten years. To illustrate the point, Prudential and Reed Elsevier both made investments in their internet businesses of around £200 million at the turn of the century. These investments were earnings diluting but the stock market rewarded their enterprise and ambition. The share price rose significantly. And these two companies are not just a couple of rare exceptions to prove the rule. Others in both the US and Europe have experienced the same encouragement to go for the long term opportunity and invest now in building their e-commerce capability.

It is a bit like staking out the ground for the future and the market recognises that to survive companies need to do that and to do it now. Like the gold rush, there is only going to be so much territory, so companies need to stake out their share. Some of that will be proactive and aggressive stake-building. Some of it will be more defensive and based around: 'If we don't do it, others will'. But it's an essential part of transitioning to, and exploiting, the new economic order.

Figure 1.1 Putting Stakes in the Ground for the Future

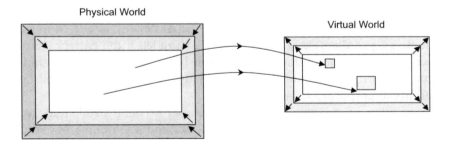

Rule 2 – Forget PE ratios when valuing an e-business. Market investors then are prepared to take a long-term view when backing e-investments. They are in the market for growth. Their immediate measure is revenues, not profits. As a result, all the major New Economy stocks are being valued on revenue multiples. And these multiples can be significant. Even after the hype of early 2000 when valuations began to settle down, the average multiple according to a *Business Week* analysis of Nasdaq stocks had halved but was still at c. 40×. Even if it halves again, that still offers an extraordinary shareholder value opportunity which just cannot be ignored.

Look again at companies like Amazon and the other emerging major e-commerce companies. Amazon, of course, is taking its time to start delivering profits because of its urgent and demanding investment goals. But even if it didn't make profits for another five years, valuation models built by the likes of Wasserstein Perella and Morgan Stanley still demonstrate the company can have a substantial value and certainly reach the c. $10 billion valuation mark that the company has had. It's all down to the assumptions that get made on growth, in terms of numbers of customers it can attract and make stay loyal and how much those customers can be expected to spend with the company. Believe in the assumptions in the model and you'd back the company. But after all, you don't have to invest!

Rule 3 – Consider internet flotations as part of the formula for delivering shareholder value. The stock market may be speculative, with fortunes won and lost, but it is an opportunity not to be ignored. If it is possible to convert investments or part of them or other business initiatives into sizeable gains for shareholders, why not take advantage of that? It is not a traditional economic value added (EVA) measure of shareholder value, but it certainly plays to the market value added (MVA) view of the world. Obviously, the timing has to be right, the business must be developing, and the proposition must be clear.

The opportunity here is basically to separate out new e-commerce initiatives, put them on a stand-alone basis, unleash the entrepreneurial energies and let the business team establish independent recognition for what it is doing, untrammelled and unchained from any old, established, traditional corporate cultures.

A number of companies, like Wal-Mart, Tesco and Prudential, have seized this way of organising their businesses and are looking to capture this shareholder value gain. In particular, they are following their instincts on how best to organise for success. But there is also compelling research to support this approach in Clayton M. Christensen's book, *The Innovator's Dilemma*.

In that research Christensen examines how winning companies in the past have responded best to 'technology discontinuities'. His conclusion is stark. The only way is to establish a separate business unit to enable it to think afresh about the new market challenges. He cites IBM's now legendary failure to adapt its mainframe computer business to the new fast-growing PC sector. Cut the new team loose or watch it be constantly hampered by entrenched attitudes.

Rule 4 – Alliances are key. It could be argued that they always are, but in internet space they are a *sine qua non* – there's no success without them. The pace is so rapid it is impossible to try to build everything organically. Internet space is so vast that companies need partners to help navigate the way through. That also means sharing risks. Take the example of companies like Microsoft. They have invested heavily in building a web of alliances. Microsoft has numerous and complementary investment partners in cable (NTL, Telewest, AT&T, Comast), wireless technology (Ericsson, Nextel and BT) and internet software (Hotmail, Vermeer, Link Exchange).

Rule 5 – Networking is key. In the same vein, a company must be net-worked. On the net itself the yardstick is again Amazon.com with its now c. 300,000 affiliates. These are simple contractual arrangements which are all about customer acquisition and driving customers to each other's sites. In doing so, Amazon and others broaden their whole product/service proposition to their customers. They become quasi-portals, because they are centres of related product knowledge, access, information and purchasing.

Rule 6 – Customer knowledge really is power now. Over the past 20 years especially, companies have talked about 'the customer is king', 'customer service is important', 'we understand our customers'. But most have paid lip-service to those mantras and not actually embraced them rigorously throughout their organisations. Now, internet technologies have pro-vided a catalyst. They enable companies more easily to capture data on who's buying, what they're buying and so make it possible to start delivering one-to-one, personalised and interactive communications between company and customer. Companies like Experian, the business information services group, therefore, are extraordinarily well placed in this arena, because over years they have collected this market information and can help other companies build it and exploit it.

Rule 7 – Data must move real-time. The new technologies make it easy to move large amounts of data in seconds. Netcard shot to prominence in the US with its 35-second credit card approval process on the net. Other companies like e-Loan are moving to quick approval processes that instantly check an applicant's credit worthiness. Onvia.com, based in Seattle in the US, is another company that is using rapid response technologies to create a fast-growing business. It operates an on-line marketplace with more than 31,500 registered sellers. Small businesses can purchase everything from computers and furniture to debt collection and web page design. Put in a 'request for quote' on say, a $2 million property insurance policy, fill in some details about what's to be insured, specify whether you want 10 or 15 bids, and click 'submit'. Odds are you'll have your quotes within the hour; for a web page design, you'll have quotes in just 20 minutes. Onvia.com's founder and president, Glenn Bellman, contributing to an issue of *Fortune*: 'The marketplace of the future will be like this – minute-to-minute, second-to-second transactions.'

Companies are building competitive advantage through this rapid integration and transmission of information. Today such enabling systems are more easily achievable. But they do require substantial commitment and investment to see them through and achieve the pay-back.

Rule 8 – Implementation must be in weeks, not years. The days are gone when a major SAP implementation exercise would often take two years and an army of people and consultants to complete. Internet technologies now enable things to happen more quickly, more cheaply and with less resource. Another example from Experian illustrates this graphically. When Morgan Stanley Dean Witter decided to launch their credit card in the UK they wanted to do it quickly and provide real time data processing and credit checks. All they wanted to bring to the party was their marketing and funding. They sought out a partner who could provide everything else and build their entire back office infrastructure and processing systems. Experian managed to complete the entire project in 87 days.

Rule 9 – Take a portfolio approach to risk. GE (General Electric) took a little while to get going in e-commerce. But when it did, it moved with a vengeance. As it mobilised resources it also set up an e-investments team. Its job was to investigate other companies that could help build up GE's e-commerce know-how, access new technologies, link into complementary products, provide additional value-added services and exploit the internet. But rather than evaluate each investment opportunity as an individual project, GE set up an e-investment fund to take a portfolio approach. GE recognises that internet space is unpredictable. By definition it is more speculative. GE appreciates that some investments will win and some will fail. So success can be measured not by the fortunes of each initiative, but by the return of the whole portfolio spread. In the first nine months of establishing the e-investment team, GE made 50 investments and contrived to build quickly and aggressively on the same basis.

Rule 10 – Share the rewards with employees. The upsides are potentially so substantial for companies that do get it right in this area that employee expectations are changing. Once again, organisations have spent years paying lip-service to employee share ownership and have often come up with schemes which are so bureaucratic and burdensome that employees feel little incentive. But many surveys indicate that sharing the benefits can be highly motivating and drive employees to go that extra mile. So today to get the best people, stakes in the future or heavily geared bonuses that share the success are becoming a pre-requisite. Not surprising then, top US performers like GE, but also the likes of Cisco and Microsoft, consistently appear high in the Employee Ownership List – the list of companies where more than 4% of the stock is owned by the workforce. And there's no doubt that creating millionaires can have a powerful and motivating effect!

The Ten Rules for Retailers

1	Be ready to cannibalise
2	Be prepared to become a multi-channel operator
3	Reappraise the property portfolio
4	Get on interactive TV
5	Think in terms of convenience, convenience, convenience
6	Content is key
7	Create a sense of community service
8	Measure the metrics
9	Invest 10% of your capital expenditure now in e-commerce
10	Test, trial and learn

Rule 1 – Be ready to cannibalise. The natural reaction of a retailer, who already has a substantial chain of stores, is to resist going onto the internet. The retailer may well consider that embracing the internet and encouraging customers to switch their buying habits by going on line might be undermining the traditional bricks and mortar business. Store staff may well feel they could be doing themselves out of job in the long run. Therefore, there needs to be a change of mindset within the company – an attitudinal acceptance internally that it is perfectly all right to cannibalise. The new mindset, to be effective, should pervade the whole organisation. It should involve the senior directors down to the most junior staff, although the tone is obviously set by top management. The reason Tesco, for example, has gained such a leading position in the forefront of electronic shopping is that it has told its staff that it does not matter if it ends up shifting some of its volume sales from its stores to the net. At the end of the day, if the company does it right, 1 + 1 will equal 3 and everyone will be better off, the company will be stronger and in fact jobs **more** secure. The bottom line for the leading stores group is that it has to take advantage of the new medium, that the net is going to develop and it is better that it should make its move early rather than late so that it can learn the lessons in good time.

Being ready to cannibalise means being prepared to allow sales to switch from one channel to another – from the bricks and mortar stores to the internet. In actual fact, the retailer can probably be fairly cavalier about it in the current situation in which electronic shopping only relates to around 1% of retail sales. But now is the time to recognise that it will only need a 10–15% shift in the number of customers switching to the net for stores to become unprofitable. It may not be an immediate threat today because nobody is going to notice a 1% shift. But when it starts creeping up to 5%, 7%, 10%, it could suddenly have a major impact.

Management needs to ask itself at what point it should take the switch seriously. At what point will it decide to make changes in the organisation to cope with the escalating drift to the internet? Several of the major retailers interviewed for this book believed it would take no more than a 10% shift in retail sales from bricks and mortar to the net for their traditional stores to become unprofitable.

The trend to internet shopping will probably happen more rapidly than most retailers realise and the ones that are slow to take account of its repercussions are going to be caught out. There are already examples of where this is happening. Barnes and Noble, the leading book retailer, has been overtaken by Amazon.com largely because it has been relatively slow to grasp the internet opportunity. Amazon, the relative newcomer, has exploited the internet to the full and reaped the rewards. Similarly, Compaq, the computer manufacturer and distributor, has been overtaken by other players because it was quite slow to recognise the benefits of the internet. Compaq held back because it was unhappy about the idea of unsettling its established distribution arrangements.

Another example is Merrill Lynch, the stockbrokers, which has seen other companies like Charles Schwab move into the market and capture quite a lot of its business. Schwab grasped the nettle and was prepared to move its bricks and mortar operation straight on to the internet, whereas Merrill Lynch was far more cautious and insisted on sticking to its traditional way of doing business for some time. Because it wasn't prepared to accept cannibalisation as a *de facto* part of the environment, it has seen some of its business eroded by more enterprising competitors in its market place.

Rule 2 – Be prepared to become a multi-channel operator. This follows on from Rule 1. Once an organisation has accepted the need to cannibalise, it should be prepared to see itself not just as a bricks and mortar company but as a company that is going to operate across a number of channels. In addition to traditional store trade, it must also operate on the net. It may also decide to operate through interactive TV home shopping channels. It could at the same time find itself having to operate through the mobile phone. It may also communicate with some customers simply by mail or fax. Companies have to think about becoming a multi-channel capable player. One way of thinking about it is summed up by the phrase: *clicks 'n' mortar*.

Probably the supreme example of a multi-channel operator is Coca-Cola, which adopted the principle long before the internet became a commercial reality. If you think about it, Coke sells the same products in different packaging forms, at different prices, in different channels and nobody complains. It sells through pubs, clubs, restaurants, supermarkets and vending machines. It sells the same quantity of Coke at different prices and in different shaped bottles and cans from a variety of outlets and everybody is happy. The consumer continues to purchase it readily, the retailer or distributor at the point of sale continues to stock it. All accept the different value propositions that Coke has developed. That is a model multi-channel operation and it doesn't happen overnight. It has taken Coca-Cola some time and a lot of effort to reach that stage in its marketing strategy. It has effectively segmented its channels of distribution and developed separate channel propositions for different consumers.

Another approach is to think of it in territory terms. Companies like Nationwide Insurance in the US evaluated its marketing strategy and concluded that in some states it had well established channels of distribution through agents, but in other states it hardly had any business at all. Where it was physically thin on the ground it was unlikely to be challenging any *status quo*. In those areas, it reasoned, it made sense to go straight onto the net.

Similarly, Asda in the UK recognised that it had a low penetration of supermarkets in the south east of England. It made sense to focus on that as a pioneering experiment for electronic shopping rather than immediately impact on areas where it had a high density of well-established bricks 'n' mortar supermarkets.

This whole approach can be summarised by the concept of *ubiquity*. Companies need to be wherever customers want them to be – and that might be in all these different channels. It's just not possible to be precious about it and not be there because it might cannibalise traditional sales or because the necessary internet skills haven't yet been acquired. A company must develop the ability, otherwise it's going to be left behind and will lose business.

Research by McKinsey shows that those retailers who effectively combine bricks and mortar with the internet actually find that on average they are doing more business with their customers than before. The research revealed that the retailers who took this double-pronged

Figure 1.2   Multichannel Vision

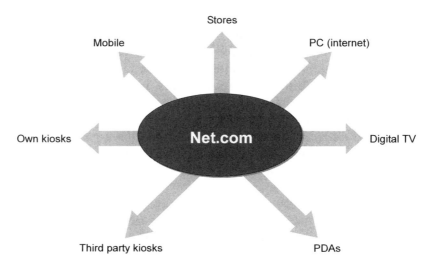

approach were 10% better off with individual customers. That was because individual customers were making some purchases through the traditional bricks and mortar stores and some through the internet. The customer was spending on average 10% more with that company. This goes to illustrate that by positively combining the two channels, retailers can very productively persuade their customers to spend more money with them. Another recent example is Wehkamp, the Dutch catalogue company. In its first two years of internet activity it found that 18% of its customers were new and generating significant incremental business.

Rule 3 – Reappraise the property portfolio. Once the idea of cannibalisation has been accepted and the need to become an effective multi-channel operator internalised, then retailers should start evaluating whether they have the appropriate property portfolio to meet future needs. They need to ask whether it is necessary to hold on to all the shops currently owned. Maybe the New Economy won't require the same number of physical outlets in the future. Maybe they don't need to be the same size or should be in a different configuration. Perhaps they need to be presented differently or in different locations. What property portfolio will be needed in ten years time? What steps need to be taken now to make sure that in the future there is the right balance when e-commerce is a serious part of the business? Is the organisation geared up sufficiently well to be able to make the necessary adaptations to the property portfolio? A number of leading retailers are already engaged in reviewing where they stand in this regard.

It is necessary to plan quite far ahead because many shops are accustomed to taking on lengthy leases with upwards only rent reviews, particularly in the UK environment. Without foresight, there won't be the flexibility to move quickly when the drift to the internet starts to accelerate. There is already every indication that a growing number of consumers are embracing the idea that staple grocery items, for example, can be delivered to their home, reducing the time and effort they need to devote to shopping. It is, therefore, reasonable to assume that the number of shopping aisles found in typical supermarkets today will shrink in the future, freeing up extra space. What can this available space be used for? Should it be re-merchandised for other products? Or will the store of the future be quite different from how it is today? Maybe in future it will no longer consist of people pushing trolley carts up and down endless rows of aisles. Maybe it will be conceived as something entirely different, fulfilling a completely different social need (see Chapter 9 and 'store of the future').

Rule 4 – Get on interactive TV. Because so much of the approach to electronic shopping is US driven, debate tends to focus on the internet. There is also much discussion and hype about mobile phone commerce. There is nothing wrong with that, but it should not be forgotten that Europe – and the UK in particular – is a pioneer of digital interactive shopping on TV. There is every indication that interactive TV is in itself going to become a powerful medium for home shopping in the future. There are a number of leading UK companies developing the technology, such as News International's Open, Telewest and NTL. Retailers need to keep abreast of these developments and ensure that they are well placed to reap the benefits when the technology is sufficiently advanced to turn the potential into mass market appeal (see Chapter 17 and the case study (p. 291) for more interviews and detail).

Engineers are already developing set-top boxes for TV, which will give access to the internet and will feature special buttons to link users, for example, to the local pizza take-away or their preferred supermarket. These hot buttons will operate automatically and bypass having to specifically log on and dial up the internet.

Rule 5 – Think in terms of convenience, convenience, convenience. The sophism or motto that retailers have lived by in the past decade has been 'location, location, location'. The internet has turned that on its head. Location is irrelevant on the internet. Everybody starts in the same cyberspace location. It's all about convenience, convenience, convenience. It is now all about making it easy for customers to reach out, access your website and enjoy the experience. It is all about making it convenient. Convenience is at the heart of what fundamentally drives the demand for the internet. It is because it offers services in a more convenient way that people have become attracted to it. The retailers who are going to be successful are those who recognise this essential fact and are able to turn it to their advantage.

'Companies that deliver products with the greatest convenience are those that will prosper in the New Economy,' suggests *Business 2.0* in an article looking at the new success factors for e-commerce. 'Whereas traditional merchants are open during so-called business hours, limited hours of operation will soon be an anachronism for many types of business.' The on-line store stands ready to provide sales and service 24 hours a day, seven days a week. The Gap advertises that its on-line store is 'always open'. Banks once ran on what was called the 3-6-3 system: Borrow at 3 per cent, lend at 6 per cent, and make it to the golf course by 3 o'clock, giving rise to the expression 'bankers' hours'.

Electronic banking has changed that forever. Now Citibank tells us 'the Citi never sleeps'.

A lot of observers insist the reason people shop on the internet is because it is the place to find bargains and it is all about price, price, price. This is a fallacy. The McKinsey study shows that most people shop on the internet for the sake of convenience and that price is in fact some way down the list of benefits. Amazon also argues that heavily discounted prices are not the main factor in its success. The internet book supplier insists that it is its excellent customer service that persuades people to shop with it. Its success is attributable to the provision of a totally satisfying customer experience. While it is true Amazon is using discounted prices today to grab some headlines and to give a fillip to its market share performance, this is only a short term strategy. Like all businesses, whether on the internet or not, Amazon will ultimately need to settle on sustainable prices in order to achieve sustainable margins. It believes that its customer service model – striving toward 'customer ecstasy' – will enable it to achieve that goal.

There is a lot of debate about what constitutes fulfilment or delivery in the context of internet shopping. One of the issues most frequently raised concerns how an efficient delivery to the door service will be achieved, which many people argue is at the heart of the focus on convenience. It is early days and logistics companies are still trying to work out the most practical way to achieve home delivery. At the moment there are lots of delivery vans dashing about all over the place, getting in each other's way and finding it difficult to deliver on time because of traffic congestion and other obstacles. However, there is a whole raft of experiments being pioneered. The US is in the forefront of this innovation and its successful experiments will inevitably transfer to Europe. The focus is on how to reach the consumer in the most leveraged way. That has led, for example, to an experiment in Manhattan called 'Urban Fetch', which is also scheduled to cross the Atlantic. It offers within Manhattan delivery within two hours of things like pizza, basic shopping items, videos, books and CDs. To overcome traffic congestion, deliveries are being made by people on roller-blades, bicycles, motor-bikes – anything that ensures a trouble free delivery. This is essentially a solution for urban areas where the density of population is such that suppliers can achieve economies of scale. It is probably not the answer nationwide.

Other suppliers believe that to overcome the complications of delivery to the door, it might be more efficient to deliver to a neighbourhood pick-up point. It could be a local petrol station, the convenience store on the corner of the street or secure deposit boxes – typically places that are manned 24 hours a day anyway. These are yet more aspects of convenience that are being explored. Ways to make home delivery more economical will continue to be looked at. At the moment each company providing an electronic shopping service has its own delivery arrangements, but this is likely to consolidate so that eventually we will get single service provision operating in a particular locality or sector of a town and a few leading major operators working nationwide with the necessary drop densities and economies of scale to deliver a very profitable business.

Rule 6 – Content is key. If companies are going to develop a web business they need to create an environment where it's about selling more than just the product range. It's about providing a website that can also be an informative and worthwhile experience. Just having a list of products on a page can be extremely boring. It needs to include, for example, a facility for providing product knowledge. Where groceries are concerned, a list of products is perhaps all that is required. It doesn't need to have that much elaboration. But when it comes to travel, books, CDs, holidays, financial services products, and that kind of thing customers want to find out more. They are seeking information and the internet is an excellent environment for providing all that. It can be provided in a fun, user-friendly way. It then develops what is called a *stickiness* to the site. It is a site that people want to access, to linger with and come back to time and time again, because things are happening on the site which are informative and are of benefit to them in planning their lives.

CDs are a good example of how this expanded service can be provided on the internet. Reviews of latest issues and samples of tracks can be downloaded. If it is a classical recording, different versions can be compared on line to help the potential purchaser make up his or her mind about which suits their particular taste. So don't simply put the brochure on line. Consider the net as a channel, a medium, in its own right, which requires the development of its own customer value proposition.

Rule 7 – Create a sense of community service. While getting on-line and learning about the net environment, try in effect to create a sense of community, so that those who log on feel they are coming to something that is more than just a list. Excite their interest and instil in them the feeling that this is the place to come to find out what is going on. A car dealer, for example, can establish a motor club with an abundance of information about cars in general – make it the place to come to chat to people about the experiences they have had with various models of the car the site is selling. Maybe provide a site for do-it-yourself enthusiasts who want to converse with like-minded subscribers about how to go about their own car repairs. It provides an opportunity to exchange ideas and experience. Currently, this is done in written form, but there is already the technological means to do it verbally. It will soon be possible to have an interactive dialogue with a call centre representative, for example, who will be able to answer queries via a video picture in the corner of the PC screen. All that is part of community service.

There are a growing number of internet companies that have already seized the opportunity to exploit the on-line potential for creating a community service. One of them is called *Motley Fool*, which is in the financial services arena. Subscribers come on site to learn about financial services products, stocks and shares, among other things. The information is presented in a relatively fun environment with the emphasis on tailored and personalised communication. It's the place to find out what is happening with net stocks and shares in a club atmosphere. It has created a buzz of excitement about its up-to-the-moment, easy-to-use facilities. It's good at generating word of mouth so potential customers feel this is *the* site they should subscribe to rather than other competitors. Another community site is *ivillage*, which essentially is targeted at working women and families who want to learn about issues affecting their lives. Another is *Seniornet*, which is for senior citizens, and deals with issues affecting them. For example, members can also club together to buy computers and other products at discounted prices.

These community sites are again more than just a product list. There is something else going on that makes people feel it is the place to visit. It's very intangible and a bit emotional. It's somewhat contact-driven. It's a bit about brand values, which makes participants feel it is a comfortable, warm place to be, where they will meet others for a friendly chat to exchange ideas and information and learn about the latest developments in a particular product range. Another obvious possibility would be a site for mothers and babies, where parents can learn more about bringing up children, while at the same time buying on-line all the clothing and equipment for their offspring. This could even be extended to take advantage of the changing nature of bricks and mortar establishments. Mother and baby clubs could be launched in the product-vacated space where parents can meet each other physically and compare notes. It needn't be only a virtual experience!

Rule 8 – Measure the metrics. How to measure the progress of an internet business? Before even starting to grapple with earnings and profit, companies need to focus on a much more immediate set of metrics. In some relative order, these are:

- number of page impressions
- number of visits
- number of unique visits
- number of orders
- number of customers
- number of repeat customers
- individual customer value
- average basket/transaction value per order
- length of time visiting the site
- average clicks to order
- e-mail response times
- delay/drop-out rates per page
- delivery lead times
- customer survey satisfaction scores.

There are other measures of course. But what companies must learn to do is to monitor these key trends, develop the statistics and, most importantly, actively respond to them. It means trying to encapsulate and capture centuries of retailing and merchandising experience into just a few short years. It is about learning how to optimise and make most effective an internet business. It was never going to be easy but today's information technology environment means this data *is* available and the more determined management teams can learn to exploit it.

Obviously, in the long run, no company can ignore a lack of profits, but in the early stages when retailers are beginning to build up their internet trade they can use these new metrics to boost their confidence that things are going in the right direction and to pinpoint weaknesses in their approach. These measurements can also be used to benchmark against other on-line competitors and rival companies in general. If the metrics are more favourable than those of rivals, it would suggest the organisation is doing better than them. They might also be fed to the City via the annual report to assure investors that even if there are currently no profits, developments are progressing in the right direction.

These kinds of metrics have typically in the past been buried in the marketing department. Today they should receive wider exposure, because if a company is not making profits, how else do you evaluate it, estimate when it might become profitable or whether it is capable of becoming a success in the future? There is now this new approach to the way companies in the internet space are being evaluated, particularly pure plays that are losing money.

Rule 9 – Invest 10% of capital expenditure now in e-commerce. Today, e-commerce may be no more than 1% of sales, but it can be expected to grow rapidly and it is necessary to create the circumstances in which a business can compete in that environment. If it only invests 1% of total capital in developing the on-line business it is not going to be able to achieve very much. It needs to start thinking about spending 10% of the capital expenditure now to create a viable e-commerce environment for the future. It is not uncommon to find US-based companies spending $30 to $50 million a year developing one web business. That is a significant amount of money. Some are spending more, some are spending less. But as the game shifts, as companies get better at exploiting on-line opportunities, the idea of getting on the web for $50,000 by just posting a brochure on the screen and listing with Yahoo! as a search engine is entirely inadequate. Current trends demand something far more enterprising. Consumers' expectations are beginning to rise and the functionality of the information technology employed in the business needs to grow in parallel with these expectations. To be successful, companies must, for example, personalise the experience so that when particular individuals log on they can indicate that they recognise them and are aware from previous occasions what their special preferences are.

Restricting investment to 1% is short-sighted. A business needs to engage in a more aggressive spend to keep pace with the internet's rapid growth. If it doesn't invest ahead of the game it won't be in a position to ride the wave and reap the undoubted benefits to come. On the contrary, it will be caught out by others who have invested more daringly. It will also be in a weak position to compete against all the new entrants that are streaming onto the internet. While it has become less easy for new plays to attract venture capital nowadays compared with the end of 1999 and early 2000, good propositions are still managing to raise the money and will continue to do so.

Rule 10 – Test, trial and learn. Waiting to see how electronic retailing will develop in the future is a dangerous game. The cautious-minded may think they ought to bide their time and see how things pan out and perhaps review the situation when e-commerce has become a more significant force in the market place. But by then they may well have missed the boat. Better to follow the example of Tesco for one which took the plunge early on in the game to learn important lessons that are keeping it in the forefront of latest developments.

In the beginning people scoffed at Tesco for manually downloading the on-line orders and re-keying them into their existing systems – an approach that seemed the very height of inefficiency. The lack of automation came in for a certain amount of derision. But the last laugh may well be with Tesco, because it had made up its mind to learn in easy stages. It was not prepared to ramp up too quickly sophisticated electronic links in its back-end information systems environment. It shrewdly decided to test the waters and try to measure the level of demand there was out in the market place for on-line shopping. Tesco was prepared to become part of the game and to learn from trial and error, trying out different approaches. It has proved to be a sensible route to take because by the year 2000 its internet home shopping business had become the biggest in the world with annual sales of £125 million plus. Its internet business – including its home shopping operation Tesco Direct and its own internet service provider – has now become so significant that it has decided to spin it off as a wholly owned subsidiary. It was reported in 2000 to be investing £35 million into Tesco.com in the current financial year. If it were to float Tesco.com on the stock market it would probably find that it had created £1 billion plus piece of shareholder value, which will of course become even more valuable as time goes on.

The Ten Rules for Manufacturers

In this section we look at the ten new rules applicable to manufacturers and suppliers of consumer goods. They are equally applicable to the providers of services, such as banks and building societies. Manufacturers generally have been slower than their retail counterparts to take advantage of the net and to exploit it as a medium. The main inhibiting factor has been that they have not wanted to upset their retail distributors. Manufacturers have feared that if they disintermediate their retail distributors they will retaliate by cutting them out of their order books and that, naturally, is something manufacturers are very anxious to avoid. This understandable caution compelled manufacturers to tread very carefully in the early stages of e-commerce. Between 1995 and 1998 they hardly embraced the net at all. If they did anything it was to place some general information about their products on a website, maybe mentioning the retail outlets they could be obtained from.

There are signs, however, that this cautious attitude on the part of manufacturers is beginning to change, for two basic reasons. One is that they have seen other more adventurous competitors taking advantage of the web and stealing a march on them. Secondly, manufacturers are beginning to see that others of their ilk have developed much more of an internet presence and still managed to retain good relations with their retail distributors. In this section we explore the ten new rules manufacturers should adopt based on current experience that will help them to pursue best practice in this area. We firstly look at five market-facing opportunities for manufacturers and then at five rules to help them take advantage of new internet technologies in the supply chain.

Five market-facing rules for manufacturers:

1   Get the product on the web

2   Get networked

3   Establish direct on-line links with customers

4   Develop a net-differentiated value proposition

5   Sell selectively on the net

Five supply chain rules for manufacturers:

6   Joint venture with other manufacturers

7   Link with own suppliers

8   Join an exchange

9   Use the net to improve productivity

10   Outsource

Rule 1 – Get the product on the web. It is pointless taking no action for fear of upsetting retail counterparts. The fact is manufacturer suppliers just cannot afford to ignore the challenge of the internet. They don't necessarily have to use it as a selling medium. But at a barest minimum it is essential to be present in the e-world and make as much of that presence as market conditions will allow. At least describe the product and make information about it widely available.

Take the examples of Sony and Toyota, which have both created very informative and entertaining websites. Sony's website incorporates games, competitions, kid zones. Even though there are only limited possibilities to buy a Sony product on line, there are still powerful reasons for visiting its website. Sony has created the sense of community and 'stickiness' we referred to earlier in this chapter. It has given Sony the chance to learn about being on the net, how to create an effective website. It has also given Sony direct access to its customers, because each customer who visits the site provides Sony with detailed information for its customer records, which is invaluable for future marketing campaigns and provides immediate market intelligence and consumer research.

Long before Toyota began to think about selling cars on-line it decided that, rather than do nothing, it would create an on-line environment that would not upset its dealers. So when it offered car promotions they were advertised on-line, not just on the telephone. People could dial 1-800 to hear the commercial or go to Toyota.com. In fact, Toyota found that with some of its promotions more people went on-line to obtain the information than used the telephone. This consumer interest prompted Toyota to go a stage further and it has since set up Gazoo.com, which has become one of Japan's most popular cyber gateways, peddling everything from brake pads to hit compact discs to horoscopes. According to *Business Week*, Toyota's Gazoo.com division 'boasts more than 50 vendors, 500,000 members and 2,000 new subscribers every day. It's so popular that almost 13,000 convenience stores want Gazoo.com terminals to go in their locations. Consumers will order stuff at Gazoo kiosks, then pay and pick up their deliveries later at the store.'

Manufacturers like Sony and Toyota have gone beyond just sticking their brochures on the web. They are providing information and entertainment and hot links to other relevant sites. It could actually be hot links to their retail partners. So, while retaining good relations with their retail partners and dealers, they are learning about the web, picking up customers and reinforcing the brand name.

Rule 2 – Get networked. There is no point keeping the website passive. Wherever possible link up with other people, while still maintaining current distribution arrangements. Link up with affiliate partnerships, as Toyota does, so that, while not necessarily selling on line, a manufacturer can still actively engage with and through other people who, for example, do sell complementary products on-line.

It is possible through the network to develop new promotions and sponsor other people's sites. The decision of Unilever and Procter &

Gamble to back teenage websites is a good example. Unilever has invested in *Wowgo*, a new on-line Europe-wide lifestyle brand for teenage girls, which was launched in 2000. The internet venture is targeted at girls aged between 12 and 16. It features a customised homepage and links to separate microsites covering issues such as health and beauty, relationships, music and entertainment. It is also being used to collect generic, non-specific data on users and trends in the teen market, which is then being sold to third companies. As a further revenue stream, Unilever is looking at potential sponsorship tie-ups with 15 to 20 partners for specific parts of the site. The Unilever initiative is expected to use the site to go head-to-head with rival Procter & Gamble, which also announced plans in 2000 to launch a teenage-focused website in conjunction with portal, Excite@Home. It was reported that the site would have a budget of several million pounds and would provide community, chat and other interactive services alongside content secured through third-party networked deals.

Rule 3 – Establish direct on-line links with customers. Manufacturer suppliers can now use the opportunity, not just to reach customers on line in the way Unilever and Procter & Gamble does, but actually to build up their own customer on-line data base. This can be valuable not just for marketing campaigns, but maybe eventually, if it is appropriate, for direct selling. The latest internet technologies facilitate this. The advances that have been made in this area were outlined in a special report in *Business Week*: 'The latest advances in software technology make it possible for companies to amass detailed profiles of customers, offer them just the things they're likely to buy, reward them for loyalty, and quell their frustrations. And, thanks to the web, companies can keep all of their information about customers in a single electronic storehouse, easily accessible through web browsers for executives at headquarters, salespeople on the road, and service reps in remote call centres. It's all about delivering TLC (tender loving care) – internet style.'

David Caruso, a vice president at market researcher AMR Research, told *Business Week*: 'Everybody is scrambling to grab the customer and not let them go.' The *Business Week* article goes on to point out that the latest internet technology promises to transform the way companies do business. 'Gone are the days when they could afford to build products without knowing for sure if customers would snap them up. Now they can learn precisely what their customers want before they design a single widget. Manufacturers can even let buyers specify the key features they would like before a product is assembled. And by using technology to track their every encounter with a customer, companies can easily separate out the best from the bad – and focus their marketing muscle on customers who are likely to buy often and pay their bills on time.'

For example, Cozone.com, an on-line computer retailer, has taken full advantage of the latest internet technology to glean data about its customers. Using Silknet's new virtual sales assistant, Cozone.com has created 'Jill – the Notebook Advisor'. It's a piece of software that walks customers through a series of questions about their lifestyles and what they're looking for in a computer – then makes recommendations. Cozone.com gathers a vast amount of data from cybershoppers and uses it later to target them with e-mail promotions. But mostly, 'Jill' is about making customers feel good about their experience so they want to come back for more. Other internet-based software packages, like Siebel, enable companies who are new to the game to develop better links with their customers, understand what their customers' needs are and manage the customer relationship more efficiently. There's no excuse for not getting close to customers.

Rule 4 – Develop a net-differentiated value proposition. When potential customers visit the net to understand more about what's on it they have certain expectations. It's not like walking into a shop. They will want a different experience, because it is a different medium. And so different value propositions need to be established (as Coca-Cola did). Think through what needs to be said and how to package it. What sense of community needs to be achieved? What contents? What games and competitions? It may be appropriate to set up distinctive websites for kids and a separate one for older customers. Again, it may not be essential to sell to them, but it is essential to come up with ideas to attract them.

One way to achieve this is to use personalised software. A company called Netperceptions, for example, has developed highly personalised software that enables companies to tailor their response to a customer's individual needs. If, for example, a company is a supplier of CDs and learns that one of its customers is interested in classical music, it can direct that person to the latest releases the minute they arrive on the website rather than making them wade through a lot of other selections before arriving at particular preferences. Companies can get customers to buy things they might not have intended to purchase if they personalise those customers' experiences enough through a developed value proposition.

Rule 5 – Sell selectively on the net. Manufacturers may have been inhibited about upsetting retailers through exploiting the net, but that does not mean manufacturers need be excluded from selling direct on line, provided they go about it in a subtle and shrewd manner. Procter & Gamble, which sells its Hugo Boss perfume over the net, illustrates how the softly, softly approach can work. Procter & Gamble's research shows its mainstream retailers that this particular line of perfume appeals only to a certain target niche and so it wants to use it for a pilot experiment. It wants to develop a community and selling environment on the net for Hugo Boss, but one where both P&G and its retailers will win because it will enhance awareness, build brand values and so total sales across the whole market will grow. P&G is attempting to create a life-style website, while at the same time selling its perfume. It reassures its retailers that it is not competing with them or trying to disintermediate them. It's a tactic that helps companies like P&G learn more about the net, little by little, rather than burying their heads in the sand, saying they are not prepared to risk upsetting their traditional outlets.

Another good example of this approach is to look at how Quaker Oats dealt with a poor selling cereal called Quisp. For a decade, the crunchy corn cereal could only be found in five and a half US cities. The half was Buffalo, where Quisp showed up in one or two groceries. With only 92,000 boxes sold over a 12 month period, the brand was barely a blip for industry-data collectors. But Quaker couldn't bring itself to pull the plug. Quisp, a cross-eyed cartoon character with a propeller on his head, whose popularity peaked in 1968, inspired nostalgia at Quaker's Chicago headquarters, reminding old hands of a time when the cereal business wasn't so competitive. So the cereal survived, albeit barely – until Quisp began its quirky quest on the internet.

It turned out that veterans at Quaker were not the only ones to feel nostalgic about the offbeat cartoon character. Quaker, which maintains websites for each of its cereal brands, noticed that www.Quisp.com was drawing far more attention than bigger brands like Cap'n Crunch and Life. Quaker's marketing department sensed an opportunity. But it needed a way to satisfy Quisp lovers without taking precious grocery-store shelf space from other Quaker cereals. To solve the problem, Quaker built a link between Quisp's website and www.netgrocer.com, an on-line retailer that sells only nonperishable grocery items and delivers them throughout the US within two days. Quisp quickly became NetGrocer's best-selling cereal, outselling even the industry titans, Cheerios and Frosted Flakes, often by ratios of two to one.

The outcome could hardly have been better for Quaker. Provided it keeps Quisp in a contained environment, it is learning a great deal about selling on-line without causing much concern among established outlets.

Rule 6 – Joint venture with other manufacturers and suppliers. As we've discussed, anything that looks to directly disintermediate retail customers is viewed as threatening by them. Often that perception among retailers is just that – a purely emotional reaction without real consideration of the underlying economics and actually how both parties can win. Because manufacturers can't stand still, what other ways are there to respond to the e-commerce challenges and opportunities?

One way might be to collaborate and joint venture with other manufacturers in the same industry. Co-operate rather than compete. Establish a joint approach that is so compelling that retailer customers just cannot resist it. They might be able to delist one brand in the category, but they can't delist them all. It's always possible as well to start to do this in a less confrontational manner and choose relatively small product categories to test the ground rather than putting the entire business range on the line.

With this approach no doubt in mind, Ford and General Motors have each launched initiatives to sell cars directly to the buying public on line. There is no suggestion there was any collusion between them but, because these two major car companies are both moving in the same direction and more or less at the same time, it becomes an industry-wide trend which defuses some of the opposition that might have come from established car dealers. They can say to their dealers that the industry is changing and they have got to change with it. By moving in this way, Ford and GM are creating an industry-wide dynamic that gives them the muscle to leverage the internet in a more positive way. Of course dealers are pushing back and even using political lobbying to assist their cause, but there's no doubt the likes of Ford and GM are putting their stakes in the e-space.

Similarly, a UK plastics manufacturer, looking for ways to avoid upsetting its traditional wholesalers, decided to create what might be called a plastics portal on the web. Visitors to the site, including its existing customers, can obtain information about plastics and other manufacturers can exhibit their plastics-related wares on it. The plastics portal is an example of a manufacturer trying to establish new routes to market and potentially new markets of distribution, but through collaboration with its supply chain, strengthening its own market position.

Rule 7 – Link with own suppliers. The Matsushita Industrial group recently announced it will set up a vast internet bazaar for most of the materials and components it buys from thousands of suppliers, in one of the biggest moves by an Asian industrial group to tap the web for efficiency gains. By March 2001, Matsushita – a conglomerate of 11 makers of products such as fax machines, VCRs and digital camcorders under brand names including Panasonic and National – expects all its manufacturing-related purchases in Japan to go through the new web-based marketplace. It is planning to bring overseas suppliers into the system at a later stage.

Given Matsushita's clout as one of Japan's dominant electronic equipment makers, the move may well inspire similar steps at other Japanese companies, which have been struggling to restructure but have been slow to weave the internet into their manufacturing operations. Matsushita plans to switch 3,000 large-scale suppliers of parts and materials to the new web-based system by March 2001. Those suppliers account for more than 98% of the parts the group procures from a total of 7,000 suppliers in Japan.

IBM is another company that is exploiting the internet to achieve greater efficiency in its dealings with its suppliers. A new on-line procurement system has eliminated five million pieces of paper a year, among other things. IBM bought $13 billion worth of goods and services over the web in 1999, saving more than $270 million. Still, IBM continues to look for ways to improve efficiency. It is getting smarter about saving money on computer parts too. It buys from suppliers who may build only a small part of the machine – say, the motherboard for a personal computer. But in the case of a motherboard, scores of microprocessors from other manufacturers go into making that part before it is delivered to IBM. So IBM asks the company making the motherboard to supply it with a list of all the chips, along with their prices and their suppliers. To do that, IBM has wired up some 12,000 suppliers to its network. All the information IBM gathers is then placed in a huge database that includes what IBM pays for every microchip or part to make other products the computer giant sells.

IBM uses data-mining software to drive down procurement costs and improve efficiency. It can see whether, for example, chip X used by its motherboard supplier is also used elsewhere in the company. The software compares the price IBM pays with what the motherboard maker spends. If IBM is getting a better deal on chip X, then IBM will go to the manufacturer of chip X and demand the motherboard maker get the same price. The motherboard maker has to lower its prices to IBM by the same amount.

Rule 8 – Join an exchange. There has been a significant new development in the B2B market during 1999 and 2000 that has seen major companies joining together to form buying exchanges. The collaborations have mostly been between corporate giants, mainly the market leaders in their respective fields. These industry giants have realised that combining their strengths leaves them less vulnerable to dotcom start-ups looking to break into their market. The trend began in the autumn of 1999 when General Motors and Ford announced plans for electronic-based B2B procurement systems. GM – together with Isuzu and Suzuki, its Japanese affiliates – teamed up with Commerce One, a leader in e-commerce software, to form TradeXchange, while Ford partnered with Oracle, the US software group to form AutoXchange.

The potential for both these systems was quickly seen as huge, reports the *Financial Times*. Both manufacturers interact with about 30,000 suppliers and the GM-Isuzu extended supply chain is thought to total about $500 billion annually, while Ford's is around $300 billion. Comments Nikki Tait of the *Financial Times*: 'Not only would the car companies' own purchasing requirements be pushed through these systems, but suppliers could also use the on-line facilities to do their sourcing, for anything from nuts and bolts to stationery.'

The car industry initiative was followed in early 2000 by the launch of a global B2B on-line exchange for the retail industry by Sears and Carrefour, two of the world's largest retailers, and Oracle, the US software group. The exchange, GlobalnetXchange, will enable retailers to buy all types of goods and services over the internet. It will handle Sears' and Carrefour's combined $80 billion annual purchases from 50,000 suppliers and will be open to all retailers – a $50 billion world market. The retail exchange, observes the *Financial Times*, provides further evidence of the rapid growth of B2B business e-commerce, which is expected to reach $2,000 billion by 2004. 'Establishing a single industry-wide exchange rather than numerous competing exchanges was critical to achieving cost savings', the retailers said. Often alternative exchanges have also been set up in this space as companies scurry to find appropriate partners.

Rule 9 – Use the net to improve productivity. Re-engineering was all the rage in the mid-1990s. But the vast and speedy internet is ushering in an even bigger wave of business transformation and cost restructuring. *Business 2.0* magazine suggests it might be called E-engineering.

'Companies realise that it is not enough to put up simple websites for customers, employees and partners. To take full advantage of the net they've got to re-invent the way they do business – changing how they distribute goods, collaborate inside the company, and deal with suppliers.

Technology companies like Intel, Dell and Cisco Systems were among the first to seize on the net to overhaul their operations. At Intel Corp, for example, web-based automation has liberated 200 sales clerks from tediously entering orders. Now they concentrate instead on analysing sales and pampering customers. Cisco Systems, for its part, handles 75% of sales on-line. And 45% of its on-line orders for networking gear never touches employees' hands. They go directly from customers to the company's software system and onto manufacturing partners. That helped Cisco hike productivity by 20% over the past two years.'

Rule 10 – Outsource. When thinking about going onto the net, take advantage of the fact that internet technologies are enabling application service providers (ASPs) to help a company make it work. Rather than investing in the software and hardware involved and having to upgrade the software at regular intervals, let the ASPs take care of it, saving the hassle. A case study reported in the *Wall Street Journal* illustrates the advantages of taking this route:

Jim Dybalski, chief executive of LoanCity.com, an on-line mortgage company based in California, set up his operation from scratch by outsourcing to an ASP. His business plan was ambitious. He wanted to build up a customer base of more than a million within a few years. Any on-line operation of that scale would require a sprawling computing centre, which in turn would require a sprawling set of resources costing millions of dollars. Dybalski decided to let someone else worry about that problem. He hired an ASP to set up and run the various enterprise resource planning (ERP) business software packages that LoanCity.com would need to handle such areas as sales, accounting and human resources. Instead of making a huge technology investment upfront, he uses the internet to connect to the applications he needs located at his ASP. 'I had six months to go from a mom-and-pop start-up to a world-class system. I don't think I could have done that myself.'

A growing number of outsource providers are vying for a piece of the on-line customer support market. Though web-based support systems are quite expensive, they can be a very worthwhile investment. For example, Cisco Systems has used on-line outsourced technical support to reduce its technical support staff by 1,000 people – most of whom were highly-paid engineers who were transferred to more complex and suitable tasks. In the past four years Cisco's sales have quadrupled, while support staff only doubled.

Outsourcing, utilising the latest internet technologies, can solve a lot of headaches, but never forget that the most important assets will remain the people. They are the intellectual capital and they will be the key in managing the relationships and driving future business success. As Don Tapscott, also writing in *Business 2.0*, puts it: 'In an economy like this, the only assets that really count are the intellectual assets – knowledge contained in the brains of knowledge workers.' And this asset needs to be nurtured even while the company is pursuing all the opportunities to capture further internet-enabled efficiencies.

*   *   *

What these 'new rules of the game' add up to is a blueprint for doing business in the twenty-first century. It is not that brands and service and customers and price and product features have suddenly become less important. They're just as critical. It's that there is now a new context in which they need to be applied, a new economic and business framework. And organisations generally need to become keenly aware of this new environment, embrace these new and additional opportunities and disciplines, and ensure they are continually evaluating their progress. The new game in town means some of the traditional barriers and boundaries are breaking down and new ones are taking their place. Understand these new rules and win. Ignore them and die.

2 Overview: The Key Conclusions

It's all happening very quickly. In just a few years since it went commercial the internet is proving to be one of the biggest phenomena business has seen. Bursting onto the scene in 1994 it has caused a major rethink on how to sell products and services to consumers. Many companies are rushing to explore this new opportunity. What potential does it hold, will it impact and if so, when?

After the initial excitement there has been an inevitable period of trial and experimentation, a gradual awakening and appreciation of the realities of electronic commerce. It can provide many advantages to the consumer, it can be a new growth vehicle, it can offer a lower cost/higher margin route to market. But it's going to take significant investment; there will be structural difficulties like payment security to be overcome and despite the hype existing technology is not yet up to the communication challenge. But how long till it will be?

The coming era of electronic commerce is in the early stages of growth. Like the VCR, the computer, the microwave and satellite TV there is a necessary period of acquaintanceship and improvement before it really takes off. This essential development is now taking place. The beginning of the twenty-first century is seeing the massive investment being made (estimated by industry observers at c. $200 billion), innovation in technology, education and awareness building with consumers, government intervention and support (especially in the USA by President Clinton and Al Gore) and the necessary experience and expertise gradually being established in operating and marketing electronically.

As we shall see, it's no longer a question of whether electronic shopping will come to change our lives. It's now simply a matter of when, and to what degree. When will it reach critical mass? Is it within existing planning horizons or can it be ignored and shelved for a few more years yet? Who will be most affected? Are all retailers vulnerable to electronic shopping trends? Will they simply be disintermediated or can they respond and not just survive but build on this new opportunity? What about manufacturers – how can they exploit the situation? And consumers – to what extent are they interested in shopping in this new way, will they *all* eventually become dedicated electronic shoppers?

There's so much change going on, the impact is so wide-ranging that we need an early summary of the specific messages and themes in this book to set the scene and establish the context. This chapter sets up the main ideas and summarises what amounts to the thirteen major research findings and insights. They are introduced here by way of initial sound-bite and brief illustration only. They are then explained in detail with case studies and the research more fully examined through the subsequent chapters of the book.

These are the key findings and conclusions:

1. The revolution in electronic shopping *is* going to happen
2. It's going to have a major impact on the shopping and retailing scene
3. Already c. 15–20% of consumers say they'd prefer to shop electronically rather than visit the shops
4. It only takes a drop of c. 15% in store traffic to make many stores unprofitable
5. This revolution will achieve critical mass by as early as 2005
6. As store visits reduce, some shops are in danger of dying out; mid-sized high streets and malls are the most vulnerable
7. From supermarkets to banks, nearly all retailers will be affected
8. Companies should quickly assess the potential impact on their business using the 'ES Test' set out in Chapter 6
9. Not all is lost! Retailers can survive and succeed but need to decide which of the ten identified strategic options they are going to pursue
10. Manufacturers can seize the opportunity to decide whether to establish their own direct consumer distribution and bypass existing retail chains
11. The electronic environment will demand new marketing skills
12. Future success urgently requires the development of a clear long-term strategy . . .
13. . . . and rigorous implementation and communication.

Let's now consider in a little more detail each of these key messages:

1. The revolution in electronic shopping *is* going to happen

All the evidence points to an unstoppable momentum, an inexorable force that will drive electronic commerce forward and reach out to make it so pervasive and accessible that it can't fail to impact shopping habits:

- 'President Clinton has announced his personal support for a five year programme to develop the internet as a universal medium open to everyone. The White House will fund the program in its first year with a near $1bn commitment.'

  (*Reuters News Service*)

- VP Al Gore is targeting every classroom in the country to be connected to the internet. 'It's an enormous effort, comparable to building the nation's roads and railways but it's essential.'

  (*Reuters News Service*)

- 'A new generation is growing up digital. In 2001 there will be more than 88 million people in US and Canada between the ages of 2 and 22. They are the kids who are leading the charge using the new media that's centered around the internet. This Net Generation is developing and imposing its culture on us thereby reshaping how society and individuals interact.'

  (*Don Tapscott, author of 'Growing up Digital'*)

- 'In 1999, 28 million US households were wired to the net. Through 2000 this will rise to 40 million.'

  (*Business Week*)

- '40% of households in the major Asian economies will be connected to the internet by 2002.'

  (*NUA internet survey, 2000*)

- 'Communication bandwidths will rise exponentially and hardware equipment will become simultaneously more powerful, sophisticated, easier to use, affordable and portable. Once the hardware and telecommunications infrastructure has been established, an enormous range of services can be exchanged at nominal incremental cost, such as location-independent shopping and banking.'

  (*Jagdish Sheth, Professor of Marketing, Goizueta Business School, Emory University*)

- 'There's no doubt that over the next five years, electronic shopping will become an important facility for customers. Too many people are investing too much money for that not to happen.'

  (*VP of former Burton Group, UK $4bn clothing retailer*)

2. It's going to have a major impact on the shopping and retailing scene

Commentators on the marketplace have no doubt about the potential. It's not going to be just another distribution channel or an experience confined to 35-year-old male computer nerds. It's going to become a mass medium for communication, interaction and all forms of buying and selling:

- The internet is a tidal wave. It will wash over nearly all industries drowning those who don't learn to swim in its waves.'

  (*Bill Gates, CEO of Microsoft*)

- 'It won't be too long before 20 to 30% of households will be buying electronically. This will mean boundless potential for bypassing traditional distributors.'

  (*Andrew Grove, CEO of Intel*)

- 'Retailing will never be the same – home shopping will revolutionise retailing'

  (*Business Week*)

- 'Virtual stores are the future. They are the natural extension of the ECR [Efficient Consumer Response] initiative to streamline the logistics of getting products from manufacturers to consumers.'

  (*Raymond Burke, Professor of Business Administration, Indiana University*)

- 'One third of consumers interviewed said they expected to do most of their shopping in the future via the telephone, internet or television.'

  (*Bossard Consultants research*)

3. Already c. 15–20% of consumers say they'd prefer to shop electronically rather than visit the shops

Consumer research shows significant numbers of people instinctively appreciate the benefits of shopping electronically. Many have busy lives and struggle to find enough time to do things. Shopping is often a hassle and regular purchases are commonly seen as a chore. In this era of time poverty many would prefer to have the opportunity for leisure, sport or relaxation. The underlying convenience of electronic shopping is just too tempting to ignore:

- '– 13% of consumers actively hate going shopping
  – In total 16% of consumers said they 'generally dislike shopping'
  – As many as 31% of all consumers would classify themselves as "reluctant shoppers" finding the experience "not really enjoyable".'

  (Mintel research)

- '19.4% of all shoppers said that "if there was a grocery shopping and delivery service in my area I would use it".'

  (A. C. Nielsen research)

- '32% of people who say they don't have enough time to go shopping – a group classified in the research as "frenzied copers" – said they would be interested in home delivery.'

  (A. C. Nielsen research)

- 'Consumer acceptance of non-store retailing is already high. 45% of US households and 58% of UK households purchase products from catalogs or buy via television each year.'

  (Verdict Home Shopping report)

4. It only takes a drop of c. 15% in store traffic to make many stores unprofitable

Retail margins are often wafer thin. 2–3% is quite common and UK averages of 5–6% plus are not the international norm. In these circumstances retailers are very vulnerable to relatively small shifts and reductions in the number of people who visit and shop at the store:

- 'It will only take a 10–20 percentage point shift in the retail market from the high street to home to eliminate most retailers' profit margin.'

  (Goldman Sachs research)

- 'Even a 10% loss in consumers visiting our stores would be a worry. For many of our outlets that would push us below breakeven.'

  (Managing Director of $2bn plus retail group)

- 'Average retailer margins will be eliminated by a 15–20% reduction in consumer traffic through their stores. It is far from clear that this margin loss can be made up by capturing the electronic purchasing instead. Consumers may buy from an alternative provider.'

   (*CSC Kalchas research*)

- 'Even a small shift in purchases from traditional to virtual stores will have dramatic implications for retailers and manufacturers.'

   (*Professor Raymond Burke*)

5.   This revolution will achieve critical mass by as early as 2005

Forecasters vary widely in their predictions on the growth of electronic shopping. Many foresaw an explosion of interest reaching significant levels by as early as the end of the twentieth century. Since the initial hype more measured assessment has taken place. Most now agree that it is in this decade that the real growth will come. It will happen as the electronic environment begins to move out of its experimental phase into its first era of maturity. The infrastructure will be much more widespread and technology will have reached a greater level of sophistication offering much easier to use yet higher quality electronic communication Companies will have begun to learn how to make real the convenience and added value of electronic shopping:

- 'Through 2000 a third of the most attractive households will be ready to buy on line.'

   (*McKinsey*)

- 'The combination of technology sophistication, equipment power and ease of use plus the supporting infrastructure will make electronic purchasing widespread in the US by the year 2005.'

   (*Jagdish Sheth, Professor of Marketing, Goizueta Business School*)

- 'According to the CBI [Britain's major industry association], the internet technology available in 10 years [2007] will be sufficient and widespread enough to outstrip the high street in terms of sales.'

   (*Internet Business report*)

- 'There will be a new wave of growth around the middle of this decade responding to new user-friendly easy access low cost technology. It will enable the 15–20% hard core of "reluctant shoppers" who dislike going to the store to become near dedicated electronic shoppers instead.'

(CSC Kalchas research)

● 'Electronic retailing will grow inexorably thru this decade. By 2010 it may account for as many as 25% of US retail sales.'
(Professors Louis W. Stern and Barton A. Weitz)

● 'Non store retailing could account for as much as 55% of "total retail sales" by 2010.'
(Kurt Salmon Associates)

● 'In 30 to 40 years time (around 2030) there may be no shops at all.'
(Maurice Saatchi)

6. As store visits reduce, some shops are in danger of dying out; mid-sized high streets and malls are the most vulnerable

As it gets easier to purchase electronically so by definition the number of store visits will reduce. When consumers do go out to shop the basics will already have been delivered. They'll be looking for a new type of shopping experience. Expectations will be different. They'll demand new things, a wide range of choices, the opportunity to relax and enjoy themselves combining that with other leisure, social and entertainment activities. In that regard the big supermarkets, the larger malls and high streets have more space and more flexibility to respond. Small high streets and shopping areas just won't be able to meet consumers' widening needs and expectations:

● 'A quarter of British people believe the traditional local high street is bound for extinction because of the growth of home shopping.'
(Bossard Consultants research)

● 'The internet will drive half of today's retailers out of business.'
(Research by International Business Development Corp.)

● 'By 2010 there may not be much left of the high street.'
(Eat Soup magazine)

- 'Shifts from traditional to virtual stores will have dramatic implications. I expect you'll have left warehouses and then you'll have 7–11s and that would be it. All the major stuff would come out of these central locations. You'd be interested in the cheapest cost for the product that you want. Then you go to the convenience store for the last minute things that you need.'

  (Research input to Professor Raymond Burke)

- 'Consumers are clearly looking for a way to divide shopping for staples distinct from browsing for fresh/novelty/impulse/luxury purchases.'

  (Financial Times Management report)

7. From supermarkets to banks, nearly all retailers will be affected

The electronic shopping phenomenon is not restricted just to grocery. It cuts across all retail consumer sectors, with financial services one of the most vulnerable areas. Basic banking and insurance have already proved popular sellers not just on the internet but simply by using phone or fax. The number of new entrants dedicated to electronic selling is growing rapidly and can be found in just about every area of consumer activity:

- 'Products and services bought on line range from software as currently the most popular through to books, music, electrical and electronic goods, food and clothing.'

  (Verdict Electronic Shopping report)

- 'Clothing sales already dominate mail order shopping, evidence that clothing can also succeed on line and that consumers are prepared to buy *before* trying.'

  (Verdict)

- 'Consumers are flocking to us and some of our most popular food lines are fresh fruit and vegetables ahead of other packaged goods.'

  (US grocery/food distributor offering electronic shopping services)

- 'Direct Line (the UK insurer) have demonstrated the attractiveness of selling insurance over the phone. Their fast rise to market leadership shows consumers are happy buying over the wires.'

  (Internet Business)

• 'First Direct telephone banking is growing new customers at more than 20% per annum and many are now describing their banking as a "pleasurable experience".'

(*Marketing Week*)

• '$8bn worth of entertainment and travel tickets will be bought on line in the US in 2001.'

(*Jupiter Communications research*)

• 'Computer hardware company Dell reports selling $20 million-plus worth of computer products a day over the internet.' This is increasing all the time.

(*Forrester research, 2000*)

8. Companies should quickly assess the potential impact on their business using the 'ES Test' set out in Chapter 6

In Chapter 6, the 'ES (Electronic Shopping) Test' is described. It sets out a framework to decide which products and services are most susceptible to being sold electronically. The test provides a guide to retailers and suppliers. Are they in a product/service field which will be untouched by the electronic revolution? Or are they operating in an area which will be particularly attractive to the would-be electronic consumer? Is there a need to change urgently or can they simply wait and see? The ES test offers a simple and practical way of determining the impact of these new market forces. It has three components examining: (1) Product characteristics of touch, taste, smell, etc; (2) Consumer familiarity and confidence with the particular product/service and (3) individual consumer interest and demand for 'convenient shopping':

• 'Products which traditionally need to be **touched**, **tasted** or **smelled** are prima facie less likely to sell well on line. But products and services without those characteristics or where they are of low importance will have electronic appeal.'

(*CSC Kalchas research*)

• 'Where consumers are **familiar** with the product or trust the brand name they'll be more comfortable buying by phone, PC or TV.'

(*Professor Sunil Gupta, University of Michigan*)

- 'The search for **convenience** will be a major driver. The modern consumer is often described as overworked, stressed and time-poor. But they are demanding. Those for whom convenience is important will respond to the virtual store that can deliver satisfactorily.'

(*FT Management report*)

9. Not all is lost! Retailers can survive and succeed but need to decide which of the ten identified strategic options they are going to pursue

Research and testing has shown there are up to ten alternative strategies that are available to retailers in choosing their response to the electronic revolution. In Chapter 8 these ten strategies are described and evaluated. They range from a relatively low-key response through to aggressive investment in the new medium. But there are also options to 'buck the electronic trend' and reinvent the role and value-added of the physical retail estate:

- 'Retailers are allegedly frightened by the implications of responding to the threat of electronic shopping. If they set up their own websites will they simply cannibalise their store sales? . . . they have made massive investments in their physical infrastructure. Should they now jeopardise all that and undermine long-established customer relationships?'

(*Verdict*)

- 'Retailers can continue to develop and transform their existing retail channels. For example the four main UK grocery multiples have aggressive store expansion plans. These will provide competition to the internet.'

(*FT Management report*)

- 'Retailers must decide what are the innate characteristics for their products or services and whether they are easily susceptible to being bought electronically. With that input they can decide whether they need ultimately to abandon their real estate or whether they can still make it work.'

(*CSC Kalchas research*)

- 'Retailers do have the choice whether to be active or passive. Either choice has however to be creatively and comprehensively followed through.'

  (*Professor Fred Phillips, Oregon Graduate Institute*)

10. Manufacturers can seize the opportunity to decide whether to establish their own direct consumer distribution and bypass existing retail chains

Manufacturers have spent the past twenty years dominated by their retail customers. They have been pushed for bigger discounts, squeezed on shelf space, seen private label initiatives copying their own product innovations even down to similar looking packaging. Electronic shopping presents them with an opportunity to fight back and re-establish their links with their end user. Rather than continue to struggle with retail distributors they could deal direct. In evaluating their options a further set of ten alternative strategies, this time tailored for manufacturer suppliers can be identified. They range from 'sticking to their knitting' through to establishing their own home delivery operation as their principal means of distribution:

- 'If your company deals through agents, wholesalers or retailers it's time to do some serious strategising . . . All those roles can be disintermediated . . . food producers won't need supermarkets when customers can replenish supplies weekly by accumulating entries in their shopping list database and take delivery at home . . . . hotels won't need travel agents.

  Take the case of consumer goods manufacturers being squeezed by giant retailers like Wal-Mart. They could use the new infrastructure to sell direct over the net. An electric tool and appliance company like Black & Decker could provide interactive programs for a fee on say home renovations featuring their tools and offer an immediate purchasing facility.'

  (*Don Tapscott, The Digital Economy*)

- 'Manufacturers are reacting to the pressure tactics of traditional retailers by seeking direct links to end-users through the internet and mail order operations . . . Apparel and accessory designers such as Donna Karan, Giorgio Armani and Liz Claiborne . . . Nike and Sony . . . Airlines for example, are letting consumers book reservations bypassing travel agents . . . many consumer products manufacturers have created sites on the web, hoping this link to consumers will ultimately permit them to reduce or eliminate their dependence on retailers and dealers.'

(*Professor Nirmalya Kumar, IMD*)

- 'Some manufacturers will start building up their direct capabilities (Procter & Gamble and Unilever are two examples) and retailers will have to play to their strengths if they are to compete.'

(*FT Management report*)

11. The electronic environment will demand new marketing skills

Consumers will have much greater choice. They won't be dependent on buying from those shops they can physically access within reasonable drive times. They can buy whenever and wherever with a choice all over the globe. In addition, electronic shopping offers them the chance to set up a very personalised relationship with their internet or other electronic provider who can respond by tailoring their offerings to individual segments of one. Marketing will have to become more selective and segmented, general mass advertising and communication may be too generic and miss the target. But brand awareness will remain vital. Guiding consumers to the specific website will be a new challenge and making it easy once they get there the most critical point of leverage:

- 'Marketers who are unprepared for this sea change we're about to experience won't survive. But those who do grasp the implications and get ahead of the curve will emerge more competitive. They'll be forced to build relationships with consumers that are deeper and more enduring than any we can create today.'

(*Bob Wehling, Senior VP at Procter & Gamble*)

- 'Companies still have a lot to learn about effectively marketing on the web. Currently it is hard to find retailers' websites. They can only work if customers know exactly where to go to find the products they want. Try looking for "retailers of groceries" in the web's best search engines and you're going to be disappointed ("no matches" is the response). Try searching for "food and detergent in Birmingham" and you will suffer the same fate. Being in exactly the place where most consumers will look for what you sell is the essence of location,

location, location. Being available on line but impossible to find falls a long way short of that.'

(Verdict electronic shopping report)

- 'The expanding global electronic marketplace has powerful implications. The introduction of interactive media and the on-line environment has made real-time, customised one-to-one advertising, marketing and commerce possible. Interactive multimedia can no longer be considered an afterthought when developing an integrated marketing campaign.'

(Margo Komenar, Electronic Marketing)

- 'Almost 30 years ago, AT&T pioneered the first steps in electronic marketing with the invention of the 800 number. Now the merger of the communications and computing industries is transforming the way the world works, sells and gets its information and has created a platform on which marketers can create new value for their businesses.'

(John Petrillo, Executive VP, AT&T)

- 'The web gives us an immediate global reach but also the opportunity to customise what we offer to a market segment of one.'

(Jeremy Silver, Virgin Records)

12. Future success urgently requires the development of a clear long-term strategy ...

This new market challenge in one respect is no different from any other. Success can be achieved only if companies confront it and determine to work on developing a clearly thought-through plan of action. Immersion in the market place, understanding customers' needs and wants in a comprehensive and rigorous way, identifying the various options and evaluating which will have the best leverage – these are all critical steps any current player in the retail scene must now go through:

- 'Companies that plan their way through emerge as winners. "Visionary companies" outperformed their industry rivals on average by a factor of six on the basis of stock market returns on investment.'

(Collins and Porras)

- 'Nowadays we are having to make ever bigger bets in our investments
. . . we can't afford to back one direction and then find out five years
later it was wrong . . . so strategy is our most important management
issue.'

  (Chairman of United Parcel Services)

- 'The market place has become saturated with competition. New
products and new market channel opportunities are emerging with
increasing frequency in every industry. Mapping the way through this
market maze is an enormous challenge. Winning companies are ones
who are seizing that challenge firmly in both hands and with every
effort. They are developing a long term plan and vision of what they
want to achieve and in detail how they are going to get there.'

  (Foreword to Strategy in Crisis, 1997)

- 'Key to growth is the development of a clear, long term strategy.'

  (Coopers & Lybrand/Sunday Times research)

- 'Those that do well in the electronic market place will be those who
best understand their customers . . . and develop an effective game
plan to evolve and meet their needs.'

  (Professor Joseph Hair, Institute of Business Studies,
  Louisiana State University)

13. . . . and rigorous implementation and communication

Strategic thinking and planning, setting the framework and plan for the
future – that's the first half of the equation. Next comes the most difficult
task of pursuing it forcibly, getting the workforce to buy-in to the targets,
feel motivated and involved and wanting to go the extra mile, then being
able to stick to targets and hit milestones – all part of the challenging path
of making things happen and adapting to change. For some companies
this may result in significant upheaval and new investment in systems and
skills. But given the way electronic commerce is moving and the speed of
its development there may be no choice:

- 'Corporations are learning that handsome returns come directly from
a superior combination of strategic planning and strategic execution.'

  (Professors Bartlett and Ghoshal)

- 'Effective business leaders of today communicate a compelling and believable strategy and vision of where they want the company to go and understand what role and responsibility their workforce has in getting the company there.'

  (*Charles Handy*)

- 'If people are to put out the extraordinary effort required to realise corporate targets then they must be able to identify with them and share in the ideas and goals they represent.'

  (*Jack Welch, GE*)

- 'All the things in the value chain need to work effectively to deliver the best possible experience for our customers . . . to add customer value a firm cannot just sell a product, it must also service what it sells.'

  (*Kenneth Hill, VP, Dell Computer Corporation*)

- 'Existing mail order companies have a head start in electronic commerce. They already have a well-developed highly experienced infrastructure experienced in dealing with customers remotely, handling any complaints, packing goods safely and delivering reliably. In effect they have developed a high performance fulfilment operation which will set a benchmark for others moving down this path.'

  (*FT Management report*)

*   *   *

Electronic commerce *is* clearly going to be part of everyday business life. It will be one of the primary dynamics as this first decade of the twenty-first century unfolds. Even today the pace of change is extraordinary. Every week there is a new improvement being announced in the technology, equipment is getting cheaper and the reach of the internet is widening through TV as well as PC access. Consumer life-styles are becoming if anything more pressurised for time not less, thus accelerating the search for convenience and the need to find enjoyment in what little spare time can be carved out.

The present relatively low levels of purchasing on-line cannot be used as an excuse for inaction. They are a temporary state of affairs while the technology improves and the investments poured in during the last few years begin to bear fruit. The analysis described in this book shows that the middle of this decade will be a key period in the development of electronic buying and selling. 2005 is the date being pinpointed. By that stage many of the experimentation and teething problems will have been sorted out. Business generally will be in a far more capable state to exploit the new medium and find new sources of advantage and business growth with target customers.

No business can afford to stand still. The 'ES test' can be used to pinpoint the extent of the 'danger' – but also the opportunities. The 'ten strategies' evaluation can be reviewed to help fix on the most appropriate and leveraged course of action. As always the winners will inevitably be those who grasp the nettle most firmly, develop the most rigorous understanding of their customers and end-consumers and be so in touch with their marketplaces that they can almost anticipate what initiatives and moves will work. Combine clear planning with rigorous implementation – in theory at least a straightforward formula – and the potential is there for growth and success in the electronic marketplace.

*   *   *

Structure of the book

Following this Introduction and overview, Chapter 3 stands back for a moment to set some context for this electronic shopping review. Some definitions need to be made for the terminology employed and some emphasis and priority described in considering different industry sectors.

Chapter 4 is one of example and illustration. There's a lot going on in the electronic arena. Traditional mail order houses are not standing still and are rapidly developing their on-line capabilities. Many manufacturer suppliers are quietly but determinedly establishing their websites and learning how to market over the net. The retail community is at the forefront of many new initiatives and is trialling electronic ordering. New entrants, unencumbered by existing physical infrastructures, are emerging with exciting and dedicated on-line offerings. What's the extent of all this activity and what learnings are already accumulating in the market place?

Chapter 5 examines the evidence and looks to pinpoint when electronic shopping is likely to reach critical mass. While the USA is some way ahead, the UK and Germany are setting the pace in Europe and the major Asian economies are not far behind. The middle of this decade, c. 2005, is likely to represent an important stage in the evolution of the technology and the infrastructure.

How can a retailer or manufacturer analyse if its products and services are vulnerable to these forces of electronic shopping and if so, to what degree and how immediate is the threat? Chapter 6 sets out the 'ES Test' which provides a framework for defining the need and extent of the response required.

In this new era, the challenge facing established retailers is enormous. But they have had a history of successful evolution. They have been pioneers of developments in the supply chain. Through self-service in the 1950s through to hand-held scanning and bar code terminals they have themselves fundamentally changed consumer shopping habits and expectations. Are they now equipped to respond adequately to electronic shopping developments? Does their leading position in the distribution chain make it easier for them to evolve and retain the consumer relationship? What kind of platform do they have to build on in responding to these new challenges? This is examined in Chapter 7.

Chapter 8 sets out the range of responses retailers can choose from. There are ten alternative strategies that can be defined. The message is that no retailer can afford to ignore these market developments.

One strategy moving forward is for retailers to stick with their real estate but transform it so consumers still want to visit, despite the home shopping temptations. The successful 'store of the future' – Chapter 9 – will need to represent a completely new experience. It is unlikely to be just about getting the goods off a shelf and paying for them at the check-out. If the real estate is to continue to add value, retailers must rethink the way the space they have can be utilised. How can it meet changing needs and expectations? How can it be evolved to provide a new and exciting experience? Can major supermarkets, for example, establish and capture some role that continues to lock them firmly into the hearts of their 'local community' and catchment area? In fact, can they achieve an even more entrenched position? We can illustrate by looking at one kind of 'store of the future'.

Chapters 10–12 set out in more detail what's driving the developments of electronic shopping and why it appears unstoppable. Executional difficulties such as individual privacy and security of payment are gradually being resolved. Indeed the view has been expressed that 'payment for goods over the internet will soon be more secure than the regular use of credit cards for ordering over the phone or in the mail'. Chapter 10 especially looks at how the technology and infrastructure are moving forward and how improvements in what can be transmitted over ordinary telephone cable, the possibility of using the electricity grid and developments in satellite communication will all accelerate reach and penetration into more households as well as enhancing the visual quality of what can be communicated.

In Chapters 13 and 14 there is a review of how manufacturer suppliers could now look to take advantage of the new medium. Like their retail counterparts they have a range of options and a further set of ten alternative strategies can be defined and described.

The final Chapters 15 and 16 consider what it will take to be a winner in the new electronic environment. Responding to the changing scene will require investment and carry risk. Some tough decisions will inevitably have to be made, some sacred cows abandoned. Key to determining the most leveraged response will come from being market and customer rooted, so understanding the market place that the company is totally in touch with its customers. Rigorous assessment will help determine whether and how critical it is to respond electronically. Market opportunities can be prioritised and clear plans and strategies pinned down. As understanding crystallises so companies can better determine when to start changing and how best to transition from where they are to where they will need to be.

Mapping the path through the new market challenges is going to be critical. Clarity in thinking and in direction-setting will naturally help the workforce appreciate the new direction, get them more involved and motivated behind the new targets and more committed to go the extra mile to achieve them. Electronic commerce is likely to be one of the most fundamental changes business will face and there will be an additional premium on putting the necessary time and resources into developing the best response and way forward.

3 Definitions and Consumer Trends

Some brief definitions and explanations are required before moving into the detail of what retailers and manufacturers are doing about the electronic revolution and how they can best respond.

This chapter looks at:

- a definition of electronic shopping
- the products and services included
- underlying themes behind all the changes.

Definitions

In defining the various terms and expressions, it's important to immediately set out what is meant and included in 'electronic shopping'. In fact it incorporates a wide range of different media or what can be described as different electronic connections (Table 3.1). The internet is but one of these, though emerging as by far and away the most prominent. (For reference the term 'electronic shopping' will be used frequently through the book and will sometimes be abbreviated to 'ES' .)

Table 3.1   Electronic Shopping Connections

• Communication/access devices	TV, radio, PC, phone, fax, ATM, interactive kiosk, pager, personal digital organiser
• Content media	catalogue, CD Rom, teletext, world wide web, terrestrial and satellite broadcasts

Products and services

These 'electronic connections' cover a wide range of commercial transactions but the focus here is on the consumer. The aim is to look at the interface and interaction between retailers and end-users, how that might be changed by these new market forces and the role and opportunity for manufacturer suppliers in that context.

55

Consumer shopping covers almost every retail product area and a number of specified retail services. The detail is set out in Table 3.2. In principle, all the areas listed will be exposed to some electronic selling and buying and so need to be investigated.

Table 3.2   Consumer Products and Services

Products	• Grocery including meat, fruit and vegetables • Clothing • Footwear • Music • Books • Computer hardware, software • Household appliances • Brown and white goods (e.g. HiFi and washing machines) • Sporting goods • Camera and photographic supplies	• Confectionery • Bakery • Home improvement and building materials (DIY) • Garden products • Furniture • Furnishings • Motor vehicle and bike retailing • Auto supplies • Pharmacy and OTC (over the counter)
	– Eating and drinking places are excluded	
Services	• Retail banking • Personal insurance • Financial advice • Stocks/mutual funds • Travel • Holidays • Entertainment tickets • Home education	• Real estate • Consumer information • General information services

The grocery sector will often be used to provide examples and illustration. This is for a number of reasons:

- Grocery sales are a substantial part of all retail sales. In the USA some $400 billion is spent on grocery, about 20% of total sales. In the UK the proportion accounted for by grocery is closer to 25%.
- It is estimated that around half of the world's population is involved in the production, distribution or sale of food products.
- Time spent by consumers in buying grocery products is considerable, on average making 2.5 trips to the store each week.
- Research shows c. 80% of items bought are simply replenishment purchases (e.g. milk, bread, paper towels, soft drinks).
- According to a 1990 University of Michigan study, consumers ranked grocery shopping as one of the least enjoyable daily activities!

Underlying themes

A number of case studies will be discussed through the book. They will illustrate and reflect a set of underlying trends in the marketplace which are fuelling not only the development of electronic shopping but also a transformation in commerce and daily life. These underlying trends (Table 3.3) will often be referred to in more detail but some brief introduction and explanation is also required early on.

Table 3.3   Key Underlying Trends Behind Electronic Shopping

- Consumer time poverty
- Consumers looking to take control
- Convergence of technologies
- Shift from physical to digital
- Shift from assets to knowledge

Consumer time poverty

In today's pressured environment it has been well documented that people suffer from 'time poverty'. There is luxury of choice but chronically less time to indulge. 'Spare time' is more precious and consumers are constantly searching for products or services that help save time, improve life-styles or make it easier to do things. Shopping electronically once it's made easy may be just what consumers have been waiting for.

Consumers looking to take control

In the context of time poverty, consumers don't want to be dependent on shop opening hours or physical location of the retailers. They want to be able to buy what they want when they want it. As *USA Today* pointed out in a recent article, we are moving into an 'I want it now' society. Consumers of today are now better educated and more sophisticated than their predecessors. They are more demanding, expectations of service and convenience are high and they search restlessly for new ways of meeting these needs.

Convergence of technologies

The overall structure of the economy is changing. A new industrial sector is emerging from the convergence among computing, communications and content companies. It's creating a multimedia industry of more than $1 trillion with computing companies leading the way. It's the combination of these technologies and skills, the alliances and partnerships between companies from the different sectors and the billions of dollars of investment that is going to revolutionise what can be achieved in electronic commerce.

Shift from physical to digital

Information flows used to be all physical, typically on paper such as cash, cheques, invoices, catalogues and shopping lists. In hard copy form transmission and processing times are slowed. Now the information superhighway is seeing the conversion of what was physical into bits stored in computers that are inter-networked across the globe and can communicate instantly.

Shift from assets to knowledge

Retailers' current business is built upon their assets. Their leasehold or freehold sites are often in high-cost real estate and interiors have been expensively kitted out. But the new electronic economy is based upon knowledge not assets. It's about the exploitation of information and know-how without reference to physical location. Now companies can enter the market place and transact with consumers without the expensive infrastructure. It's going to put increasing pressure on existing real estate distributors.

*   *   *

These terms and definitions form part of the basic lexicon of electronic shopping. There's a whole new world taking shape and as it does so a new vocabulary for commerce will develop with it. We will all become increasingly familiar with dotcoms, websites, interactive media, search engines and browsers. We will all gradually become wired up and on line and in touch with a new electronic age. It's already a recognisable and fashionable *lingua franca* among the new generation of net kids and others are latching on. The general mass media of press and TV is typically quick to embrace and popularise new ideas and soon large numbers of consumers will be going 'electronic' .

4 Learning from the Pioneers in Electronic Selling

The retail shopping scene is already changing. At the leading edge it's moving from casual flirtation with electronic shopping to much more serious investigation. It's developing in profile from a pet project for the marketing department to an opportunity that the whole organisation (especially in the areas of marketing, logistics and systems) will need to come to terms with and integrate into future plans.

There are a number of companies who are beginning to emerge as leaders in the new arena, pioneering change in their industry sectors and looking to establish new forms of advantage and differentiation in their market place. They see electronic commerce as exciting, not as a threat. They are innovating and ready to take 'constructive risks'. They are proactively investing and investigating. They want to be recognised by their customers as being at the forefront of their industry and doing all they can to strengthen their product service value proposition.

Who are these industry pioneers and adventurers? How are they changing the rules in their sectors? What are their strategies, what lessons can be learnt for others who are looking to come in and explore these new electronic opportunities? This chapter investigates those companies who are among the most innovative and proactive. It also considers the impact already being achieved through the general level of trial and experimentation.

Industry pioneers

There are some eight corporations who stand out in the field of consumer electronic commerce. Several of these did not need the advent of the internet to awaken their interest. They were already tapping into consumer needs for convenience and added value by exploiting very successfully the 'old-fashioned' electric connections of phone, fax or TV. Others have taken the internet as their catalyst and are at the forefront in their direct to consumer interaction.

The eight companies which deserve the accolade of 'pioneers' are:

- Direct Line
- 1-800-FLOWERS
- First Direct
- QVC
- Dell
- Levi's
- Amazon.com
- Tesco.

These eight companies will now be discussed in turn.

Direct Line

Direct Line was established in the UK in the mid-1980s and in the fifteen years of its existence has rocked the insurance industry, driving former market leaders into share decline and profit loss. It has changed the way consumers buy auto and household insurance. Insurers in other countries have watched these developments with growing anxiety and many have been investigating what strategy they might adopt if and when the same phenomenon takes place in their own domestic arena. Direct Line's former CEO Peter Wood is planning a new assault on the US market, focusing in on certain states and consumer segments and looking to accelerate the revolution in the US domestic insurance market.

What did Direct Line do that was so revolutionary? Simply, it dealt direct with the consumer. The company advertised on TV and in the press and encouraged consumers to phone or fax in. By cutting out the middle agents, brokers and distributors it saved costs on infrastructure and third-party profit share. It translated those cost savings into aggressive advertising to build awareness and supplemented that with sophisticated consumer targeting techniques, eschewing high-risk policies and majoring on age groups with safer track records.

By the mid-1990s, just around seven years after launch Direct Line had achieved UK market leadership. Its competitors, initially slow to respond on the basis this would be 'just another marketing channel', have all now rushed to set up their own direct operations. They have realised that it's no longer just about alternative channels – 'direct' has now become the principal way of selling and buying personal lines insurance.

What were the reasons behind Direct Line's success? Its key was to fully fund and resource its market initiative. It realised it had to change consumer buying patterns, it recognised that that was a tough but feasible target in the market circumstances and that it would need to create high levels of awareness and reassurance. As a result there was considerable investment in advertising, building up the brand and establishing an accessible and friendly direct phone operation with consumers. Direct Line knew that half-hearted efforts in this direction would lead to failure. It had to break through the noise barrier. It had to break the mould if it was to succeed. What was also in Direct Line's favour was that it could enter this market greenfield. It had no established branch and agency infrastructure resisting the change and pulling it back to 'old ways' of doing business. It could set its sights, exploit its full investment and inexorably grow its direct operation.

Direct Line's rivals, the long-established insurance groups, have not had this greenfield luxury. While they have not sat idly by, many have struggled to make their direct initiatives a success. They find themselves stuck with conflicts of interest – established intermediary channels pulling one way, 'direct to consumer' opportunities pointing them on an alternative path. A main challenge now is learning to manage this 'channel conflict': how to take advantage of the new market opportunities without totally cannibalising or undermining existing operations.

Can that be achieved? There is learning and experience to suggest it can and this will be examined in detail in Chapters 7 and 13. But the key will lie around segmentation, around so understanding different customer needs and desired ways of purchasing that a targeted differentiated marketing and distribution programme can be confidently and persuasively pursued.

1-800-FLOWERS

1-800-FLOWERS is another electronic success that did not need the internet to get started. It has built a flourishing business on the back of the 1-800 free phone number ('the first truly electronic marketing tool' according to its inventors at AT&T).

Its goals have been to build a fast but friendly service operation 'making human contact and connections'. It has grown rapidly ('we didn't need to build a nationwide chain of stores'). Since it was set up in

1985, 1-800-FLOWERS has become the world's largest florist. It has more than $300 million in sales and over 2000 employees.

Jim McCann, the company's President, has often been described as a pioneer ready to 'break business rules'. He realised that a major challenge would be to get people comfortable with buying flowers over the phone, when they couldn't see, touch or smell the product beforehand. With that in mind he established and heavily promoted the '100% Quality and Assurance guarantee' that promised the flowers would be fresh and last a full week or money would be refunded. The company went out of its way in its early days to build up consumer comfort and confidence. It added follow-up telephone surveys to check on satisfaction with both customers and recipients and set up a substantial programme of local education classes about flowers as a way of finding out what customers wanted, what was working and what needed improvement.

Once the internet started developing as a commercial network, 1-800-FLOWERS was in a prime position to take advantage. It had the electronic shopping know-how. It had the infrastructure in place. There has been little room for any new comers to try to usurp the company's position as the 'electronic seller of flowers'. In its first year of marketing its website, 1-800-FLOWERS added an additional $30 million to sales. 'We are truly interactive . . . our stores on the web are as important to us as brick and mortar retail stores in local markets. But we have found that people consider us a more convenient location.'

First Direct

First Direct Bank (a UK subsidiary of the Hong Kong and Shanghai Banking Corporation) has been a patient and steady developer of telephone banking services, following in the footsteps of leader Citibank in the USA.

While rivals stood by or offered basic call-centre services, First Direct has built up a sophisticated telephone and PC banking operation and a customer base of nearly 1 million UK households. It offers a low cost 'bank when you please' service. It's particularly targeting the 'frenzied coper' (see Chapter 10), the busy executive or 'person on the move' who doesn't have time to visit the branch between 9.30am and 4.00pm Monday to Friday.

Its success lies not just in the convenience of its service but most particularly in the way that service is carried out: 'it makes banking a pleasure', 'I can call up any time and they always answer immediately and are friendly and efficient', 'they've got a good database and know what I need'. It is principally a result of their service excellence that their reputation and business is growing. 'We're currently adding new customers at the rate of 20,000 a month and much of it is word of mouth recommendation.'

Other banks competing in the UK market have examined setting up rival operations and some like Lloyds TSB and Barclays have taken steps to do so but their initiatives have often been too tentative. They, like the insurance companies, are struggling with the conflict around channels of distribution. Would encouraging their customers to bank by phone, fax and mail or via their PC simply accelerate the demise of the physical retail branch? If that happens does the bank lose its value-added role in the community? Can that be sustained or replaced in a 'virtual' selling environment?

These questions are growing in importance as electronic commerce develops and their resolution cannot be postponed indefinitely. The closer we get to the 2005 'critical mass date' the more important it will be to build up the learning of how to succeed electronically and manage these channel conflicts.

QVC

QVC (Quality Value Convenience) is *the* TV home shopping broadcaster. Established in 1986, it has demonstrated the extraordinary reach and potential of TV home shopping. It reaches into 54 million homes across the USA – more than half of all US households – and currently receives more than 70 million phone calls a year for products ranging from jewellery, household and hardware through to health and beauty and clothing fashion brands. In 1999, it shipped around 60 million packages in the USA.

QVC opened in the UK in 1993 and took time to establish itself. Its breakthrough came in 1995 when it negotiated with the British Satellite Broadcasting company (Rupert Murdoch's satellite venture) to be an integral part of that company's multimedia channels package. As a result in the UK it was able to get the access to consumers it had previously been denied. It now reaches into more than 5 million homes (25% of all households), has a customer base of over 1 million and is seeing sales grow at 30% plus a year.

As with First Direct, QVC has worked hard to make home shopping an easy, reliable and pleasurable experience. It has developed a sophisticated telecommunications network able to handle 50,000 purchases an hour and offers a 24-hour next-day delivery service. It ensures the product quality meets consumer needs, makes the shopping experience enjoyable and offers full guarantees and refunds. It looks to provide all the key ingredients converting uncertain consumers into becoming TV shoppers and paving the way for others to develop their own successful TV shopping operations.

Dell

Dell are pioneers in telemarketing and selling. They have broken the mould in their industry sector by consistently and persistently selling computers direct to the consumer, bypassing the traditional network of electrical wholesalers and retailers. In 1999 Dell's turnover reached $25 billion, up 27% from the previous year and with sales continuing to grow each month.

Dell started out twelve years previously confounding industry experts who claimed it would be impossible to sell something as complex as a computer over the phone. But Dell's argument was that everyone had a phone, many sat next to one all day long in their offices, it could provide immediate connection not just for selling but to handle queries, provide after-sales service and 'keep the customers satisfied'. Many industry commentators also believed no consumer would provide their credit card number over the phone for security reasons. Again, Dell showed that this was not the case once consumers could believe in the company and trust its professionalism.

In that regard Dell put its faith in its front-line employees and saw them as the source of its competitive advantage. It has made enormous efforts to ensure they are educated about their products, can easily access and assess the technical specification data and interact efficiently with customers: 'We will use our employees to deliver the personal touch that many customers desire – you don't need physical contact to do that.'

Dell not unexpectedly was one of the first companies also to pioneer marketing and selling over the internet and does an increasing part of its business on line. Its vision is to have all its customers eventually do business through this medium, but that vision assumes that phone and video facilities will be integrated to ensure communication can remain personal and interactive.

As it develops its internet business Dell is also experiencing its own form of channel conflict with its existing salesforce and telemarketing operation querying whether their jobs and customer relations are under threat. But the company's view is that the internet simply enhances the total customer communication package and that if less time is required for selling or information-giving over the phone, then more time is available for customer account management, relationship building and after-sales service.

Levi Strauss

Levi Strauss has long been one of America's most admired corporations despite more recent price and competitor pressures, and has made its name in the world of blue jeans and casual clothing. But as a traditional manufacturing company, Levi's often felt too removed from its end-consumer and felt frustrated that its consumer connections only got as far as its factory gate.

Levi's has shown what manufacturers of consumer goods can achieve by pushing out into the consumer arena, opening its own stores and working hard to build stronger customer relations. It is this greater proximity to its marketplace that helped Levi's realise its customers still weren't satisfied. They wanted still better service, better fit, better value. In a world where many products are perceived as commodity-like, Levi's consumers expected something extra from a market leader.

As one response to this challenge Levi's have made their whole sales, marketing and distribution much more electronic. For its distributors it has developed an interactive operating system that automatically allows reordering and enables other retailers to tap into Levi's own internal manufacturing processes, track where the order is and even alter order configurations within certain guidelines. (Fedex and UPS are other leading-edge examples in this.) Distributors as a result feel they have much better relationships and are more in partnership with Levi's.

In Levi's own stores, the company has introduced a simple interactive kiosk which enables the store assistant or customers themselves to input their personal measurements and get a 'Custom Fit' pair of jeans made up and ready for collection within a couple of weeks. Lead times for this service are already reducing and a one-week turnaround is already being targeted.

Levi's have been testing the possibilities of offering some of these same services over the internet so consumers can shop with even greater confidence. After all, for many of Levi's consumers buying a pair of jeans is simply a replacement for a worn-out pair, there is no need to visit the store to try them on and a measurement facility can be easily offered on line.

Amazon.com

This virtual bookseller ranks among the most famous sites on the internet. Founded as recently as 1995 it has set the pace in electronic shopping generating more than $40 million of sales in the first six months of 1997. By the first quarter of 2000 this had risen to $574 million, giving Amazon a market-leading 7% share of US book sales. It has created a mini revolution in its industry sector forcing once sleepy chains like Barnes & Noble to wake up to the realities of the electronic age.

As a pioneer Amazon.com has enjoyed enormous publicity, helping to create awareness and also quickly establishing its brand name among the book-buying public. Jeff Bezos, the company's founder, was convinced from the outset that consumers would enjoy the experience of browsing books electronically, reading reviews and excerpts from a particular book and being able to have it delivered within a day or two. For Bezos it wasn't just about providing a convenient service, it was also about being able to offer a one-stop shop making available the widest possible selection of titles – 'if it's in print, it's in stock'.

Amazon.com's early trading saw significant losses and when Barnes & Noble and Borders, the established book retail giants in the USA, woke up to the electronic opportunities, many believed Amazon.com would simply be muscled out. But Bezos has stuck to his guns, milked the TV and press publicity about his site, marketed and priced aggressively and is emerging as the dominant on-line bookseller.

In fact bookselling over the internet is now one of the more sophisticated industry sectors to have developed in this way. Market commentators have moved on from debating whether virtual book shopping will survive to examining the next stage of its development. Competition between booksellers on the internet is intensifying. We've already seen head-to-head internet pricing wars with companies outdoing each other to offer greater discounts. But on a more long-term basis, issues of branding, service levels and tying up on-line distribution deals will become more prominent. For example, Amazon has secured deals with America On-Line and search engines Yahoo! and Excite to guarantee on-line traffic and ensure high prominence.

What Amazon so admirably demonstrates is how quickly a business can develop and grow in the internet environment. In Amazon's case from $500,000 of sales in 1995 to $80 million in 1997, realizing about $400 million for 1998 and approaching $1 billion in 1999! It also shows how easy it can be in this new electronic age to bypass established physical retailers and reach directly to the consumer. The key, as demonstrated by

Bezos, is the conviction and belief in the potential of this way of buying and selling and the pioneering determination to make it succeed. Right now this 'pioneering spirit' can be seen as the domain of the romantic and the adventurer. How long before it becomes essential for survival?

Tesco

Tesco is Britain's largest food retailer and has been leading the trial and experimentation of electronic shopping in its sector. Its website is one of the most frequently visited by the UK consumer base and it has been steadily building sales. At c. £150 million of turnover it now claims to be the world's largest on-line grocer!

Its latest moves include the extension of its home shopping service throughout London and further extensions across the whole country. Its internet superstore offers customers the ability to purchase any of the 20,000 product lines typically available in its stores. Tesco mails all would-be electronic shoppers a CD Rom with the shopping list and orders are made on a return path on line via CompuServe. Each month in addition Tesco mails consumers a full-colour catalogue detailing special offers and highlighting particular product categories: 'We're constantly looking to improve our offering and we have to keep thinking about the future and what our customers will demand.' Next-day delivery is the usual arrangement but shoppers can also order goods up to 28 days in advance. Deliveries are made by a sub-contractor with a fleet of refrigerated vans.

Tesco acknowledges it still has much to learn about internet shopping and home delivery and that the service levels and interactions that take place are a long way from their potential: 'We have a history of innovation and we're learning on this one at every step . . . it's important to be at the forefront as the internet develops . . . there would be nothing worse than having to play catch up.'

Tesco certainly still sees its physical real estate as its principal distribution channel and, while it is treating internet opportunities more seriously than many of its rivals, it's a long way still from seeing that as its future direction. What Tesco is already experiencing though is growing levels of interest on the back of the publicity for its home-shopping service. It is also currently enjoying getting new customers who cannot get the same electronic shopping service from their own regular supermarket.

Tesco is actively putting itself in a prime position to benefit from increasing electronic shopping interest. Most importantly, it is learning how to make that route to the consumer work, is establishing itself in the consumers' eyes as being the leading edge exponent and will thus be best able of all its competitors to effectively respond and see through the inevitable evolution of its existing retail estate.

General trial and experimentation

Aside from the major pioneers there is a wealth of trial and experimentation taking place across the whole retail shopping scene. This can be categorised by looking separately at what steps different players in the distribution chain are taking and how they see their interest in electronic commerce. There are many case examples with considerable innovation taking place. We can consider:

- Manufacturers
- Retailers
- New intermediaries
- New entrants
- Consumer clubs.

Manufacturers

Manufacturer supplier companies are considered in more detail in Chapters 13 and 14 but to date they have mostly kept a low profile. They are concerned that they may disturb existing channels of distribution and undermine currently important customer relationships. This has dampened their enthusiasm and caused them to downplay any initiatives. Only a handful of companies have announced their plans:

- Unilever is looking to develop its own direct links with its end consumers:

  'We're looking at diversification into new service-related methods of channelling our food and personal products to the consumer. Because of fundamental changes in the retail market we are seeing the emergence of alternative channels of distribution . . . unless we are careful we will find ourselves boxed in to what is sold through a consolidating block of retailers.'
  (*Sunday Times interview with Niall Fitzgerald, Chairman of Unilever*)

- All the major car manufacturers from Audi to Volvo have set up websites and are experiencing tremendous interest. One specific example is Vauxhall Cars, the General Motors subsidiary, who have been experimenting with selling over the internet. The company has set up a point and click facility to demonstrate the features of the cars and includes full motion video sound and graphics which can change colour and specification. There is also a price list based on various finance deals. The system is used particularly by the dealers as a high-speed ordering link, demonstrating cars not in the showroom and expanding the range of information available. Consumers can access this site on line but lack of sufficient bandwidth in many home PCs means downloading times are still slow and picture quality not yet up to acceptable levels. Vauxhall nevertheless say they are committed to strengthening this way of doing business.

- Guinness and Allied Domecq are both examples of manufacturer brewers who have set up on line. While their sites are relatively well developed they are still at the stage of providing information to consumers and haven't yet progressed to proactive electronic selling. They are still exploring how to develop electronically without upsetting existing distribution channels. Guinness's site is nevertheless so popular that many have downloaded their on-line advert for the product as a screen saver. The site also sells related merchandise like sweatshirts and has received orders from all over the world.

Retailers

This group will also be considered in more detail in Chapter 7 but while Tesco has been taking the lead, other retail groups from grocery to banking to betting shops have also been trialling new approaches:

- Sainsbury, the major UK rival to Tesco's food stores, has established an 'Order & Collect' operation. This involves customers ordering by phone or fax from a catalogue, having the goods picked for them in store and then coming to collect later in the day or at some other prearranged time. The service costs an extra £2 and customers need to sign up to take advantage. It's done on a local store basis and there are presently limits on the number of 'order and collect' customers per store. Sainsbury will also help customers develop their own shopping lists. Appointments are made with customer service representatives who will then spend around 2 hours walking with the customer around the store compiling a standard list of basic shopping items which can then be ordered by simply quoting a reference number over the phone.

Sainsbury also have an internet/home delivery option and are in talks with British Interactive Broadcasting for a store offer on the new digital TV shopping platforms (see Chapter 10).

- Waitrose, another UK grocery chain, has launched an Intranet shopping scheme with ICL Computers. The initiative will allow the 500 ICL staff to sign up, order their shopping from their desks in their office and pick up from the office lobby area on the way home.

- Lloyds TSB, the UK retail banking group, has set up a 24-hour telephone banking service to rival First Direct: 'We want to move with the times and a growing number of our customers are looking for this kind of service.'

- Barclays Bank relaunched its website again in 1999. Its first effort set up in 1995 was 'an important experimental test bid' but did little business. Its relaunch involved a fundamental reworking and an easier-to-use format, 'We have seen stunning growth with over one and a half million visitors and we are looking for the J curve of performance as we come out the learning curve.' The site itself is still seen as an incremental growth opportunity and Barclays will not yet acknowledge that it will have any meaningful impact on their branch business.

- Major UK betting shops like Ladbroke's are trialling new websites and are offering trackside betting on horse races all over the world from the comfort of the home. Ladbroke's for one has announced that it is set on developing the on-line operation but is still working out how to ensure the betting and payment can be kept secure and confidential and there is an effective shield preventing children under the legal age from betting. The security and confidentiality side they expect to have resolved and they plan to prevent under-age gambling through a mix of personal subscription and credit vetting.

New intermediaries

The arrival of electronic shopping has created opportunities for new companies to come in and capture a part of the restructuring value chain. This is particularly in the area of home delivery. Existing manufacturers and retailers don't have such an infrastructure in place and typically sub-contract transportation and warehousing. This has facilitated new dedicated home delivery companies to enter the market place and start taking over the previous role of the retailer as distributor closest to the end-consumer:

• Peapod is an on-line grocery shopping and delivery service. It's been through a number of learning pains to finance its development, but throughout its consistent aim has been to 'relieve Americans of the time and trouble of buying groceries'. They are looking to capture just a small share initially of the $400 billion US grocery market but 'even a 1% share in the next two or three years would turn us into a substantial grocery distributor especially if concentrated in our five target regions'.

Peapod takes order by phone, fax or computer and delivers to the door. Their Vice President Thomas Parkinson says they want to change the way people shop. Peapod are encouraged in their ambitions by independent research organisation Forrester whose early forecast saw a growing rise in home delivered food and drink sales (Figure 4.1). Peapod have already found that barriers to buying fresh produce can be overcome and its top five selling product lines include fresh fruit and vegetables. Vice President Parkinson has said that Peapod is rapidly proving its reliability on product quality, 'shoppers are flocking to us'. Future development is now underpinned by 20% shareholder WPP, the global marketing services group, who can bring funding and advertising muscle to complement Peapod's activities.

Figure 4.1 Projected Food and Drink Sales on the Internet

Source: Forrester/Jupiter Research (2000).

• Shoplink is another venture looking to attack traditional distribution channels and facilitate new ways for customers to shop. While Peapod are working with a range of different stores like Wal-Mart or Kroger, Shoplink has set up greenfield. Started in 1997 the company aims to establish its own refrigerated warehouses to service the eight major cities across the USA, starting in Boston. Bankrolled by parent Elcom

International, CEO Robert J. Crowell is not surprisingly an enthusiast:

> 'Our aim is to take the grocery stores out of the equation. We will receive deliveries direct from the manufacturers with our own onward home delivery operation. We can save on all those retail real estate costs and can therefore afford to deliver to individual homes at the consumer's convenience for only a small delivery charge.'

- Streamline, another US operator set up along similar lines, has announced a target of 1 million households buying grocery direct through their operation by 2005.
- In the UK, similar dedicated home-shopping intermediaries are busily establishing themselves. Flanagan's works presently throughout the western side of London and has links with Sainsbury, Food Ferry is more like Shoplink, targeting certain areas but buying in product into its own warehouse. The Cotswold Shopping Service provides an example of a neighbourhood home-shopping service, buying goods on order from any store and organising their home delivery.
- In the business to business arena, new info brokers like Chemdex.com are inserting themselves in the value chain between manufacturers and purchasing. They will become the place to go to buy or sell commodity and other chemicals.

New entrants

Amazon.com have paved the way but others are following hard in its footsteps setting up as dedicated on-line providers:

- In the last few years a plethora of new sites have been set up in the Financial Services field. New companies are providing information and transaction services so that it is possible to deal in company shares on the screen but also to buy motor insurance or shop around for a mortgage. Such services can be cheap both to set up and run. Indeed there are so many sites being established that the regulating authorities are struggling to control those enterprises that appear to be operating in their jurisdiction.
- Music sales are another rapidly growing internet category. Research consultancy Jupiter Communication forecasts on-line music sales in America to be worth $2.5 billion by 2001 – that is 13% of the US music market. Companies like Boxman, CDNow provide informa-

tion, band details, discographies and track listings. There are audio samples for many different albums and the whole website is easily laid out enabling would-be shoppers to follow the categories of music they are most interested in. Pricing in the USA is the same or cheaper than in-store and delivery can be within 48 hours.

- New sites offering travel and holidays mean there may be no need to deal through travel agents and certainly no need to visit their shops. Most of the major airlines, for example, have their own websites with clear on-line booking facilities. All the major car rental companies and large hotel chains now have excellent arrangements to book direct with ever-better information and display on the product and services being offered. For holidays, a number of destinations e.g. Skiing in Vail, have come together to set up their own websites that can then take the consumer into general resort information or individual hotel room availability.

Consumer Clubs and Communities

This is a new phenomenon and recent times has seen the emergence of a number of examples like letsbuyit.com. They are discussed later in Chapters 8 and 14. But they are likely to represent a growing force in the distribution chain. Once consumers begin to become comfortable with the internet as a communication and transaction device they'll begin to learn not just how to use it to get information and buy goods, they'll also begin to see it as a means of taking greater control for themselves for what they buy, when they buy and the price they buy at. They will no longer be dependent on the few stores they can reasonably drive to in their neighbourhood. As this consumer awareness grows, so the internet will enable like-minded consumers to 'club together'. Some of this clubbing will be for social purposes, some of it for lobbying or political ends, but some element of it will be to get better buying terms from manufacturers or distributors. A 'mother and baby club' is an obvious example where mothers in a neighbourhood get together, organise collectively their total weekly diaper requirements, for example from Procter & Gamble, and order direct from the manufacturer themselves, expecting next-day delivery and on better terms than available from distributors.

These 'buying groups' will develop through this decade and we will likely see pioneers spotting this as a new business opportunity and being at the forefront in encouraging and exploiting it.

*   *   *

There is certainly a vast amount of electronic shopping activity. Some of the more notable examples have been described but it's worth also referring to some of the more broadscale initiatives. These aren't limited in their impact. They affect all parts of the distribution chain and so challenge not only retailers but also manufacturers and other existing distributors.

One example can be found in Palo Alto, California. There's an initiative to wire up the whole city with full two-way internet capability as part of a 'Smart Valley' project. The aim is to establish an electronic community, linked by high-speed networks, able to communicate and conduct commerce with ease and reliability. Project initiator was the Palo Alto mayor Liz Kniss who has commented how this investment will 'open up possibilities and potential we haven't even imagined'.

Similar projects have been established on a smaller scale in France and in Spain. Finland has capitalised on its already sophisticated telecomm infrastructure to accelerate internet connections and activity. A few streets in London have been converted by way of experiment, in one case sponsored by Microsoft, to test out consumer interest and responsiveness.

As these community-wide initiatives take root so electronic sellers will be encouraged to increase their own investments and so it will be easier still for consumers to buy what they want. There's a virtuous circle that will gradually take shape and solidify (Figure 4.2).

Figure 4.2 Electronic Shopping: The Virtuous Circle

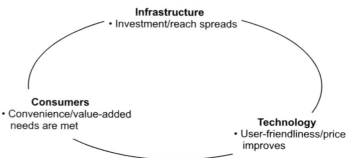

5 Future Growth of Electronic Shopping: Look Out for 2005!

There's so much activity and investment going on, but when will it reach critical mass, when will it truly begin to shape mass consumer shopping habits? All the evidence is pointing to around the middle of this decade, to c. 2005. By that stage it looks as though there will be sufficient infrastructure and technology in place, experimentation and improvement will have reached a point of maturity – though still far from complete – and consumer purchasing will start proving notably easier, more enjoyable and more rewarding.

In this chapter, the evidence pointing to 2005 is examined, describing some of the key dynamics bringing this critical mass date so near in time. For the reader searching for more detail, Chapter 10 drills down further, looking at both the impressive range of technology and infrastructure options that are being developed and at how consumers are already impatient for these kind of innovations.

As we begin to examine the shape of things to come, let's first envision what the brave new world of electronic shopping might be like. How will life-styles and habits change, how will it save time and improve the quality of life? Here are a few possible scenarios:

- It's Friday, it's 6.30pm and Deborah is just finishing work. Up till the end of last year Deborah used to have to rush to the supermarket to do her weekly shopping. She likes to keep her weekends free but spending Friday evenings after a hard day's work pushing her shopping cart up and down the crowded aisles was a bit of a nightmare. Recently, however, it's all changed. She can leave the office on Fridays and head straight out with her friends. What's happened? Simply that her local supermarket has at last expanded its home-shopping service to her area. They've got her regular list of basics and each Friday she can just phone, fax or e-mail them, quoting her reference number, and it automatically triggers the reorder. There's also the opportunity to add on the specials she wants that week – fresh strawberries and cream because it's summer and

Wimbledon. While she's now out relaxing and enjoying herself someone else is walking round the food warehouse picking her order. It's then all delivered to her, as arranged, freshly picked and packed on Saturday at 10.00am just as she's finishing breakfast. Next year her supermarket have announced they'll be providing her with special food-supply bins for free. They'll be fixed in a suitable place to the side of her house and there will be a digital lock on the lid. The supermarket delivery van can then deliver whether she's at home or not. Only they will have the digital key code and the food will be packed in special chilled containers keeping things fresh.

- John has never liked shopping much. He always felt a bit embarrassed standing in the middle of a shop trying on new clothes and shoes while passers-by ogled and no doubt thought his choices ill-suited and inappropriate. To some extent, those days are gone. For example John has just discovered the new Custom Shoe Shop. It's in that great big shopping centre that's opened. You can drive there and get just about anything. In the new shoe shop, John is shown into a personal cubicle and invited to sit down in front of a computer screen. The instructions tell him to place his feet on special plates. He touches 'start' and his feet are photographed from a variety of angles and detailed measurements taken. There's a new global standard issued by the Shoe Manufacturers' Association and John is pleased to see they've approved this particular equipment. While he's waiting a shop assistant has brought him some coffee and croissants and the daily newspaper. It's all so civilised. John has seen some of the Custom Shoe Shop's adverts but he now goes back to the screen and scrolls through the range of shoes and accessories. He can put any buckle or bow on any shoe in any colour. If he needs help the assistant is on call. But it's all very easy. He chooses a pair he likes and the computer shows pictures of what they would look like on and he can look at different colour suits and trousers to check they match. Now he has the choice of a 2-hour express service, he can go and check out the rest of the mall and come back and collect or he can have them delivered next day. Because it's John's first time he says he'll come back later. When he does the shoes fit very comfortably. Now they have his details and preferences, next time he needs a pair of shoes he could access their website and do all this from home or the office.

- Peter has just received an e-mail telling him the interest rate on his mortgage is going up next month. Peter is concerned and is sure he can get a better rate. He goes on line and uses one of the search engines to look at different mortgage rates that could be available and to find the one that offers him the best value. The search engine looks all over the world and identifies one bank in San Francisco and another in London that might have what he wants. Peter fills in a basic form on line setting out details of how much he wants to borrow, the equity in his house etc. and the search engine automatically notifies the two banks, informs the banks that their offers are being matched and compared and asks each for its best counter offer. The London bank seems more flexible and starts setting out terms that Peter likes. It will be cheaper than his current mortgage and there will be no switching costs. The bank makes Peter an offer subject to the usual conditions and Peter e-mails his financial advisor to send through the necessary documentation to the bank. The whole process took just half an hour and Peter can't help but remember the first time he went to get a mortgage, had to wait in the bank to see the manager, how long it took, how many banks and brokers he had to visit and call. He can now get on with enjoying his weekend.

These scenarios are no longer stories from science fiction. The technology exists and suppliers are advanced in experimenting with it. It is already possible to shop from home, have clothes and shoes measured automatically (look at Levi's 'custom jeans') and search the internet to compare prices. Given the rapid pace of development these services can only improve in speed, quality and price. In fact there is a further evolution already being developed in the lab, though further off in terms of its mass commercialisation. It's going to be yet a further step forward, making electronic commerce not just more convenient but also exciting and fun. It's 3-D virtual reality and while it hasn't yet impacted the world of shopping it's already on many internet companies' horizons. We can get a view of how 3-D will work with this extract from Michael Ridpath's *Trading Reality*. With 3-D graphics, consumers can use their extensive knowledge of the physical marketplace to shop for products in the virtual store:

'Most of the break-throughs in computer technology over the last twenty years have come from getting more and more power on smaller and smaller chips . . . But you remember I spoke about Graphical User Interface, how people will talk to computers? That's where the next strides will come. And virtual reality is the ultimate user interface.

When a person is actually in a computer-generated world, can talk to it, point within it, then the computer disappears as a barrier. Computer and user become one. I'm convinced that a whole new range of human activity will become possible. Anything to do with communicating between people in different physical locations will be vastly improved.

You will need a computer with special software to run the virtual world. Then a head-mounted display with two little screens, one for each eye, earphones to give sound in stereo and a sensor that tracks where you're looking. So when you turn to the left the image you see changes to the view to your left in the virtual world. Special gloves can recreate a sense of touch. With the senses of sight, sound and touch all totally immersed in the computer-generated virtual world you really are in virtual reality.'

We can see this future world rushing at us, about to change our experiences and perspective and expectations of what can be done and what can be achieved. To some extent we can't imagine it, yet ideas and images come from movies we've seen, books we've read, news features on the latest computer product innovations. What's so extraordinary is that it's now coming alive – it's the fast-approaching reality.

One of the major forces driving its reach and penetration into our lives is the rapid spread of the internet and the number of people that can access it. It's coming into homes through both the PC and the TV. It's coming over telephone wires, cable and satellite. It's available in most offices and often at each person's desk through their own PC. It's available while people are travelling at airports and at kiosks. It reaches across the world, its messages are universal, its products and services the same. There are no barriers. Payments can be in local currency, software can be used to translate an English-language website into the local dialect, everyone can in principle get everything. Of course, there are social and cultural hurdles. Some countries and people would never be able to afford the equipment but there's no doubt that across the western hemisphere at least commerce is going global on the internet.

A look at some of the statistics provides compelling evidence for how quickly things are expanding. We can consider in turn:

- infrastructure development
- size of the internet economy
- who's using the net
- consumer acceptance
- country snapshots.

Infrastructure development

There are several dimensions here:

- The number of host computers on the net (the computers that deliver information and services to users) grew from 100,000 in 1990 to 40 million by 1998 and is projected to grow to more than 100 million in 2000.
- The number of commercial websites grew from 350 in 1994 to 414,000 in 1998. Estimates for the year 2002 are for more than 1.6 million.
- In terms of the number of households on line, Table 5.1 shows the extraordinary growth and penetration in such a short amount of time.
- Another way of seeing this household penetration is from research in Table 5.2, showing the growing percentage of households with PCs and in Table 5.3, the growing number of PCs that are wired to the internet.

Table 5.1   On-Line Households, 1998 and 2002

Country	1998 (Actual mn)	2002 (Forecast mn)
USA	28.5	42.1
Europe	10.2	37.5
Asia	7.8	16.0
Japan	4.1	8.0
Australia	1.0	2.5
Germany	3.6	15.2
UK	3.2	9.7
France (excl. Minitel)	0.8	4.0
Scandinavia	1.5	3.8

Source: Jupiter Communications.

Table 5.2   Growth of European* Households with PCs, 1994–2000

Year	% households
1994 (actual)	17
1995 (actual)	22
1998	30
2000	40

Note:* Western Europe only.
Source: The European Information Technology Observatory.

Table 5.3 Penetration of US Households with Computers and
Internet Connection, 1995 and 2000

	1995 (%)	2000 (%)
Home PCs with Internet	21	43

Source: The Internet Society, Computer Industry Almanac.

As a specific example of infrastructure development, Verdict research
has set out (Table 5.4) its view on how the UK especially will become
wired up to the internet. They foresee higher levels of penetration and
usage and forecast that more than one-third of the UK population will be
on line by the year 2001.

Table 5.4 UK Growth in Internet Connections, 1997–2001

Year	Home Internet a/c holders (mn)	Growth (%)	Corporate Internet (mn)	Growth (%)	Satellite digital TV (mn)	Growth (%)	Digital terrestrial TV (mn)	Growth (%)	Total (mn)
1997	1.55	–	0.8	–	–	–	–	–	2.35
1998	3.11	100%	1.9	150%	0.04	20%	0.01	35%	5.2
1999	5.45	75%	4.6	130%	0.09	125%	0.01	150%	10.2
2000	6.81	25%	9.1	100%	0.27	200%	0.02	200%	16.4
2001	7.49	10%	13.7	50%	0.88	225%	0.90	400%	23.0

Source: Verdict.

A sophisticated infrastructure is gradually taking shape around the
internet which will facilitate and accelerate the increasing levels of
electronic commercial activity that are predicted. Rapid PC penetration is
combining with fast cable and improving telephone wire links to enable
quick net access and the downloading of richer material with higher video
and visual content. Developments with digital and satellite broadcasting
promise to bring net access to millions more households, avoiding the
expensive laying of fibre optic cable. The emergence of open standards in
development tools and at the network protocol level has made it cost
efficient for software developers to create interoperable products.
Payment security systems are now enabling website operators to make
data transmissions on credit cards safe. Data encryption software is
improving and spreading, providing further reassurance on confidentiality and privacy.

There is a growing maturity following the early days of hype and
exploration and there is an impressive gathering of companies providing

hardware, software, telecommunications, media and content racing to provide an attractive buying and selling environment for the twenty-first century.

Size of the internet economy

Total commerce over the internet – both business-to-business and business-to-consumer – is forecast to reach up to $1 trillion through the year 2000. In the USA alone internet revenues approached $300 billion by the end of 1999, setting the pace that other countries will doubtless follow.

These revenue forecasts are drawn from an extensive series of interviews with over 40 CEOs whose companies do business on the internet today. They highlight five major industry segments with the biggest on-line revenue potential: infrastructure, access, content, financial services and consumer retail. These CEOs say the key drivers of electronic commerce are the number of households and businesses going on line and the increasing availability of effective technology solutions from the vendor community.

Spotlighting business-to-consumer internet revenues, most forecasters now see $20–$30 billion of revenues by the year 2000 (Figure 5.1), with a recent *Business Week* survey reinforcing views that the top end of this

Figure 5.1 Total Internet Spend, 1996–2000

Source: *Business Week*/Forrester.

range will easily be reached. These figures exclude catalogue home shopping sales and other established phone/fax operations. In 1999 those longer-established forms of electronic shopping accounted for c. $85 billion of sales, just taking into account North America.

The same *Business Week* survey (Table 5.5) named the top ten selling product and service areas.

Latest reports show further headlong developments in internet sales, with *Business Week* finding that growth is coming in every product category – from 'airline tickets to tennis rackets'. American On-Line President Robert Pittman commented that consumers are getting increasingly familiar with the idea of the internet and beginning to learn they can shop satisfactorily through it: 'people are beginning to move from window shoppers to buyers . . . few companies of any size haven't now got some kind of web site'.

Table 5.5   Top Ten Internet Shopping Categories

1.	PC hardware
2.	Travel
3.	Entertainment
4.	Books and music
5.	Gifts and flowers
6.	Apparel and footwear
7.	Food and beverages
8.	Jewellery
9.	Sporting goods
10.	Consumer electronics

Source: *Business Week*/Forrester.

Who's using the net

Traditional home shopping by catalogue mail-order or by phone and fax has always been especially popular among women who are the majority users. The internet, however, was originally the preserve of men and in its early days had a very skewed demographic roughly equating to the computer nerd. Times are changing though and the latest surveys on who's using the internet show a much more representative balance emerging with people of all ages, backgrounds and of both genders.

GVU, a US-based research organisation, has carried out widely read surveys on internet usage. Among other things this shows that 43% of internet users are now women. This proportion rises higher in the USA.

In Europe it is around 30% on average but growing since the previous year's research.

Other studies by NUA and Lexmark International show that women are increasingly using the PC for a variety of applications ranging from planning the family's finances, running educational programs, e-mail, newsgroups and bulletin boards to a growing interest in shopping facilities. Researchers predict that increasing comfort and experience of using PCs among all members of the population will lead to greater investigation of internet options and thereby more trial of what can be purchased. This development is now being fuelled more particularly by a number of print magazines, some targeted specifically at women and featuring web home pages and bringing attention to what's available. In addition there are a wider number of specialist websites such as Hearst's HomeArts Network, Women's Wire and Village Parent Soup which are targeting new women readers.

For would-be internet providers other demographics also look appealing with good acceptance across most age ranges and social/ income groups (Tables 5.6 and 5.7).

Table 5.6 Internet Electronic Shopping, by Age

Age group*	(%)
15–24	39
25–34	34
35–44	29
45–54	22
55–64	18
65 +	9

Note: *Average age is estimated to be 34.
Source: GVU, FT Management surveys, Healey and Baker.

Table 5.7 Internet Electronic Shopping, by Socioeconomic Groups (USA)

Social group	(%)
AB	35
C1	24
C2	19
DE	19
All adults	26

Source: GVU, FT Management surveys, Healey and Baker.

Internet users are spread all over the world but the energy and leadership is firmly rooted in the USA. This is consistent with US corporate attitude to IT investment generally which has traditionally been significantly more progressive and proactive than all other major trading nations (Figure 5.2).

Figure 5.2   Average IT Spend per Worker per Year ($)

Source: *Business Week*/IBM.

Such is the lead the USA is establishing that some commentators have expressed concern that other leading western countries are in danger of falling behind. More recent initiatives in both the UK and France, for example, do however show a heightened awareness of the investment gap and plans are being put in place to catch up (see 'Country Snapshots' on p. 89).

Consumer acceptance

Some 60% of adult consumers have shopped remotely and satisfactorily from home. There is a comfort and confidence in using established devices such as phone, fax or the mail. It is widespread and part of the shopping scene. Familiarity with many products and services makes it easy to buy without having to visit the store again. In principle any improvement to this home-shopping experience should be appealing. This is especially so if it can enrich the quality of interaction and information communicated. In this regard no one doubts the potential of the internet to fulfil that goal, but all recognise the technology has some way to go. A key question in this book is when will it reach a sufficient level of maturity and capability that a critical mass of consumers will become engaged and involved in it on a regular shopping basis.

Consumer interest in the internet is already high and it appears there is a strong platform on which would-be internet sellers can build. Tables 5.8 and 5.9 show there is an established level of confidence in general use of new technologies and significant numbers of people prepared to consider different forms of remote shopping.

Table 5.8   Confidence in Using New Technologies, by Age Group

Age group	% confidence
16–24	51
25–34	40
35–44	38
45–59	26
60+	11

Source: FT Management report; Henley Centre.

Table 5.9   Proportion of People who would Consider Remote Shopping

Shopping method	% of respondents
Postal system/mail-order	50
Telephone	34
PC Internet	28
Cashpoint	25
Fax	25
TV	24
PC CD Rom	14
Electronic kiosk	9

Source: FT Management report, BMRB.

A recent study by Motorola in association with the *Wall Street Journal* found that this platform of consumer confidence applied to a wide variety of electronic goods and services (Table 5.10).

Among certain target segments, acceptance of remote shopping is especially high. A recent survey among 25–45 year-old males suggests that this segment already represents a highly attractive marketing target for electronic sellers (Table 5.11).

Table 5.10   Comfort in Conducting Services by Computer

Service	% respondents
Ticket/Travel reservations	63
Home Banking	51
Education/Training	42
Shopping	32

Source: Motorola.

Table 5.11   Attitudes to Electronic Commerce

Question	% respondents answering Yes
Ever bought via Internet, multimedia kiosk or interactive TV?	33
Ever ordered and paid over the telephone?	98
Would pay a premium to have goods delivered to the home?	78

Source: IMRG.

These are remarkably positive levels of interest and acceptance among consumers at large and in certain segments in particular, all the more so because electronic commerce is still in its relatively early days and still grappling with inevitable early teething troubles. It appears that many see internet shopping as simply a natural evolution from more traditional phone/fax/mail-ordering. Comfort with the PC, familiarity with brands, readiness to rely on suppliers and providers with a solid reputation all leads to a quiet comfort with the new medium.

Business at large has naturally also observed these same consumer trends and indications and has a growing awareness of their long-term potential. For example, a *Forbes* magazine survey of chief executives in 500 top US companies found over 50% of executives believing that 40% of all transactions would take place over the internet in the future. They also saw consumers becoming more sophisticated shoppers using the internet first, to obtain product information, then to compare prices and then interactively consult company sales executives before then ordering – a series of steps which the internet readily facilitates.

These predictions among company executives on the impact of the internet are spread wide across all sectors of industry. For example, an IDC research study asking how many felt electronic commerce would be 'critical to very important' in the coming years generated strong

Table 5.12 Importance of Electronic Commerce

Sector	% respondents saying High Importance
Retail	32
Banking	29
Insurance	32
Process manufacturing	26
Transport	29
Healthcare	14
Business Services	43

Source: IDC.

responses with executives in the business services arena especially showing an acute consciousness of the shape of things to come (Table 5.12).

Country snapshots

With so much of the internet development taking place in North America and in the English language it provides a useful perspective and contrast to examine two of Europe's non English-speaking powerhouses – France and Germany. We can also take a snapshot of Singapore, showing the remarkable strides being made in one of Asia's leading economies.

France

France was the first country in the world to get wired up. During the early 1980s, the French government through the state-owned French Telecommunications company issued to millions of households for free a 'Minitel'. A small simple low-power computer terminal, its original purpose was to give French consumers direct access to an electronic phonebook with the Yellow Pages and phone numbers that could be scrolled through on the screen.

Business quickly realised there was a wider opportunity not just to advertise in Yellow Pages but additionally offer a range of business services. As a result the Minitel is now regularly used to buy plane and train tickets, make reservations at the theatre, opera and restaurants and in simple detail access product/service information on items ranging from insurance, retail banking through to shop opening times and prices. What Minitel cannot cope with as it is so under-powered is any detailed or complex transaction.

There is no doubt that the Minitel has successfully introduced all French consumers to the world of electronic information-gathering and purchasing for basic services. Use is widespread and knows no age or social–economic barriers. In fact technophobia has been replaced by a form of technophilia. The French generally love their Minitel and don't want to see it replaced. French businesses, too, are keen to preserve the Minitel operation as it keeps French consumers focused on French providers and keeps them away from the global competition found on the internet.

Indeed the French government initially reacted with hostility to the internet seeing it as another form of Anglo-Saxon invasion into French culture and the French way of life. In 1995 France's Centre for European Studies received wide publicity for its claims that 'French values are under threat . . . we cannot build Europe around the language of America'. At the same time France's Ministry of Culture hired staff to set up a special department to create and promote websites in French.

By 1999, however, the French business and government communities were being forced to acknowledge the sweeping potential of the internet and that if they did not invest and get involved they were in danger of losing out in a significant way in the race to the global electronic market. French Prime Minister Lionel Jospin has now called for a 'mobilisation of the French around the internet'. Government is now starting to invest heavily in what Jospin describes as the 'information society of the future'. It's a tacit acknowledgement that the Minitel, such a successful pioneer, has had its day and it's now time for the nation to get rewired with more modern connections. As part of this drive, Jospin has 'ordered' every school in France to develop an 'internet access plan' and is setting aside funds to create an internet site at every one of France's post offices. There is a determination to adopt the internet as a standard for all public information and a desire to encourage business to embrace the medium in the same fulsome way.

Indeed there need be no fears about an English-language invasion. There is a wave of new companies such as Globalink (ironically a US organisation) who are developing software that translates English e-mail and websites into a chosen local language. While French business groups are expressing strong interest in this there will also be applications into German, Japanese and most other widely spoken languages.

Germany

Even without a Minitel system, Germany has still developed as one of the most advanced home shopping countries in Europe. This is largely due to the presence of two of the world's largest mail-order companies – Quelle and Otto Versand – being based in Germany. Both these organisations have built substantial catalogue, phone, fax, mail operations which are highly developed and popular. It's created yet another base and platform on which to more easily build a more sophisticated electronic shopping environment. CD Roms are replacing bulky paper catalogs, TV interactive shopping is developing well and Germany is one of the leading European countries wiring up to the internet.

Clothing is the staple home order product, accounting for more than 50% of sales. Quelle and Otto Versand have learnt to target different consumer segments with tailored offerings that appeal to their needs. Like Next in the UK, they realise that mass mailing and communication has much less impact than getting into the real underlying detail of what will work with individual consumer groups and responding accordingly.

German home shoppers say their key reasons for buying in that way are: (1) convenience, (2) the opportunity to choose at leisure, (3) shopping is stress-free, (4) comparing prices and products is easy and (5) they can get a customer-oriented individual service.

Home shopping has received a further boost of interest with the arrival of Quelle's own TV station called HOT (Home Order Television) which was launched in 1996 transmitting 24 hours a day. It has found a great freedom to broadcast as the German TV authorities have concluded that HOT is not television in the formal sense requiring regulation: 'It is a merchandising procedure and therefore subject to different laws.'

HOT is proving successful. It reaches into nearly 10 million German households and is encouraging further the German addiction to TV. Planning restrictions have long controlled German retail-store opening hours and forecasters predict the convenience of 24-hour, 7-days-a-week shopping will have particular appeal. Estimates are that at least 10% of all German retail turnover will be electronic by the middle of this decade.

Singapore

Singapore is a compact island with a population of only 3.6 million. Computer penetration is high and the *World Competitiveness* report places Singapore among the top nations in the world in terms of strategic exploitation of IT, computer literacy and telecommunications infrastructure.

Since extensive privatisation of the telecoms network in Singapore, the industry is now well developed. The IT2000 master plan, set up by the National Computer Board (NCB) in 1991, seeks to develop Singapore into an 'intelligent island'. An integrated and extensively connected National Information Network (NIN) is being established to link computers and other information appliances in homes, offices, schools and factories.

PC ownership has risen from 27% of households in 1994 to 47% in 1999. Approximately 50% of these households are connected to the internet. Public access to the internet first became available in 1994, and there are now three internet service providers to home users, namely Singnet, Pacific and Cyberway (Table 5.13).

The Singapore government is looking far ahead in its commitment to the latest network technology. Singapore ONE (One Network for Everyone) combines two distinct but integrated levels. The first is a broadband infrastructure of high-capacity networks and switches which will break the current bandwidth barriers of current internet technologies. Using the latest technologies, the Singapore ONE Network will easily handle high-resolution video, sound and 3D graphics, presenting businesses with the potential to develop fast services for customers. Connections will upgrade from the current standard of 33.3kbps to 5–10 Mbps.

Construction began in 1996, and the network reached all areas of Singapore by the end of 1998. The government aims to have every home in Singapore connected to Singapore ONE through the year 2000, with around 20,000 households currently being cabled each month. At present, the programme is running as a pilot scheme, with over 100 applications developed and around 5000 homes and businesses actively using the network.

Table 5.13 Singapore Internet Growth, 1995–9

Year	No. of Internet dial-up accounts	Growth
1995	25,000	
1997	230,000	920%
1998	516,000	224%
1999	872,000	169%

'The implementation of Singapore ONE makes Singapore the leader in the Asia-Pacific Region in establishing a nation-wide broadband network. In the next five years we will focus on establishing network linkages between Singapore and the rest of the world.'
(*Teo Chee Hean, National IT Conference and Minister for Education*)

＊   ＊   ＊

When will it all reach critical mass?

From Germany to Japan, Mexico to Malaysia, business and consumers are getting wired into the electronic economy. Where there was initial reluctance as in France it has been replaced by a concern not to get left behind. Where there was hesitation as with grocery shopping (would consumers buy fresh fruit and vegetables?) there is now a growing recognition that the search for convenience, time-saving, leisurely, hassle-free shopping has strong appeal. Initial perceptions that this is just another distribution channel, like putting products into vending machines, are gradually changing. There appears little doubt that the appeal of electronic shopping will be far more widespread and will gradually become mass and mainstream.

When will it impact and take meaningful effect? In the research in this book the date of around 2005 has been established and this section examines that prediction in more detail. Certainly no company can now afford to ignore these developments and while some may argue the impact will be delayed in their particular industry sector, there will be few arenas that ultimately will not be significantly affected.

Ignoring predictions can be a dangerous pursuit. This is especially so with the wealth of activity and investment in electronic commerce that is taking place. As history records and as Professor William Keep has pointed out, there have been some famous gaffes as various technological innovations in the past have been dismissed, their potential doubted, only for them to go on and fundamentally change society:

- 'The phonograph is of no commercial value.'
(*Thomas Edison, 1880*)

- 'Everything that can be invented has been invented.'
(*Charles Duel, Director US Patent Office, 1899*)

- 'There is no likelihood that man can ever tap the power of the atom.'
  (*Robert Milliken, Nobel Prize winner in Physics, 1925*)

- 'Who the hell wants to hear actors talk?'
  (*Harvey Warner, 1927*)

- 'I think there is a world market for about five computers.'
  (*Thomas J. Watson, Chairman, IBM, 1943*)

- 'There is no reason for any individual to have a computer in their home.'
  (*Ken Olson, President of Digital Equipment Corp., 1977*)

Electronic technology has been a major driver of change throughout the twentieth century and it's achieving impact in the market place at an ever quicker pace as supply-side competition rushes to translate ideas from the lab into commercial reality at affordable prices. Table 5.14 shows the increasing speed with which technology changes lives.

Beside technology, there are an extraordinary number of other factors fuelling the growth in electronic commerce generally and shopping in particular. Consumer time poverty, the general shift from a physical to digital world based on knowledge rather than assets, the convergence of companies from different sectors as multimedia develops, unusual levels of government intervention and support from the USA to France encouraging investment and providing central funds and resources, a rapidly developing infrastructure, with the USA again especially leading on PCs in the home plus internet connections and advanced optical fibre cable links, and finally a new generation of people growing up computer

Table 5.14   Time for Technology to Penetrate the Mass Market

Interface	No. of years
Telephone	38
Cable TV	25
Fax machine	22
Microwave	13
VCR	11
Cellular phone	9
PC	7
CD Rom	6

Source: Info Tech, Pac Tel Cellular, Coopers & Lybrand.

and 'net literate' for whom using the technology is as commonplace and institutionalised as the telephone has already become. As a VP of Burton Group, the UK clothing retailer (already quoted), has recently commented: 'too many people are investing too much for it not to happen.'

With this bandwagon rolling, with this increasing momentum for change and advancement in commerce and life-styles, it is no wonder forecasters in the know are predicting significant impact in just a few short years. A number of forecasts have already been mentioned but we can remind ourselves of perhaps some of the most compelling:

- 'Through 2000 a third of the most attractive households will be ready to buy on-line.'

(McKinsey report)

- 'Once the hardware and telecommunications infrastructure is in place an enormous range of services such as location independent shopping . . . will likely be widespread by 2005.'
  (Jagdish Sheth, Professor of Marketing, Gouizeta Business School, Emory University)

- 'Electronic Retailing will grow inexorably . . . accounting for as much as 25% of US retail sales by 2010.'
  (Professors Louis Stern and Barton A. Weitz)

- 'On-line services will replace at least half the US citizen's average number of monthly shopping trips to grocery and related outlets by 2007.'
(The Consumer Direct Consortium of 31 US consumer goods companies)

In addition to the research conducted in this book, some 38 different forecasts and predictions on electronic commerce have been reviewed and assessed to understand how other market commentators see the future evolving. These other forecasts come from a range of different individuals and organisations including practitioners and observers. The mean date that emerges from this combination of research is around 2005 (Figure 5.3). By around the middle of this decade a majority of forecasters see electronic selling and buying reaching critical mass where a significant part of the population regularly shop electronically. The inputs come from information technology research companies like Gartner Group, International Data, general trend-spotting firms like Forrester and Jupiter, consumer market research organisations such as the Henley

Figure 5.3 Predicting when ES will Reach Critical Mass*

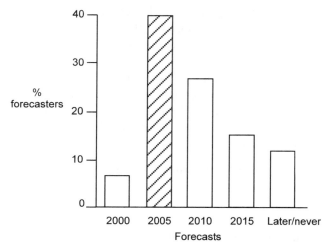

Note: *Defined as c. 15% plus of consumers regularly shopping electronically.

Centre and AC Nielsen, consultancy firms like Ernst & Young, CSC and Andersen, companies such as IBM, Cisco, Karstadt and Chrysler and individual commentators like Professor Fred Phillips, Professor Jagdish Sheth and Dr David Diamond.

Of course no one can be absolutely certain as to when electronic shopping will really take off and achieve mass volume penetration. It does seem unlikely that retail sales over the internet will have reached substantial levels by as early as the year 2000. But with technology developing at an exponential rate there is confidence that this decade will begin to see the new electronic world taking shape, with business and consumers becoming increasingly familiar and comfortable operating in that way.

This development can be mapped out into five stages of evolution and maturity (Figure 5.4). It naturally follows the 'S'-curve pattern of investment leading to a wave of growth. That is typically followed by a period of consolidation and then further investment fuelling the next rise in growth and acceptance:

Stage 1: 'Initial hype': this was the period of early excitement and interest. It saw universal media comment and established high levels of awareness across the mass consumer base. But access was limited and so usage still low.

Figure 5.4   Growth in Electronic Shopping: Key Stages of Growth, 1993–2007

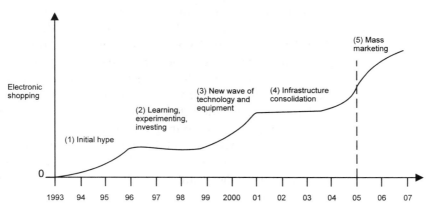

Stage 2:   'Learning, experimenting, investing': after the hype a gradual settling-in period has taken place where companies are learning how to make electronic shopping work for their consumers, establishing and finding the essential investments and setting up experiments and trials.

Stage 3:   'New wave of technology and equipment': the supply side is beginning to get its act together, the internet begins to reach into the home through improved web TV facilities, digital TV broadcasting allows a range of new home shopping channels to broadcast, more user-friendly equipment becomes available, mobile/hand-held technology develops bringing with it Smart Phones and PC Phones, PCs become cheaper and prices reduce rapidly following the pattern of other electrical equipment for the home. But it's all still not at mass consumer acceptance levels!

Stage 4:   'Infrastructure consolidation': companies can begin to meaningfully define the size of the opportunity – consumer expectations and demand are growing now the infrastructure is rapidly improving. The 1990s generation of net kids is growing up, starting to shop more widely and setting up their own homes. Efficient and widespread home delivery operations are built up and fine-tuned, equipment is designed for simple home usage (a typical equipment breakthrough being the remote control for using the TV), cable networks are extended, TV and satellite communication links enhanced.

Stage 5: 'Mass marketing': equipment is low-price and user-friendly, access is via the PC or TV or phone but is now sold as part of the package with every new TV, marketing is widespread, promotion levels are geared up for mass consumer appeal, it becomes the next piece of electrical gadgetry to have in every home, technology has learnt how to get speed and quality of transmission to acceptable levels through existing telephone wires, other communication links through satellite or the electricity grid are also now coming on stream, home delivery operators are well-recognised and developing a role as part of the local community, people are getting used to shopping where they want, how they want, when they want and they like the extended choice.

As internet and other forms of electronic shopping reach wider levels of consumer acceptance so the user profile is changing. It's no longer the obsession of a few computer buffs, it's graduating beyond the hobby of the IT/PC-literate individual. By reaching into the home it reaches the family. It's not just dad upstairs in his study or den but mother and kids too.

It becomes part of the fabric of living, woven into life-styles, accepted and adopted as an essential tool for information-gathering, communication, obtaining services and helping with the shopping. It's the global version of a more sophisticated Minitel. It doesn't turn us into a nation of couch potato zombies, it doesn't leave us marooned at home, it doesn't destroy social activity, it doesn't stop people going out. On the contrary it gives us more time to be more sociable. It simply removes hassle and makes shopping more convenient. Why shouldn't that appeal to the mass consumer base?

What the 'S'-curve analysis in Figure 5.4 shows is that there will be clear periods of investment and consolidation leading to new waves of growth. By 2005, the supply side will probably be geared up, the infrastructure more in place, the fulfilment mechanisms better established, thus enabling the mass marketing of electronic shopping and true levels of mass consumer penetration to really begin.

By this stage we can be sure there will be a 'hard-core' user base who will be the regular and often dedicated electronic shoppers. They are the 15–20% of the population who in one research study after another – from A.C. Nielsen, Mintel, BMRB, the Henley Centre and many others – emerge as clearly wanting the convenience and time-saving. They have expressed a determined preference to take advantage of shopping electronically as soon as it becomes available and accessible to them. They will be the first to get the equipment, log on, experiment and subscribe to the home delivery operation once it reaches their neighbourhood.

But they won't be alone. Following on their heels will be other groups of users, less dedicated but still looking to take advantage of the services on a more elective basis. By 2005 we might expect the pattern of electronic shopping users shown in Table 5.15.

Table 5.15 Possible ES Shopping Profiles

Consumer acceptance (%)	% items shopped electronically
1. 15–20% 'hard core'	50–75%
2. 15–20% occasionals	25–35%
3. 15–20% experimenting	10–20%
4. All the rest still irregulars!	5%

As this pattern of usage develops then some 15–20% of all retail shopping will be taking place electronically by around the middle of the next decade. Consumer shopping habits will be changing. Many will see the old days of pushing heavy shopping trolleys around as totally outdated. A new generation will be growing up and reaching maturity with different expectations. They will be familiar with the technology and want what's new and exciting. They'll be looking to forge their own life-styles and patterns of behaviour and won't have time for quaint notions of visiting the grocery store to lug home the soap powder.

The challenge is truly set for all retailers and manufacturers. Given their positions in the market place they will be able to see this 'S' curve unfolding. Some for sure will stand back and wait and see, perhaps leaving it too late to capture the emerging consumer trend. Others will be playing a leading role, defining and shaping the future of their industry sectors. In the next few chapters we can examine the opportunities and strategies available to retailers specifically and later on we can also see how manufacturer suppliers can best respond to this new environment. Whatever the approach, the writing is on the screen.

*   *   *

For a contrasting perspective, let's stand back for a moment from electronic shopping activity and consider the development of a different home innovation – the microwave. Here's an extract from the

International Herald Tribune telling the story of how the microwave took time to catch on and be accepted but eventually became an essential feature of every home.

'Eleanor Vavricek remembers the day she came home from work and laid her eyes on the brand new, boxy-looking contraption on her kitchen counter.

"I thought, what is that, what in the world do I do with it?" Cook that's what, like never before.

The new fangled gift from her husband was the new Amana Radarange microwave oven which made its debut in American kitchens in September 1967.

"It made my life a lot easier and simpler", said Vavricek. Many now feel that way too. Americans rank the microwave oven the no. 1 technology that makes their lives better. That puts the microwave ahead of the telephone answer machine and automatic teller machine which rank second and third.

Yet Amana officials were nervous about introducing the microwave technology in 1967. Even in an age of astronauts and TV dinners they did not really believe the product stood a chance. They spent a long time educating wholesalers and retailers on how it worked before finally launching it. The company even hired home economists to make house calls to help first time buyers. Those home economists were on call 24 hours a day backed up by servicemen guaranteed to arrive within one hour in case of trouble.

It took time to develop. Ten years after introduction in 1977 it still could only be found in around 1 in 10 households. But after 1977 it began to take off to the nearly 90% penetration it has today.'

6 The ES Test: How to Tell How Much Your Business is Going to be Affected

Which products and services are going to be most affected by the trends and developments in electronic shopping ('ES')? Are there some which are so obviously susceptible that they can be readily sold on line without any noticeable loss of value-added? Can those be easily identified? In contrast are there other products whose characteristics demand such a personal involvement and physical interaction that electronic selling is never likely to make much impact, except among a dedicated few?

Where product characteristics do point in the ES direction then must existing manufacturers and retailers give up on established traditional distribution routes and move quickly into the virtual world? Can they buck the trend? What are their various options and how can retailers and manufacturers begin to make sense of these market developments? Can a framework be devised that will help pin down the extent of the electronic threat, and opportunity, and the likely strategic responses required?

The 'ES Test', described in this chapter, provides a simple three step approach to help address these challenges. It applies to all types of products and services in all industry sectors. It can be used by retailers, by manufacturer suppliers, by any company participating or looking to participate in some part of the retail distribution chain from factory gate into the consumers' home. As the test is described, 'product' will be used to refer to both product and service industries.

The three steps in the test (see Figure 6.1) are:

1. **Product Characteristics**
2. **Familiarity and Confidence**
3. **Consumer Attributes.**

- *Product Characteristics* is about the product's primal appeal to the senses. Does it need to be physically touched or tried before buying?
- *Familiarity and Confidence* looks at the degree the consumer recognises and trusts the product, has tried it before and is confident in repurchasing it.

101

Figure 6.1   The 'ES Test'

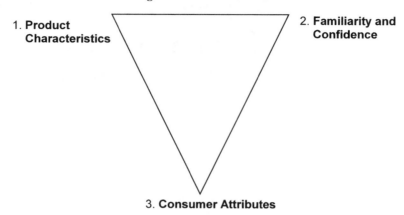

**1. Product
Characteristics**

**2. Familiarity and
Confidence**

3. Consumer Attributes

- *Consumer Attributes* considers the consumer's underlying motivations and attitudes towards shopping. Will they carry on visiting the shops even if a product naturally lends itself to electronic purchasing or will they be among the first to take advantage of the new medium?

Before describing and showing how best to use each part of the test it's worth emphasising that all three steps must be taken and checked out. A full evaluation needs to be made. Put simply, a product may seem to have obvious 'electronic characteristics' and be a familiar item in most consumers' shopping baskets. However some of those consumers may themselves just not be ready yet for electronic shopping, be reluctant to deal with new media and may respond in only a very limited way to on-line selling.

For example, a 35-year-old professional may be perfectly confident in buying insurance over the phone but a 65-year-old retired blue-collar worker may likely have a very different attitude and prefer face-to-face personal advice. Equally a busy mother with young children may relish the convenience of the family's weekly groceries being delivered to her home but a young single adult newly arrived in the city might look forward to the social interaction of a visit to the grocery store.

While superficially straightforward these examples simply demonstrate the importance of not rushing to conclusions based just on the product's characteristics. Understanding the target consumers and their likely responses and motivations will be as important and may well drive final decision-making. Not surprisingly success comes best from being market and customer-driven, rather than just being product-led!

1. Product Characteristics

Every product has an innate set of characteristics that makes a primary appeal to the consumer's senses. This appeal is traditionally ascribed to the five senses of sight, sound, touch, taste and smell. Some products appeal primarily to one of these senses such as a painting, music, perfume. Others, such as buying food, clothing, a car or a home will call up a whole mix of senses and appreciation

Each product's principal senses can be identified and at the same time categorised as lending themselves to electronic purchasing – or not (Table 6.1).

Products which appeal to the senses of touch, taste or smell are *prima facie* not suitable for electronic selling. Consumers expect to be physically involved in the purchase decision and want to handle, try and experience it before deciding. This is especially true if the product is new and has not been bought before. Other products that appeal mostly to sight and sound more naturally lend themselves to being bought over the internet or other electronic connection. Indeed as the quality of internet communication improves so sight-sound-based products can be expected to see increasing share of sales on line. The product's value-added can be effectively communicated in a 'virtual environment' and the consumer loses little through lack of physical contact or involvement.

Looking at the early consumer surveys, some of the best sellers over the internet have been basically sight/sound products that most naturally and immediately fitted into the new medium. Books, computer hardware and software, music CDs, basic financial services, information services generally all have a distinctly sight/sound appeal and suppliers have found it relatively straightforward to communicate their basic product proposition (Figure 6.2).

Table 6.1 Five Senses: Primal Product Appeal

Sample Products	Sight	Sound	Smell	Taste	Touch
Music		X			
Perfume			X		
Books	X				
Computers	X				
Autos	X	X			
Food	X		X	X	X

Higher ES potential $\Leftarrow$ $\Rightarrow$ Lower ES potential

Figure 6.2   Physical vs. Virtual

'Physical'
– Require human contact

'Virtual'
– Can be bought remotely

- Emotional content; or
- Reassurance required; or
- Purchase perceived as complex

- Purchase can be based on more rational criteria; or
- Are past experiences/recommendations to call upon; or
- Purchase perceived as simple/ straightforward

We can go further and map out (Figure 6.3) the whole list of retail consumer products defined in Chapter 3 and immediately establish an initial view of which products have a principal appeal to selling and buying electronically.

As the map in Figure 6.3 shows there are fewer touch/taste/smell-only products. The majority are sight/sound in nature and it would seem that a large part of the retail scene will likely have a basic responsiveness to electronic shopping activity.

Figure 6.3   Product Characteristics: Responsiveness to ES

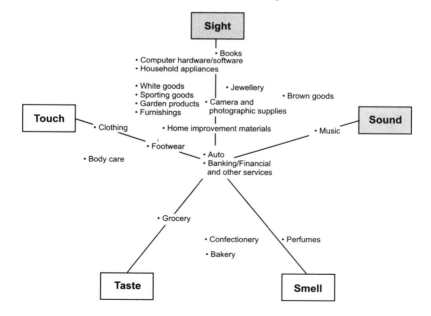

But, before conclusions can be drawn and before companies operating in any one product area rush to build their on-line franchises, it is necessary to drill down into more detail. At an individual product line level we can look for example within Grocery food (Table 6.2) and show that while some products certainly do share the generic Grocery 'Touch, Taste, Smell' appeal, others don't. Some are so packaged up that touch, taste, smell sensations are lost.

Table 6.2   Product Appeal for Individual Grocery Product Lines

Grocery products	Sound	Sight	Touch	Taste	Smell
Strawberries			X	X	X
Bananas			X		
Chicken		X	X		
Breakfast cereals		X			
Cookies		X			

Where a grocery or other product is packaged it does limit the sensual opportunity. The only criteria for purchase are 'like the look of the packet', 'have tried other products from same company', 'like that combination of ingredients'. Criteria such as these can be evaluated as easily on line or via a home catalogue/CD Rom as they can be in the store.

The same analysis can be done for clothing. Basic items like tights, undergarments, socks, handkerchiefs and shirts are often sold in boxes or wrapped up. The manufacturer and retailer are trying to make the purchase easier but in doing so they have removed much of the emotional content in making a purchase decision and made physical interaction before buying unnecessary – and with all the packaging nigh on impossible. Marks & Spencer, one of the world's leading clothing retailers, packages up many of these basic items in its stores to encourage easier purchasing. It is noteworthy that it is already experiencing demand for clothing items to be included in its home delivery services.

As suppliers and distributors reflect on the challenges of the electronic age one area they will need to re-examine is the way in which products are presented. If they still want consumers to visit the store the emotional and physical experience needs to be enhanced and reinforced at every turn. Things that get in the way like plastic wrapping and boxes may need to be removed and the product itself reinvested with a sense of fun, of being interesting and different, for example, in the way it is merchandised and the other products it is presented and associated with.

Looking again at the **Product Map** in Figure 6.3, one other important observation is how services like banking and other financial transactions don't naturally belong to any one of the five senses. It's as though their key characteristic lies with a broader sixth sense which might be described as the 'intellect'. Buying these products is typically a rational analytic process, not relying solely on sight or sound. It rather draws on a whole range of derived experiences and inputs which are then assessed in the mind and then a buying decision is made.

The more the product or service appeals to this broader 'intellectual' assessment, in contrast to something more physical or emotional, the greater its electronic selling potential. We could even redraw the product characteristics map (Figure 6.4), adding this sixth or derived sense as its centre. Where a product has a particular primary sensory appeal it can be plotted firmly along its axis. Where the product or service has this broader 'intellect' characteristic it is drawing on the whole range of sensory experiences and can be mapped across the centre.

The map can be redrawn in this way to help pinpoint as clearly as possible what are the product's basic characteristics and its electronic appeal. Any conclusions at this stage still need to be kept on hold, however, while the next two steps of the test are checked out.

Figure 6.4 Product Characteristics: Adding a 'Sixth' Sense

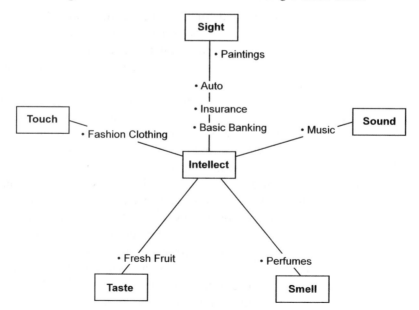

2. Familiarity and Confidence

The second step in the ES Test looks at how familiar and confident customers are in purchasing an individual product. Have they used it before? Have they purchased it previously? Have they had a good experience with it and are pleased to buy it again? The greater the familiarity and comfort with a product the less the need to be physically involved in its repurchase and so the easier to buy electronically (Figure 6.5).

Familiarity and confidence can typically be found among all types of everyday purchase:

- Basic foodstuffs   – cereals, dairy products, potatoes, bananas, cookies
- Drinks   – beers, colas, fruit juices, wine
- Basic clothing   – undergarments, socks, tights, regular shirts, and blouses, e.g. for the office, workwear.

These products are bought every week and consumed every day. An Indiana University research study showed that c. 80% of a customer's average grocery shopping basket was made up by replenishment items. There is a high degree of familiarity with much of the weekly shop. This would suggest a wide range of what's currently sold in a supermarket for example, could equally as well be sold by catalogue/CD Rom or on line and ordered from home without visiting a store.

Figure 6.5   Familiarity/Confidence Check

Table 6.3   Top Ten Brands

1.	McDonald's	6.	Gillette
2.	Coca-Cola	7.	Mercedes-Benz
3.	Disney	8.	Levi's
4.	Kodak	9.	Microsoft
5.	Sony	10.	Marlboro

Source: Interbrand.

Consumer familiarity and confidence is especially high where there is a strong brand name on the product which has a reputation for reliability and trust. Look at today's list of strongest brands (Table 6.3) – would consumers find it difficult to buy these electronically? Would they still feel the need to physically interact with the product before buying it? Isn't the product's established reputation sufficient?

Among other things, a strong brand creates a depth and breadth of consumer franchise that cuts across ages, demographics and geographies. A strong brand builds commitment and loyalty that persuades consumers to pay more money for it and sometimes go out of their way to get it because of its perceived value and reliability. It's hard to see how virtual or electronic purchasing – once the infrastructure is in place – will present any barrier to consumers buying established branded products.

Those companies who have invested in their brands over time have put themselves in an excellent position to take advantage of future changes in shopping habits. As consumers do become more familiar with buying on line and as the number of store visits reduce so there will be a premium on established reputations. For consumers learning to navigate their way through cyberspace the easiest purchases will be the products they recognise or the brand names that have the track record.

For new companies wishing to 'break in' there will be renewed emphasis on brand-building and brand-sustaining skills and investments. Even today the physical market place is crowded, saturated in some categories, with many products seen as commodity-like. In such an environment branding may be the only meaningful differentiator that makes one product stand out and become the first choice for consumers. Many companies have long struggled with the challenges of effective brand-building, concerned about how much it costs, struggling to see the pay back, often compromising with half-hearted attempts which just don't break the noise barrier or achieve any significant impact. To go further and establish a lasting reputation requires a profound and enduring commitment to brand-building which only a few companies in each sector seem prepared to make.

This branding challenge will become even more acute in an electronic shopping environment where physical interaction is reduced and where the product's qualities and benefits must be distilled and captured in a way that can be communicated over the wires. It will be more difficult because consumers will now have greater control over what virtual stores and aisles they visit. They are no longer forced to push the shopping cart up and down every aisle past every one of the 20,000 or more product lines on display. They will instead choose where to shop, what categories to explore and how much time they want to spend looking at what's available, comparing prices or getting more information on new product lines.

There is more on the challenge of building consumer confidence in Chapter 15 but there will be an undoubted correlation between strong, recognised brand values and success in electronic selling. Indeed, consumer familiarity and confidence with the product can be assessed now to see if it would stand up well in an electronic environment. Is branding an important purchasing criteria for products generally in a target category? Does the product have sufficient immediate recognition?

A set of questions can be laid out to enable those concerned with product brand strength/consumer familiarity and comfort to quickly assess it and start identifying what are the gaps and investments required to get the brand to where it needs to be (Table 6.4). These questions can form a basic piece of consumer research and act as a familiarity/ confidence check for the product in its market. The aim is to score each answer 0 to 10, with a strong Yes scoring 10 and a strong No 0. 10 would indicate the highest levels of brand strength, 0 the lowest, 5 an average. Scores less than 60 here are inadequate. The strong brand-builders mentioned in Table 6.3 would likely score 80 plus, setting a standard and benchmark for what is needed to succeed.

Building consumer familiarity and confidence is an important success hurdle in any market place, whether physical or virtual. It is likely to be even more important in cyberspace. If a product's characteristics demonstrate ES potential then there may be no choice about building consumer confidence into a recognised and lasting brand name. It may well be that branding has played only a limited role in the sector in the past but the new electronic age will force would-be sellers and distributors to move more forcibly down that path. If one company does not respond and seek to exploit this opportunity then for sure rivals will eventually see the gap and come into exploit it – in the same way that Amazon.com has muscled in to the books market and immediately given some branding lessons to sleeping rivals.

Table 6.4   Consumer Familiarity and Confidence: 'How Strong is the Brand?'

1. Do consumers, without prompting, name the brand as the leader in its category/sector?	
2. Is the lead vs the next-mentioned brand name significant?	_____
3. Have a high proportion of target consumers purchased the product at least once?	_____
4. Is there a high proportion who would count as regular users?	_____
5. Is usage of the product typically highly satisfactory?	_____
6. Would target consumers say they trust the product?	_____
7. Would target consumers agree there is no need to check the product out before purchasing it again?	_____
8. Are intentions to repurchase at high levels?	_____
9. Do consumers see a clear difference in value vs other competing products?	_____
10. Is the ongoing brand investment by the company higher than that put in by competition?	_____

This Step 2 in the ES test sets out an important check on the product's position with the consumer. It applies to every product and service. It's not just relevant for basic everyday purchases. Whatever the item, if there's ES potential then building confidence can be the key enabler to successful electronic selling and distribution. Even fresh fruit, long thought to be an unlikely electronic product, can be sold effectively on line (as Peapod and others have demonstrated) where the seller establishes a reputation of trust and reliability on the freshness and quality of products sold.

3. Consumer Attributes

If the product's characteristics have electronic appeal, if consumers are familiar and confident in buying it then its ES potential is clearly high. But would consumers *want* to make the purchase electronically? Would they still prefer to visit the store? What type of consumers is the manufacturer targeting? What's the profile of those who are visiting the store? Certainly many consumers will respond to the lures and advantages of new, more convenient ways of shopping. But it is equally sure that others will be uncomfortable with the new medium and simply prefer to stick to their old and traditional ways of doing things. While traditions may eventually die out it can take a long time and companies need to know enough about their consumer to identify their electronic market – how big it is now as well as how it might develop long-term.

Figure 6.6   The Triple 'I' Model

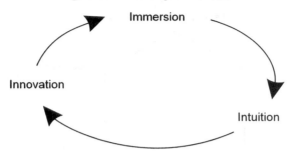

The key to building this understanding has already been referred to. It's through so deep-rooted a market immersion that a company really does understand who are its customers, what are their needs now, how they will develop in the future and the degree to which they'll respond to new purchasing options. This approach to appreciating consumer profiles and attributes can be captured in the simple 'Triple I' model in Figure 6.6.

Dig deep enough into the marketplace so that it's possible to intuitively understand the consumer and be totally in-tune with how they are thinking and behaving. Through that process it is easier to gain insights on how new initiatives will be received, what will work and what won't. With that appreciation new ideas will emerge with a stronger chance of succeeding and there will be stronger foundations on which to establish a reputation for leading innovations in the market.

This sort of approach has been adopted meticulously by leading consumer research organisations like A.C. Nielsen, Mintel and Verdict. A.C. Nielsen, for example, has a panel of c. 10,000 consumers who are regularly reporting back to the company on tastes and preferences and giving input as to what initiatives might work for them. We shall examine their research in detail in Chapter 10 but they identify a number of underlying trends when assessing the consumer base.

Consumers, for example, can be categorised into sub-groups. One such group are called the 'frenzied copers' who will be responsive to any initiative which can ease the pressure and make shopping easier and more convenient. Another group is the 'habitual die-hards' who are stuck in their ways and are reluctant to change. A third group is categorised as 'mercenaries'. They are searchers after value – either better price or better service – and they will respond to whatever proposition best offers that.

In sum, these categorisations show there are six consumer types (Figure 6.7). For each category it is relatively clear what their likely response to

Figure 6.7   Consumer Categories: ES Responsiveness

Social shoppers: enjoy shopping

Habit die-hards:
stuck in their ways

Experimenters:
ready to try new things

Ethical:
will purchase provided
it's honest and 'PC'

Convenience – 'frenzied copers':
responsive to things that save
time/make life easier

Value shoppers – 'mercenaries':
will purchase wherever
is value

Source: A.C. Nielsen, Mintel, Henley Centre, Kalchas.

electronic shopping will be. Of course consumers aren't black and white and they don't fit in just one box so they can be neatly pigeon-holed by market researchers. The categories blur, consumers behave differently, change their attitudes, will be in one category for some products and services and in another category for others. But this research does identify the main underlying motivations and provides a framework to help determine the extent to which a company's current consumer base will likely become electronic shoppers:

- **Social shoppers** – these consumers enjoy visiting stores and take pleasure in shopping. It's an opportunity to get out of the house and meet people. Some stores have identified this trend as being particularly strong among their target consumers. For example, they have set up 'Singles' Nights' where the store stays open late and encourages shoppers to meet and socialise. Commentators have also observed how the bigger stores have become meeting places for people generally – they've become the community centre, often fulfilling the role previously occupied by the church or village hall.
- **Experimenters** – they are happy to try new things and are comfortable in doing so. They have been the first to use and purchase over the internet. This category has a particularly strong representation among the growing net generation of young adults who have grown up with

new electronic connections and have already established their comfort levels in using them.

- **Convenience shoppers** – 'frenzied copers', they suffer most from time poverty and find shopping generally a chore. They represent the stereotype of the busy parent rushing to do the food shopping with reluctant children in tow on the way home from school who will grab at any initiative that can meaningfully improve their life-style, especially if there is little or no extra cost.

- **Habit-bound die-hards** – they will be among the last to change, preferring traditional means of shopping, reluctant to try things like computers. These will be the last to join the electronic revolution and will only come on board once the technology is so established that it becomes totally simple and accessible.

- **Value shoppers** – 'mercenaries' – the search for value is all pervasive but these place it at a premium. They will respond to any marketplace initiative which appears to offer the best combination of product quality, price and service. If the same product can be more easily obtained electronically at the same or lower price with similar or better levels of service back up, then they will be quick adopters of electronic shopping facilities.

- **Ethical shoppers** – there may be a minority who put ethics as their number one criteria over and above these other shopping motivations but this group cannot be overlooked. Their decision-making is likely to be indifferent to whether a product is sold physically or virtually, provided it is done in an honest and 'PC' manner.

Manufacturers and retailers can use this categorisation to evaluate their own consumer base. How many of their customers fit into each category? Is there much change between the categories and can their consumers be properly classified in this way? This type of evaluation is the start of the detailed consumer segmentation that's needed. Only by understanding their consumers in this detail can a company decide what type of electronic response is required.

The product characteristics may show ES potential, the familiarity/confidence check might get high scores but if the target consumers are all 'habit-bound die-hards' and 'social shoppers' there may be little point in rushing down the ES path. Equally product characteristics may show limited ES potential and familiarity may be low but if target consumers are experimenters and 'convenience–frenzied copers' then there will likely be interest and demand for electronic buying facilities ready to be exploited.

Figure 6.8   ES Segmentation

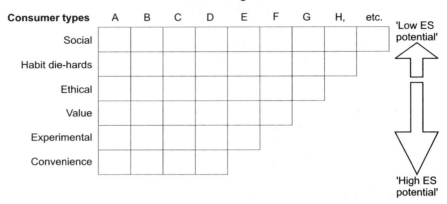

A company with a range of products should draw up a segmentation grid (Figure 6.8) to identify what types of consumers it has in each product category so it can begin to pin down the most appropriate ES response and action plan.

For each product category how many current consumers are in which consumer type? Where are the majority, who are the more frequent purchasers, which spend more or buy more of the product, which consumer types are under-exploited (e.g. are there many more 'frenzied copers' out there than the company currently attracts?) and with which group lies the greatest future potential?

These questions can be answered and the consumer base and its potential quantified. But no company can expect to succeed in the new electronic age without conducting the analysis. It can provide a clear view of the ES potential and determine whether and how best to respond to the electronic shopping revolution.

*   *   *

Summary and scoring

How should the three steps in the ES Test be brought together, the evaluation synthesised and the learning distilled? A simple scoring system can be introduced which adds up the total ES potential and consumer interest. A high score will evidently point the way for urgent appraisal of the ES opportunity and action to capture it. A low score suggests the ES potential is not yet fully formed and a different strategy will be required. The next two chapters will discuss strategic options in detail dealing with the retailer situation first. Chapters 13 and 14 will examine the position from the manufacturer supplier's standpoint. All the various strategic options require the key inputs of the ES Test.

Each of the steps in the test will contribute a score toward the total and can now be considered in turn.

1. Product Characteristics

The more physical the product's primal appeal, the lower its ES score. The more virtual its appeal, the greater potential for electronic selling, the higher its score. Scores out of 10 (Figure 6.9).

Figure 6.9   Product Characteristics' Scoring

2. Familiarity and Confidence

A research check on familiarity/confidence levels was set out in Table 6.4. The research boils down to three key conclusions around previous usage, satisfactory usage and general familiarity with the company or product's reputation (branding) (Figure 6.10).

Figure 6.10   Familiarity and Confidence Scoring

3. Consumer Attributes

As the three steps have been discussed it has become clear that the consumer's attitude toward electronic purchasing can be the deciding factor. Their interest and readiness in shopping electronically can override the conclusions from the other two steps and demand a response that meets their specific need. As a result the scoring for consumer attributes needs to be weighted so it adequately reflects the importance of the consumer driver. The suggested scoring in this part of the test is out of 30. The maximum score available then for the whole test is 50.

The key scoring measure for Consumer Attributes is the extent to which the target consumer base for the product or service is responsive to electronic shopping. How many dedicated convenience shoppers vs how many habit-bound die-hards or social shoppers? What's the overall proportion and is it of a sufficient extent that it provides a meaningful market place and level of consumer interest for selling electronically (Figure 6.11)?

Figure 6.11   Consumer Attributes' Scoring

To illustrate this scoring for different product categories, we can take a generic approach based on average market place and consumer data and provide an initial suggestion (Table 6.5) as to which categories will likely have the highest ES potential.

Any score that's significant, especially if it's over 20, is demonstrating significant future ES interest and potential. Consumer attribute scores by themselves are unlikely to be high right now given that the general development of electronic shopping is still in its early days and many consumers have yet to gain easy access to the new medium. As that consumer access grows and widens so a higher proportion will develop their electronic interests and 'attribute' scores will start rising dramatically.

Table 6.5 Products with Likely High ES Potential-Scoring

Sample products	1. Product characteristics (0–10)	2. Familiarity and confidence (0–10)	3. Consumer attributes (0–30)	Total out of 50
Basic grocery e.g. branded cereals and cookies	4	8	15	27
Basic household e.g. branded cleaners and powders	8	8	15	31
Basic clothing e.g. socks, tights, undergarments	4	7	8	19
Drinks e.g. branded beers, soft drinks	4	8	15	27
Financial Services e.g. auto insurance,	10	5	8	23
standing orders,	10	6	15	31
mortgages	10	1	4	15
Travel e.g. airline tickets,	10	6	15	31
Hotels	7	6	8	21
Books	8	7	23	38

*   *   *

This appraisal and scoring should be carried out on a regular basis. The marketplace is dynamic, things are changing rapidly and a low overall score can very quickly increase. Those who watch their marketplaces carefully and evaluate the trends rigorously can put themselves in the best possible position to respond electronically if and when demand grows. They can ready themselves now, lay their plans, set their strategies, prepare their investments. Doing nothing, unless the score is close to zero, leaves a company vulnerable to fast-moving dedicated competitors or new entrants. Laying the groundwork will build the platform on which to succeed in the new electronic age.

7 How Can Retailers Respond?

The ES test will demonstrate the potential for a product or service to be sold on line. It will help identify likely levels of demand and market size. It can be repeated regularly to watch for trends and other changes in people's readiness to buy electronically. It establishes a framework for determining right now whether and how best to respond.

If the indicators show significant ES interest then what are the response options? What can companies do about it? Must they embrace the electronic world completely, move out of existing retail distribution and deal direct and individually with each end-user? Are they tied into this strategic response? Or can they buck the trend instead and revitalise their proposition so that consumers will be content to carry on with their present shopping patterns? Are there any 'midway' strategies which do respond to electronic demand but which still aim to satisfy and serve traditional shoppers?

These next two chapters and the appendices focus specifically on the retailer dilemma and the strategies and opportunities that can be pursued. Chapters 13 and 14 look at the manufacturer supplier situation and examine their particular options. For both groups of operators there are a range of ten strategies that can be identified, each of which can provide a way through the current challenges and set a path for successful business-building into the next decade. But it's worth emphasising that the key, whichever strategy is chosen, will be its rigorous, persistent, fully resourced and funded implementation. In this highly competitive, fast-changing world, ambivalent half-hearted responses will always be in danger of being quickly overtaken by more dedicated rivals.

Retailers of any substance have already taken the first few steps in learning how to deal with this new era. They have been busy trialling and experimenting and in a low-key way are comfortable with making occasional mistakes. UK retailers like Argos, Sainsbury and Barclays Bank all launched websites with a great fanfare in 1995 only to find, through subsequent research, that the websites were seen as badly laid out, access was limited, quality of communication poor and consumers quickly disappointed with what was available. For example Argos included only a few of their household product lines, Sainsbury sold only wine out of its 20,000 products and Barclays Bank promised it would sell things but initially gave no time or indication as to when.

But retailers are using this learning positively. Websites have been relaunched, phone fax ordering speeded up with more efficient call centres and order-processing systems, home delivery improved and expanded and significant effort put into getting chilled or frozen products to arrive at the right temperature at the right time. After the initial hype and unwarranted expectations there has been a settling-down period. Retailers have established much better resourced and skilled project teams. They have realised this may be more than a small incremental distribution channel. They are going back to the drawing board.

How well placed are retailers to deal with these new challenges and what will the retail environment of 2005 and beyond look like? Do retailers have the basic skills and capabilities to develop a competitive response? Will they need to ally and partner with others to get there? And what's the likely shape of the retail market they should be aiming at in the future? Will there still be high streets and shopping centres as we know them today or will some environments emerge as more attractive than others? Can small or medium-sized high streets with only half the range and choice and experience opportunities of a large shopping mall survive?

This chapter looks at both these issues – retailers' ability to respond and the future face of shopping – and establishes some of the parameters guiding retailers' response options.

Ability to respond

Retailers should not be fighting shy of confronting and dealing with the new electronic world. Quite the contrary, for especially in the last fifty years they have demonstrated a remarkable capacity for innovation and leading edge thinking. In particular leading retailers like Marks & Spencer, Tesco and Wal-Mart have themselves shaped consumer buying patterns and behaviour and at their best have led fashion and demand. Many have a history of being market drivers.

The most far-reaching move this century was the development of self-service. It was first pioneered in the USA during the depression when vacant warehouses were converted into supermarkets selling groceries with the minimum of customer service. It was introduced into the UK by Sainsbury in 1950 (see Plate 1) and immediately impressed customers with the experience of choosing for themselves at their own pace. 'It is irresistible and seductive' recorded the journal *Home News* which reported on this new venture. Even the then British Prime Minister Harold Macmillan was moved to comment: 'it's a very clean and most ingenious way of serving the public and doing business'.

And retailers have of course continued to build on improving the supply chain. The past twenty years, especially since the early 1980s, have seen significant changes in many areas. Much of the effort has gone into improving internal efficiencies in systems, warehousing, outsourcing of transportation, enhanced stock and ordering measures, EDI (electronic data interchange) between retailer and supplier to speed up invoice and order processing, EPOS bar coding and ECR (Efficient Consumer Response) for lower costs and more efficient management of the various stages in the supply chain. All these have had significant impact in reducing costs, ensuring stock availability and providing more efficient and timely distribution of products to the store.

These supply-chain efficiencies have also been translated into benefits for the consumer. Vast improvements in freshness and quality have been achieved, sell-by dating systems have provided reassurances and guarantees of product suitability and packaging is now not only brighter but better preserves the product. In keeping with these developments the more sophisticated retailers have aggressively introduced their own private label in an attempt to further improve quality and value. In the UK especially private label has been so successful that leading retailer Sainsbury has nearly half its sales under its own banner and Marks & Spencer has an extraordinary line-up of manufacturer suppliers providing it with product under the St Michael brand name.

By the mid-1990s retailer supply chain and product innovations were beginning to peak. Where else to innovate, how to continue to excite, pull in customers and keep up the sales momentum? With the USA and UK especially saturated in many urban areas with retail selling space, retailers are in a position where they have to keep adapting, improving and changing if they are to sustain their position in the market and continue to grow shareholder value.

The latest area for innovation is utilising the total sales space to provide complementary ranges of services. Retailers now are looking to encourage consumers to begin to see the major stores as a one-stop shop, somewhere to spend an extended period of time and carry out all the basic shopping requirements. Retailers are doing this sometimes by themselves and sometimes in partnership. They are building service offerings ranging from gas stations through to banking:

- Tesco now offers its customers everything from its basic supermarket grocery food items through to Calvin Klein underwear, Armani socks, popular CDs and children's toys and board games. Its ever-increasing product range has been one of the major drivers of its growth, picking market share from other retailers' territories. Tesco is now trialling new format stores called Extra. They are hypermarket size with 105,000 sq. feet, almost double the size of the current average store. The floor plan is laid out by department and has been extended to make way for numerous new departments.

- Supermarket banks were a new phenomenon at the start of the 1990s but now they're visible everywhere. In California, for example, Wells Fargo has built a network of 700 branches and in-store kiosks, Bank of America has 200 supermarket branches. All the major food retailers have tied up with banks. Kroger is linked with Nations Bank, Publix with Sun Trust. Bank of America is tied into different food retailers in different states working with Lucky stores in California and Jewel/Osco in Illinois.

  Supermarket banking is not confined to the USA. In the UK it only really started developing through 1997 but again all the major food chains have linked up with UK domestic banks. In Germany, Commerzbank for example has 30 branches in different supermarkets and Deutsche Bank is also experimenting with the concept. As one observer put it: 'no one thought they'd ever see Deutsche Bank next to the cheese counter!'

Major food retailers are at the forefront of these developments but over the years many different retail groups have shown the capacity to redevelop and renew themselves:

- Boots in the UK is a very different store now than it was ten years ago. It had long been seen as an excellent but traditional pharmacy operation with an extended range in basic home and baby products. Since that time it has trialled and tested a number of different formats and has evolved into a total health and beauty care operation. It has a substantial amount of space dedicated to perfumery and hosts all the leading brands from Chanel through to Jean-Paul Gautier. It has muscled into Body Shop's territory with a very successful range of natural care products and in its key urban centre stores it often now dominates low-calorie sandwich sales for lunch times. With so much innovation it is not surprising to find that Boots has enjoyed record sales growth and persistently high margins over many years.

- Taco Bell faced extensive competition in the late 1980s and embarked on a long search that would clearly distinguish its operation and ensure it remained attractive. It saw an opportunity to be both aggressive on price and on food quality and set about fundamentally restructuring its supply lines and restaurant operations in order to deliver those goals. It especially invested in order-processing systems so it could serve customers fast and provide a generally higher level of customer service. It too has seen consistent sales growth whilst rivals like McDonalds have stumbled.
- Home Depot looks to keep its retail concepts fresh and alive by building its staff's product knowledge, developing help teams and enquiry desks and making service the number one goal. It has changed from outlets with racks of products to 'information stores' where consumers can go to educate themselves about the range and make the most informed purchase choice.

There are many other examples of successful retailer evolution responding to competition and changing demand patterns. Aside from the retailers mentioned, Sears in the USA, Next, Kohl the US clothing discounter, Radio Shack, Asda the UK supermarket chain and others have all made impressive recent improvements in their store operation and the proposition they make to their consumers.

Continued pressure to innovate

There is no doubt the pressure to continue to innovate will be maintained. Even without the advent of electronic commerce, Verdict – the UK consumer research house – has been reporting that consumers are generally disillusioned with the current retail scene. 'It's been somewhat samey for a number of years and consumers have become bored.' While some retailers are pushing out the boundaries many are risk averse:

> 'Retail brand identities need to be revamped . . . new ideas are needed to engage shoppers' attention . . . if retailers want success it's up to them to inject life back into their shops.'

But while retailers may have demonstrated capacity for renewal in the past they are being slow at pioneering change for the new electronic age. Particularly when it comes to facing up to electronic shopping, many retailers have remained ambivalent (see also Appendix 1). They are struggling to reconcile their physical estate with the demands and possible attractions of virtual selling and buying. As the following recent reports demonstrate, retailers at large have not yet grasped the electronic nettle:

- 'There's lots of trial and experimentation going on but scratch below the surface and we still find a mainly defensive strategy. In some cases retailers appear to be seriously under-estimating the inevitable growth of remote shopping and the key role which the internet will play. A survey of 46 retailers across Europe shows that most still think it won't make a lot of difference to how they run their business.'

  (*Pira International*)

- 'Internet shopping is a small market at the moment and we are not aware of any retailers making money in it yet. Nevertheless there is clearly demand and that will grow spurred by a variety of forces . . . It will establish a new distribution channel which will suck business – substantial business according to reputable forecasters – away from existing channels. That undermines the profitability and valuation of these channels. We believe the big weekly or monthly shop is at risk. Some commentators view the superstore as indestructible. But experts said that about the Titanic too! It's a logic that flies in the face of retail evolution. Every dominant format is ultimately replaced. We do not expect superstores to be any different.'

  (*Henderson Crosthwaite, retail analysts*)

Changing skills and competencies

Of course it's not easy for physical retailers to embrace electronic distribution. They cannot simply walk away from their developed way of doing business. They have created in the past 50 years one of the most efficient business systems to be found in any industry sector. They have built outstanding core competencies especially in location selection and management, buying, logistics and IT systems. They have invested in adding more space and learnt how to squeeze up sales per square foot to very high levels. They have sunk billions into their real estate portfolios. They either hold the freehold or have long leases, often with up to 20–25 year commitments. They have no choice but to consider – at least as a first step – every possible angle to keep that real estate profitable, maintain at minimum current levels of store traffic and ensure they get their pay back on their capital outlay.

Figure 7.1   Change in Business Systems

For established retail chains, electronic commerce has therefore initially been seen as more of a threat than an opportunity. It appears an alien world demanding new competencies and skills that they do not have, undermining their whole basic business system. When they do come to consider what will be required, it's clear that the new electronic business system for consumer selling is going to be significantly different from the current physical version (Figure 7.1). But only by confronting these changes and working out how to deal with them can they expect to turn these challenges into opportunities.

Some core competencies, such as location selection, will have limited application and relevance to a virtual world. Store operations and the management of that complexity may no longer be relevant if stores are unable to revitalise their proposition and consumers just stop visiting, ordering for delivery at home instead. New skills will be demanded – for example, in timely and efficient home delivery, handling electronic buying orders many of which may come through at 11 o'clock at night for next-day delivery in the morning. Marketing will take on a whole new significance as would-be electronic retailers learn how to reach and engage their customers and make their brand names relevant and fashionable for the new age. Relationship-management skills will be at a premium trying to forge new links with more remote consumers now with more choice, shopping flexibility and ability to compare prices.

Making the transition

Can retailers make this transition? Can they successfully migrate from a long-established way of doing business to something quite different? To what extent does their history of innovation and successfully responding to and shaping consumer shopping habits give them the courage and confidence to face up to these new changes? How long have they got to get their minds around the various options? Is there enough time left to start the planning and development so they are prepared for the critical mass point of 2005?

Certainly retailers don't have to make this transition on their own. They already have a history of outsourcing key activities. In the early 1980s there was a boom for transportation and warehousing contractors as they picked up enormous amounts of business from the major retailers either taking over existing retailer activities or building new sites and operations. Since that time outsourcing has become more sophisticated and many retailers have established joint ventures or partnerships especially in 'back-office' areas. IT has often been handed over completely to third parties, others have established large-scale call centres dealing with burgeoning phone/fax order operations, credit queries, invoice processing and in banking for example actually pioneering customer orders and confirming transactions.

There is no shortage of companies willing to offer themselves as partners to retail operations. Companies in the UK like Sitel and BT Connections offer a range of call-centre activities. Global organisations like EDS, CSC and Andersen are all moving to offer a range of outsourcing and support functions. On the home delivery side, companies like Unigate in the UK are considering how to exploit their long-established milk-delivery operation to individual homes to take on a range of broader products and services (the milk round becomes the daily or weekly food delivery service?). Sears in the USA has pioneered a whole series of home help/ home service functions and has such a solid reputation with consumers that it is in a strong position to move into the general home delivery business for others. To the extent that consumers are reluctant to allow companies to bring goods into their home wouldn't tried and trusted Sears uniformed personnel have a much warmer reception?

Organisations like UPS and Fedex are themselves extremely well placed to take advantage of this situation with sophisticated parcel pick up, tracking and residential as well as office delivery systems. Other third-party providers who might get involved in this arena include the big mail-order houses. For example, Great Universal Stores (GUS) and Little-woods in the UK have highly advanced telephone-ordering, credit-checking, order-processing and home delivery infrastructures. They could partner with others looking to embrace and come to terms with the new electronic business systems and the skills that would be required. Alternatively they could leverage their *own* home delivery competencies

Figure 7.2 Value Networks

and like Peapod, Shoplink, Flanagans, Food Ferry and others further establish their own food and other products' home delivery operation. Indeed GUS and N. Brown in UK have recently done this setting up ambitious fulfilment operations, branded respectively Reality and Zendor.

Retailers need to examine this new challenge and perhaps adopt a new kind of operating model that has been pioneered by CSC, Professor Michael Porter and others – the value network (Figure 7.2). This would put the retailer at the hub of a total solutions package. It would enable a company to provide a major response to the electronic challenges but do so in a highly leveraged partnership vehicle, bringing in a range of partners and outsourcers to provide the best expertise.

Operationally there is no doubt that retailers could achieve great success as pioneers and major distributors in an electronic environment. They have years of retail experience. They are well placed in the present value chain. And they can enhance their market position and capabilities in the new era by 'value networking'. They can bring a select range of partners and experts to help them realise their goals.

Their biggest obstacle is in their own heads. They are struggling to deal with the apparent channel conflicts. Is there an effective marriage out there that enables them to retain the viability and profitability of their current real estate while at the same time embracing the new electronic world? If there isn't then how can they migrate from physical to virtual selling without losing their customers and in the doom scenario seeing profits collapse before the electronic operation is up and running?

There is detailed discussion about managing channel conflict in Chapter 13 but it is worth emphasising right now that the transition *can* be accomplished. There are a number of 'success models' out there that point the way and demonstrate the various options. The key lies again in segmentation. There is no substitute for really understanding who are the different customer types, how many want to shop electronically and how many do not, how many are undecided and what will drive their decision-making, whether apparent interest in the electronic world is in fact relatively superficial and whether they can be kept visiting the stores if the stores can respond enough to them. The ES Test and the analyses that go with it will help determine the most appropriate response to each segment group.

Retailers have such an outstanding platform on which to build. They have great brand names, tremendous reputations with their customers, strong and often loyal followings – they are part of the fabric of society. That established position will help them withstand the marketplace changes we have described, but it provides no guarantee in perpetuity that business will keep coming through their door. They can change and are well placed to change, but the planning needs to start soon.

Future face of shopping

As retailers face up to shopping in the twenty-first century what type of environment will they be dealing with? Will there still be the current mix of giant out-of-town shopping centres and malls, large inner-city centres, small town high streets, neighbourhood stores and 7–11-type convenience outlets? Will all parts of this retail scene still attract significant customer flow and continue to be attractive and profitable? Will some shopping areas be more impacted by electronic commerce than others? Which will decline and which will gain?

Examining the trends, it seems clear the future face of shopping will experience the different forces and dynamics of the electronic age and these are bound to have a significant effect. When people do decide to go out shopping, as they surely will, many will go out with different expectations and needs:

- basic groceries and other regularly purchased items will often already have been delivered to their homes
- other products or services which in themselves have a high primary appeal to 'virtual' senses of sight, sound and intellect, will have been prescreened and ordered up electronically from the home PC or TV:
  - products such as books, music, video, computer software and hardware
  - services such as banking, travel and holidays, real estate searches.

Consumers' shopping needs will therefore take on a different emphasis. The focus will be on experiencing, seeing and trying *new* products and services rather than filling the shopping cart with the weekly shop. Some of these trends and changes are not new. Even before the advent of electronic commerce, retailers have been trying to make the whole shopping experience more fun and exciting. They have been developing new formats and searching for ways to reinvigorate their physical space:

- the large supermarkets are adding a range of services like banking, pharmacies, coffee shops to provide a stronger 'one-stop shop' environment
- big new centres are being created typically edge of or out of town which have integrated social and leisure experiences with movie centres, choice of restaurants, fitness and sport facilities – all designed to create an extended stay and family experience.

As these new, more exciting larger centres have opened so small strips and high streets or small groups of neighbourhood stores – the mom's and pop's – have been facing increasing pressure. Consumers are more naturally gravitating to the new shopping experiences (Figure 7.3). They are leaving behind the centres that are old and tired or just too small to provide for what they need. As a result many small-scale shopping areas are under increasing threat. Family-run independent outlets or small chains are suffering as the large centre category killers like Toys R Us or

Figure 7.3 Share of Retail Sales, by Location (UK): Out-of-Town/Regional Malls vs High Street

Source: Corporate Intelligence on Retailing.

Home Depot have opened and immediately penetrated through a wide catchment area with their greater range and choice. Smaller bank branches are also closing, taking away what is often seen as a commercial cornerstone of any flourishing shopping environment.

Combine those trends now with the impact of electronic commerce and there's bound to be accelerated change in the physical retail scene. Small and mid-sized retailers in small and mid-sized centres are likely to see intensified sales and profit pressures. As we move into the twenty-first century, there will be a growing trend toward shopping as more of a day-out activity. There will be even greater interest in the giant centres where the family can spend an extended period looking at new products, trying things on, buying special presents for gifts and birthdays and where the kids also can enjoy themselves.

There will, however, be some exceptions to this. Individual outlets or shops, despite being small in scale, will continue to flourish where they have developed a special appeal. This could include tourist centres e.g. the Cotswold village shopping street or Fisherman's Wharf in San Francisco. It could also include centres that feature destination shops such as specialist antique shops or factory shops where visitors can walk around a factory seeing glass being blown or chocolate made and then buy samples or gifts afterwards. Also likely to survive will be the convenience 7–11s. People will always run out of milk, bread and beer or forget certain items or need something at the last minute.

What will emerge will be a polarisation of the retail shopping scene (Figure 7.4). The larger centres will grow in attraction and the small shops and small centres will begin to die out. There will be a snowball effect, too. The less successful the small centres become, the more outlets will close, the less attractive the surviving businesses will be. And these changes are not that far away. The research is clearly pointing to around the middle of the decade as the time when electronic technology, communication and infrastructure will mature sufficiently to satisfactorily meet and encourage this polarising consumer demand.

Electronic shock! A revolution in the shopping environment is about to take place. It won't immediately affect all consumers. It won't immediately impact all retailers. The USA is ahead of western Europe, other nations are still in the process of waking up to the challenge. Not every mid-sized high street or mall will collapse in the next decade. Some will prove more resilient. Some will have a catchment area of more traditional social shoppers. Others will not have a major mall or centre that is accessible enough to seriously undermine their business. But the trends are firmly in place, the forces for change are gathering

Figure 7.4   The Shopping Environment 2005 and Beyond

momentum and there is a certain inevitability about the transformation that will occur.

Doing nothing right now may still seem a viable option because there are still many sceptics and the market change is still relatively small. But it is growing at an exponential rate. What must be concerning for all retail groups is the head of steam that is building up among the computer, telecommunication and content suppliers especially who are determined to turn business and commerce electronic as quickly as possible. Resisting that and ignoring underlying consumer demand does not appear a viable option. A response is required and the next chapter lays out the ten alternatives that could be pursued.

8 Ten Strategic Options for Retailers

If the ES Test shows that a retailer's products or services have some potential to be purchased electronically then how can that retailer respond, what options are there?

In working with companies in this area research and investigation has identified ten alternative strategies or response options. They cover a range of initiatives from taking just a few small steps to acknowledge the ES interest, through to the most radical involving a full switch of the business away from real estate to virtual shopping.

The ten strategic options are:

1. Information only
2. Export
3. Subsume into existing business
4. Treat as another channel
5. Set up as separate business
6. Pursue on all fronts
7. Mixed system
8. Switch fully
9. 'Best of both'
10. Revitalise and buck the trend.

Before we get to the definition and illustration of each of these strategic options, it needs to be emphasised that they don't all require the abandonment of the current retail estate. Even once the consumer interest and need is sufficiently understood and defined there is still a choice. There is still the option, for example, of 'bucking the trend'. Retailers can choose to review whether the real estate can somehow be so revitalised or developed that customers will still want to visit and shop no matter what the alternative ES temptations. Even moving down the ES path there are many stages of evolution and a number of the options do assume that the physical space and the stores can still play a viable and vital role.

Figure 8.1   What Path to Take?

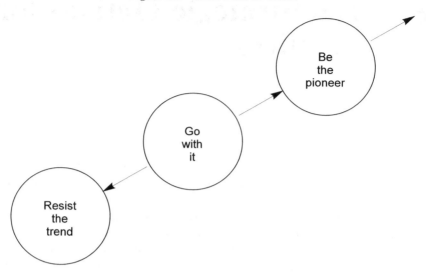

As with any strategic decision-making an organisation of course has 'free will'! It must understand its markets but need not be a slave to them. It has the opportunity to influence and shape future market conditions as much as be influenced and shaped by them. Large established retail operations like Marks & Spencer, Tesco and Sainsbury in UK and Wal-Mart, Home Depot and Brooks Brothers in the USA have been shaping the retail scene about them for many years and consumer shopping patterns are partly driven by the initiatives and changes these companies have made. So existing retail groups must be prepared to think through all the options and determine whether they want to try to resist the trend, go with it or be the pioneer (Figure 8.1).

Taking the ES Test is an important first step in deciding what path to take. But as it's still early days the test may show consumer interest still too indeterminate and uninformed. In such circumstances the middle route of 'going with the flow' is a viable approach – hedging bets till more certainty can be identified. But even that needs to be a proactive deliberate decision not passive inaction. It needs to include a rigorous and continuous monitoring of the marketplace to check when, if at all, a more forceful strategy is required.

Whichever route is chosen, as we shall examine in Chapters 15 and 16, excellence in execution will be critical. This is especially true if there is a determination to resist the trend and keep consumers coming to the store.

This cannot be emphasised too highly. As with any major market evolution the winners that we all come to talk about are those who make an exceptional commitment to ensure their chosen path works. This requires clear strategic thinking, stark milestones and targets, every $ of investment and resource made available to fully fund and staff up the initiatives and a communication and involvement of the work force that delivers an excitement and identification with the strategy and gets employees to go the extra mile in what they do and how they meet and serve their customers. Now more than ever, achieving total customer satisfaction with the shopping experience – however provided – will be a litmus test determining success.

By way of definition, options 1–8 (Table 8.1) assume increasing levels of consumer interest in ES and, with that, greater movement away from existing physical real estate toward an electronic environment. Options 9 and 10 are somewhat different. They both 'buck the trend', seeking ways to defend but also exploit the existing real estate and retail core competencies.

We can illustrate each of these options:

1. **'Information only'** – This acknowledges there will be some ES interest and some exploration by target consumers of what's available electronically in most every business sector. For this reason some presence at minimum is required, as much to respond to this consumer exploration as to protect turf against competitors taking a more aggressive approach to electronic shopping.

Table 8.1   Ten Strategic Options

Strategic options	ES responsiveness	
1. Information only		
2. Export	↓	↓
3. Subsume into existing business	Stronger	Evolving
4. Treat as another channel	the consumer	away from
5. Set up as a separate business	interest in ES	physical
6. Pursue on all fronts		retail base
7. Mixed system	↓	↓
8. Switch fully		
9. 'Best of both'	↑	↑
10. Revitalise		

This is the state which most retailers and indeed most organisations of any substance have reached at the current time. Websites largely are information-giving, indicating what's available but often referring the would-be customer to a list of existing retail outlets or other established means of purchasing.

For example, UK retailer B&Q – a leading DIY retailer – has a website which at this stage deliberately does not look to sell product proactively. Instead it focuses on promoting what B&Q offers in terms of products and services and then tells the customer *where* they can be obtained. B&Q has tried to protect this by getting the right to use the generic website address: www.diy.co.uk so any customer exploring the sector will first reach B&Q and then be told where and how to purchase. Such 'control' of website exploration could potentially cut out competitors who may have a much greater transaction-driven website but may never in practice be reached.

This B&Q example provides a good illustration of how a retailer can manage the ES potential around its products and services without potentially needing to change its retail operation. Though of course there's a point to watch and monitor for where ES interest becomes so strong that the absence of transaction facilities could actually turn the consumer away determined to find the site or electronic means that they can use to shop.

2. **'Export'** – This approach looks to ring-fence existing domestic retail establishments but use ES interest to gain access to new markets and new customers.

For example, Blackwell's is a leading UK bookseller with 82 outlets in university towns and campuses across the country focusing on academic books. For the past 100 years it has had a mail-order service offering its books to wholesalers who will in turn sell them on to individual bookshops in overseas locations or to colleges and universities.

Now with the new web technology Blackwell's is in the process of reinvigorating its entire export operation offering books not just to wholesalers but also direct to consumers. Borrowing from some of the experiences and learning at Amazon.com, Blackwell's has given its site and its transaction-processing capabilities a multi-million-dollar revamp. There is a full listing of over 1 million specialist and academic titles, reviews and recommendations, delivery anywhere in the world, on-line order tracking and account management.

To book buyers outside the UK Blackwell's is to all intents and purposes a dedicated on-line bookseller. To UK book buyers, while the on-line facility is still available, Blackwell's current strengths are its convenient retail locations close to places of learning offering a specialist destination shop.

3. **'Subsume into existing business'** – Like the previous two options this does not seek to change the existing retail operations. However it acknowledges that there will be some ES interest but that interest will, so far as it can, be subsumed or integrated within the existing retail establishment.

Safeway and Sainsbury are two leading UK grocery food retailers who have pioneered this approach – unlike one of their major rivals Tesco whom we shall investigate later. Each has established 'Order & Collect' or 'Collect & Go' operations:

- 'Since the end of the year, we have announced an initiative in home shopping. As many customers find shopping for bulk commodity items both tedious and time-wasting, Collect & Go enables ABC customers to order these products by phone or fax from a personalised shopping list based on their previous purchases.'

  (Safeway Annual Report)

First, note Safeway's recognition that 'customers find shopping [for certain items] tedious and time-wasting'. But Safeway still want their customers to visit the store. Rather than 'enabling' them to stay away with a delivery to the home service, the current strategy requires customers to come into the store even if it's just to visit the collection pick-up point. The aim is to get 'electronic customers' to still shop and walk the aisles for fresh foods and meats and other special items even if they are getting the basic commodities picked for them

The Safeway approach is built around an initial 'personalised' shopping trip where the customer together with a Safeway service representative walk the aisles establishing the 'personalised shopping list'. Once in the Safeway computer a phone call and a reference number from the customer will trigger a Safeway shop assistant into picking the order from the aisles on the customer's behalf so it will be waiting for collection at a set time.

There are executional issues still being sorted out such as managing the personalised picking and collection times so they don't bunch up at the same time of day and dealing with the common issue of substitution – what if the preferred brand or size or variant is not in stock that day? But in this period of trialling and experimentation Safeway is not afraid of making the occasional mistake if it will help to learn how to make the operation a success.

4. **'Treat as another channel'** – This is currently a common approach and many retailers are seeing ES as simply an alternative means to reach a target group of customers.

    UK retailers like Sainsbury, Victoria Wines, and Dixons are looking to exploit the new technologies in this way. Their aim is either to offer greater convenience to existing customers or to attract new customers who can't reach their stores or typically shop elsewhere. For these companies electronic selling has not yet achieved the status of being a totally separate funded and resourced business. It still shares overheads, systems, back-office functions and personnel with all the other main business activities. It's treated in the same way as other channel experiments in the past such as with mail-order or franchising. The company hasn't yet got serious enough about it to set it up in its own right.

    Part of this 'hedge our bets' experimental approach has also seen some retailers participate in others' websites rather than leading with their own. So some can more easily be located by selecting the commercial service provider's mall. AOL and Yahoo! for example each offer this service for an annual fee plus a percentage of the sales. Here it is the provider not the retailer who typically takes the lead in design and promoting the product offering and directing consumer traffic to the site and the virtual shops on it. AOL's mall included for example major retailers such as JC Penney, Brooks Brothers and Virgin music but also smaller groups such as Health & Vitamin Express, the Futon Shop and Access Cameras who can reach wider audiences that way. A further alternative is the host-mall arrangement which is to participate in an open internet web mall site such as NetMarket, Shopping.com or the Internet Mall. Each of these 'hosts' can again take the lead in establishing the site.

5. **'Set up as a separate business'** – This is an important evolution from the previous approach. It's a sign that the opportunity is seen as stand alone and significant in its own right. It also recognises that it is a 'different business' with different skills and competencies required to make it work.

    An analogy can be drawn here with Royal Bank of Scotland's (RBS) involvement with Direct Line insurance. Unlike other financial institutions, RBS set Direct Line up with its own management team, funding and operation and gave it its head. It did not seek to limit or control what Direct Line did and was prepared to live with any cannibalisation that arose for its existing businesses.

Given the general immaturity in electronic shopping at this time, there are few examples yet of retailers moving down this path. However Tesco's own direct business has a significant infrastructure of its own; Next retail has made a tremendous success of its separate mail-order business Next Directory, which works well in reinforcing the retail brand. Marks & Spencer too expects the growth in its own mail-order catalogue business to be accompanied by significant improvements and investments in infrastructure and mail-order competencies.

No doubt as we move through this current era of experimentation and trial more retailers will bite the bullet in this direction, though the cannibalisation issue is likely to be closely measured and monitored.

6. **'Pursue on all fronts'** – Some retailers are determined to pursue every channel that's open to them. They want to reach all their possible target consumers, be as competitive as possible and not allow others to steal a march in a market channel area.

Eddie Bauer, for example, sells its casual men's and women's clothing through some 500 stores in the USA, Germany, the UK and Japan. It also has a developed mail-order catalogue operation (to be expected given its parent Otto Versand's skill base) and is currently exploring on-line sales on the internet via its own website. The company has no particular prioritisation between these three channels but simply sees all three as available and necessary routes to market. If there is any cannibalisation, it's as yet immaterial as the company seeks to expand globally racing to reach as many new customers as funds and resources allow.

Great Universal Stores (GUS) is the UK's largest mail-order company and has a highly developed order-processing call centre and home delivery service. GUS also houses well known retail brand names like Argos, Scotch House and Burberrys which can be reached by mail-order, retail, and for Argos on both interactive TV and on the internet.

Levi's represents a slightly different illustration of 'pursuit on all fronts'. While still primarily a manufacturer and distributor via wholesalers, Levi's has now developed a large number of its own retail sites with some 32 in the UK alone. While living in constant conflict with other retailers, Levi's has remained undeterred and determined to explore all channels to market. It too now has its own website which strongly reflects the life-style image and presentation seen in its store outlets, with games, questionnaires and related features and information.

From the financial services sector, National Westminster Bank offers a good illustration of a 'pursue on all fronts' multichannel player. Figure 8.2 sets out how they see their business.

Figure 8.2   National Westminster Bank: Multichannel Operator

7. **'Mixed system'** – This strategy goes a long way in addressing the importance of ES but also recognises that physical retail shopping will not disappear, that there will be key malls and shopping centres where a continued presence is vital. This approach could also be called 'Flagship stores + On-line delivery'.

    As described at the end of Chapter 7, the future shopping scene does not mean the elimination of physical retail shopping. People will still go out to shop but it will be more of a day-out leisure activity as opposed to the chore job of getting in the basics. In this scenario the big malls and shopping centres will stay strong and become shopping leisure entertainment meccas which will reach out into wider catchment areas. In these centres, consumers will expect all the main retailers to be still represented.

    Retailers will want to be there too because the stores in those centres are likely to both attract a lot of traffic flow and be profitable. But also these stores will act as flagships and as major promoters of the retail brand name. It will be this brand reinforcement that will help build and sustain the complementary on-line direct electronic selling operation (Figure 8.3). This approach becomes a twenty-first-century version of hub and spoke with the flagships operating as key hubs supported by a few central warehouses supplying the stores and reaching out like spokes to support an 'on-line + home delivery' network across the country.

The challenge will be to make the capital flagships a total experience in the product and its life-style. Levi's, Doc Martens, DKNY, Disney, Warner have already established these major flagship showrooms. Tower Records currently has 7 major 'flagship' stores across the UK, its largest in Piccadilly Circus is 37,000 square feet. Tower is currently building its on-line operation to reach the many consumers who cannot get to one of its main stores. It's taking maximum advantage of the multimedia to also offer its vast catalogues electronically and has formed alliances with other commercial on-line networks so it has a highly visible, well advertised web presence. Tower does not intend to build physical stores across the country. It sees its future around flagships to promote the brand and capture a share of retail sales *plus* electronic selling and home delivery to reach out to the whole population.

Figure 8.3   Flagship and On-Line 'Mixed System' – US Example

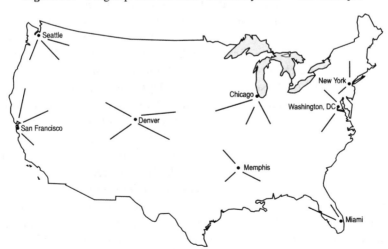

Virgin Megastore is another example in the same product category. Indeed Virgin's heritage was originally in mail-order, then branched out to its own retail outlets. Now it is building major flagships in capital cities and other large conurbations in the key shopping centres and is looking to complement that by rejuvenating its old mail-order business and turning it into a more aggressive on-line selling operation.

This mixed system approach recognises that strong brands will be key in a virtual shopping environment. It works on the premise that electronic brand strength needs to be showcased and reinforced through a select store network. Established retail operations already have a major advantage selling in cyberspace as their brand name and reputation is widespread. But as ES picks up and there are fewer visits to the store, organisations are going to have to find smarter ways to keep the brand name and awareness high. Part of this effort will go into various forms of advertising and prompting on others' websites and we shall explore this later. Part of the effort too can go into the retail operations themselves so that the visit to the shop becomes a true 'flagship' experience, more than just walking the aisles or looking through shelves or racks of products.

8. **'Switch fully'** – Will any retail operation be bold enough to switch fully, to take the path of gradually shifting away from its physical sites and becoming a dedicated electronic trader?

Certainly there are only a few examples of this happening so far. For example British Airways has been steadily cutting back on its physical travel shops as its electronic operation grows and as Microsoft's Expedia continues to demonstrate the ease of on-line ticket buying. More dramatically, UK travel group, the AA, announced the closure of all its 142 high street shops saying: 'people now prefer to do business over the telephone or website'.

As the virtual market develops might we see other retail operations or those whose products/services most lend themselves to ES gradually making the transition? Are not retail banks prime candidates (see also Appendix 2)? The branches are becoming increasingly redundant as ATMs, debit and credit cards take over the basic cash and cheque operation, telephone and PC banking continue to develop and consumers are getting increasingly used to maintaining their bank account without ever visiting a branch. At some point as electronic banking grows the economic viability of each and every physical branch will come under greater scrutiny.

How many, if any, will survive? Some banks and building societies like Nationwide in the UK do seem to have already embarked on a deliberate strategy to get customers to gradually deal with them electronically. As the switch occurs they are closing branches accordingly.

In the same context, retail chains like Blockbuster Video will increasingly see their product made available through satellite, digital TV, through cable or over the net. How long again before the number of visits to the physical store so reduce that it simply becomes uneconomic to keep it open? In such circumstances won't these retailers be forced to 'switch fully' or simply shut down?

For greenfield new entrants, of course, the choice is easier. The lower investment and set-up costs, the immediate global reach, the recognition of which products are most ES-sensitive means that the past two–three years has seen a number of new companies opening straight onto the net with an exclusive on-line offering. Companies like Amazon.com, Autobytel, Bluefly.com, The Fresh Food Company, Peapod, Internet Bookshop, Interactive Music and Video Shop, Garden.com, 1-800-FLOWERS have all set up dedicated electronic sales and home delivery operations which are slowly establishing themselves. Unencumbered by existing physical sites and with a lower cost base these organisations are learning how to take advantage of their position in the market. In certain sectors such as music, books, computers and financial services these electronic operations are already seriously challenging their established physical retail competitors.

9. **'Best of both'** – Is there an approach which can meet the electronic shoppers' needs but still retain the integrity of the existing retail operation? Is there a response which allows retailers to sustain their physical retail operations yet still takes them forward into the twenty-first century – a development path that can achieve excellence on both the physical *and* virtual dimensions?

The 'mixed system' – option 7 – goes some way in this direction but it assumes reducing to a few flagship stores supporting and stimulating a far-reaching electronic sales network. 'Best of both', in contrast, assumes that most if not all existing stores *can* be retained. It also assumes this is done *alongside* a developed electronic operation.

The essence of this approach is the physical shell of the retail outlet. Let us assume we have this sunk investment and our challenge is to move it on so it meets the new shopping environment in 2005 and beyond. What changes would we make, how would we lay out the store? Would we continue to have rows of aisles and racks and shelves or should we assume a number of our customers will already have got the 'chore buying' – the basics or the regular purchases – out of the way before they visit. Let's imagine we're a food grocery store like a Tesco, a Sainsbury, a Giant or a Kroger's Supermarket. We have all this space, now what do we do with it?

We want to achieve a store for the future, a place people will want to visit, a destination shop for the twenty-first century. We want to create an environment which keeps attracting customers and if possible gets them to stay longer, spend more money in total and enjoy the total store experience. The basic and regular purchase items must be dealt with as efficiently and quickly as possible – get them out of the way – bring out the fun side of shopping. There will always need to be a certain functionality, but can shopping now also be made pleasant and relaxing? For example, the store might feature an extended coffee shop and lounge. That could be a place where people can meet, socialise, relax *but also* place their shopping orders. They could shop conveniently and electronically via touch screens on the side of their table. Payment made there and then, so no check-out counters or long waits standing in line, no wheeling out unwieldy shopping carts to the parking lot. Simply drive out via the Collect & Go station where an assistant puts the bags in the back.

In the next chapter, a possible store of the future is described and illustrated in more detail. In planning its development retailers will need to review the combination of products, services, service and environment to find the best combination for their target consumers. They will need to test and trial what works and what doesn't and how each can best interact to serve up a totally satisfying 'best of both' shopping experience (Figure 8.4).

Ambitious retailers will want to investigate opportunities along each of these four dimensions in defining their store of the future. What level of individual customer service and services will be appropriate, what new initiatives in relationship management, product knowledge, child care, and order-processing systems will be needed to ensure that the customer experience is fulfilled and not frustrated? What environment will need to be created? Does it still look like a Tesco or a Wal-Mart late 1990s vintage? What's the buzz that lifts it into a desirable shopping experience? Is there sufficient excitement simply in the new features to the store and its new layout?

At Sainsbury's Self-service shopping is EASY and QUICK

1—As you go in you are given a special wire basket for your purchases.

2—The prices and weight of all goods are clearly marked. You just take what you want.

3—Are you a fast shopper or a slow? You can be either when you shop at Sainsbury's!

4—Dairy produce, cooked meats, pies, sausages, bacon, poultry, rabbits and cheese—all hygienically packed.

5—Meat is served from Sainsbury's special refrigerated counters. Or you can serve yourself from the cabinets.

6—Pay as you go out. The assistant puts what you have bought into your own basket and gives you a receipt.

Shopping in the electronic age

1. Shopping from the comfort of home

2. While the store staff pick your order . . . . .

3. . . . . you can be out enjoying yourself

4. Your shopping's delivered when you want it

Iceland's home delivery service

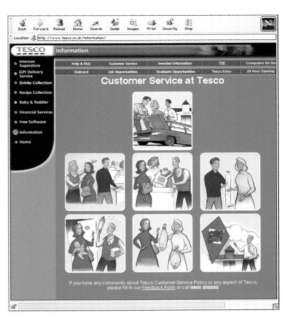

Ordering your Tesco shopping on the internet

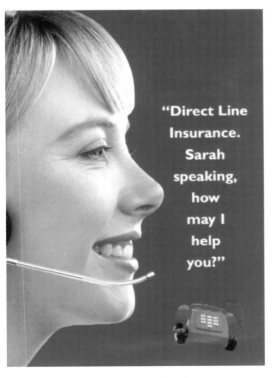

Direct Line – insurance over the phone

Lakeside Shopping Centre and Retail Park

WebTV works with the TV
you already own.

It plugs into the standard telephone line
you already have.

And you can use it from the best
seat in the house.

AsiaOne Commerce

Karstadt's My-World

Dixon's website

Abbey National website

The Information Skyway

Geosynchronous satellites orbit at an altitude of 22,300 miles.

Teledesic's satellites will be only 435 miles above the surface.

Videoconferencing
High-frequency radio waves could carry videoconferences from the surface to the satellites and back again.

Solar-powered phone booth
Remote settlements with no electricity could connect to the global telecom network via satellite.

Fiberless Internet
Telephone companies could use the Teledesic network to offer fast Internet connections in areas that lack fiber-optic networks.

The Information Skyway
© 1996 Time Inc.

Ordering from Dell over the internet

On-line Banking via Quicken at Citibank

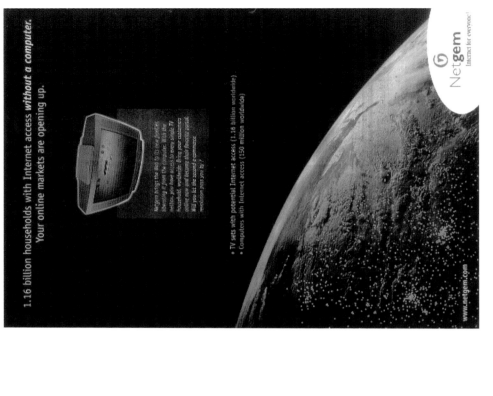

1.16 billion households with Internet access *without a computer.*
Your online markets are opening up.

Netgem brings the key to its new private
Start-up, giving more consumers will be
possible worldwide, giving your customers
online more and become really/become partial
evolution pass you by?

- TV sets with potential Internet access (1.16 billion worldwide)
- Computers with Internet access (150 million worldwide)

Netgem
Internet for everyone!

www.netgem.com

www.netgem.com

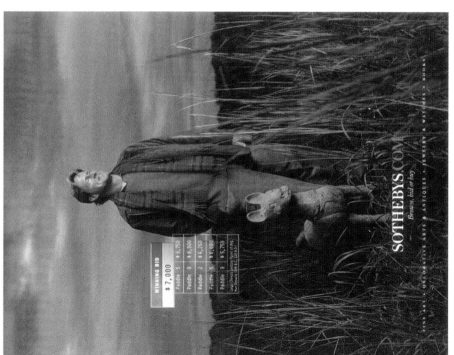

WINNING BID
$7,000

Paddle 5	$6,750
Paddle 9	$6,500
Paddle 2	$6,250
Paddle 5	$6,000
Paddle 9	$5,750

SOTHEBYS.COM
Browse, bid or buy.

FINE ART • DECORATIVE ARTS • ANTIQUES • JEWELRY & WATCHES • BOOKS

sothebys.com

www.nextcard.com

Sun microsystems

Figure 8.4 The 'Best of Both' Shopping Experience

What's the opportunity, for example, in genuinely creating a community centre where people meet and pick up their shopping later? Can that lead to the development of a strong catchment area identity and 'community spirit'? How might that be captured in-store? Does the store become like the church hall with local news, local events and meetings? Will that translate into increased consumer traffic? And where is the line drawn on the product offerings? What is showcased and what is relegated to the back of store-picking warehouse? Does it become a negotiating issue where manufacturer/suppliers can only get products into the store front on special payments and promotion terms?

Some of the challenges for building this 'store of the future' include investigating whether there is enough space – is the existing shell big enough? Which mix of services is most appropriate and if there's not room for them all then which ones have most appeal? Also for consideration will be the pace of the changes. Do stores transition in short order or do they evolve to move gradually to this new environment? Electronic system costs may be substantial, store labour may be more intensive and the economics of the store will require careful consideration to retain satisfactory levels of profitability.

As retailers consider the options there are clearly many questions to be addressed in understanding what can be achieved, what's profitable and what isn't and what will best meet consumer demand. Certainly the big food grocery chains all have large enough stores and a sufficiently aggressive new store-opening plan that in the next few years 'stores of the future' can be developed and trialled to find out what works and what doesn't. The trick will be to set out this new store at a point in time when consumer interest in ES is clearly on the increase, when technology is more readily available to make the electronic purchase experience fun and easy, and to choose a geographical area where consumers are more likely to be responsive to these sort of innovations.

Of course it requires a certain boldness to carry out this sort of store trial and development. Some of the bigger groups are in fact not that far away today from this type of set-up, with experimental 'Collect & Go' pick-up points and additional services being brought into the store. But it is the ones who continue to experiment boldly who will have the best chance of shaping and influencing how the market place develops and stealing a march on their competition.

10. **'Revitalise and buck the trend'** – This option makes no concession to the forces of electronic retailing. It takes a determinedly defensive stance toward the existing physical retail operation but looks to revitalise it so consumers want to come and continue to shop just as they did before. It assumes changes in the retail format, but unlike the previous strategy these are purposely not aimed at meeting the electronic shopper.

A likely path for retailers choosing this option is to turn their retail operation into a Retail + Leisure environment where visiting the store becomes a more rounded fuller experience. 'One view is that many retailers will also have to become entertainers,' observed the *Financial Times* in a recent survey, 'as internet shopping grows consumers may only be tempted into the shops if they can expect an environment which majors on fun.' And there are two ways to achieve this. Either each store works out its own individual solution, or groups of stores in a mall, a shopping centre or even in a high street combine and develop a total shopping and leisure solution which all can benefit from but is bigger and better for having the funding and support of a large number of different businesses.

In response there is a wealth of ideas being trialled around the world, ranging from movieplexes to a full beach and kayak racing inside West Edmonton (Alberta Canada) mall. There are also dozens of shopping centres now boasting fairground entertainment including one in Durban, South Africa which has a ferris wheel protruding through the roof of the centre. Restaurant and food courts abound and developers are now pushing out the boundaries to explore what leisure facilities will give their new shopping centre that buzz and excitement that will generate the desired traffic flow.

As electronic shopping takes off, those determined to buck the trends will face growing pressure to find the right blend of leisure and retail. Once established it will then require continued monitoring to ensure the leisure/retail concept remains up to date and endures and there is the right mix of retail tenants to complement the leisure theme. Might we begin to see retail/leisure parks targeted at different customer groups, with some aiming at the younger shopper while others target the older more sophisticated shopper whose concept of leisure is likely to be less noisy and helter skelter and geared to more sedate and subtle interests?

Achieving the appropriate retail and leisure state will require significant investment and proactivity on the part of a retail chain. It's likely retailers will want to seek experienced leisure operators as partners to both share the risk and capital but also to access the core skills and competencies required to make the leisure initiative truly work and pay back.

*   *   *

Summary

To help evaluate and compare these ten strategic responses let us draw out a couple of summary frameworks. First we can contrast the risks and potential of each (Figure 8.5).

Each option has its own risk:reward profile and will have a different appeal to each retail group depending on that group's own culture, its ambitions and its desire to resist the trend or be a pioneer.

We can also turn back to the ES Test for help in choosing which of these options is the most relevant to the specific product/consumer mix that an individual retailer is dealing with (Figure 8.6).

Now is the perfect time to be considering these ES challenges and determining the response that will prevail in the new market environment. Critical mass in electronic shopping is still some years away but the opportunity has arisen to evaluate and plan today, taking into account how the market will likely develop, using the ES Test to get a handle on specific target customer needs and determining what risk and reward ambitions are most attractive.

148

Figure 8.5 Comparing the Options

	RISKS			REWARDS	
	Size of investment	Change in business system, key skills needed	Impact on organisation/culture	New revenue potential	Pay back time
1. Information only					
2. Export					
3. Subsume into existing business					
4. Treat as another channel					
5. Set up as seperate business					
6. Pursue on all fronts					
7. Mixed system					
8. Switch fully					
9. 'Best of both'					
10. Revitalise					

○ = Low ◐ = Med. ● = High

○ Slow ● Fast

Figure 8.6   Choosing from the Ten Strategic Options

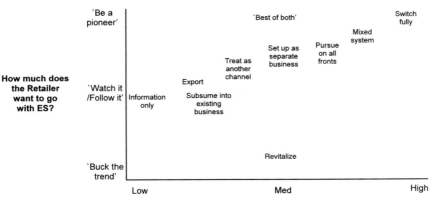

But this decision-making cannot be delayed much longer. 2005 is racing ever nearer in planning and investment terms. In the meantime new store openings are already being scheduled, land is being purchased and designs and formats defined. The new order in the next decade will not allow 1980s formats to continue to survive and succeed. Changes and redesigns can be thought through now enabling this generation of stores to be built – or the new world of electronic shopping to be created.

9 The Store of the Future

What will the store of the future actually look like? Before illustrating the 'Best of both' option referred to in Chapter 8, we should briefly examine some of the new retail technologies that are being developed and which enable the future store to take shape.

In-store technologies

Stores are now becoming intelligent. It's not just about EPOS and barcoding, the whole store is becoming smart. New technologies like wireless networks, multimedia kiosks and the internet can be integrated into the store operation. They transform what information can be communicated in-store and how quickly it is transmitted. They can link every employee not just a few sitting in the administration office. They can also, most importantly, involve each and every consumer. The whole store can be brought alive. Consumers can be electronically connected. They can be networked into store information lines and into employees for assistance as they walk around. They can do their own bar-code scanning, pay when they want, avoid waiting in lines where others tell them. They can be empowered, made to feel more in control and given the means to extract the maximum value from the shopping experience.

To facilitate this, there are two particular in-store technology innovations coming through. Each needs to be described to understand the impact they can have on future store layout and design and the services retailers can start introducing to retain and attract customers:

- Wireless networks and hand-held terminals
- Touch screens.

Wireless networks and hand-held terminals

If physical cabling is no longer a constraint then retailers are immediately liberated from a fixed store layout. While retailers have over the past ten years invested heavily in underfloor cabled EPOS systems through the store, there is no doubt that any major retailer investing in a new site would now go for a more flexible wireless environment.

There are cost benefits but more importantly significant customer service advantages as well. Sales staff can be equipped with portable PCs linked to the store server. They can deal with individual queries, check on stock availability, identify any order lead times and arrange for immediate replenishment from the warehouse. In some stores, for example, couples about to get married are invited to walk the store with a store assistant, checking what's in stock and compiling their wedding list on the portable PC. No need to wait in line at a counter or go back to the old fifth floor 'customer service centre' to be dealt with.

These wireless systems are also known as RF (radio frequency) and they can be seen increasingly in stores with sales staff wearing headset microphones attached to belt-mounted RF terminals. Most of the top US retailers now have RF systems in some form and while the initial installations were among back-office staff linking warehouse stock-picking, it's now being seen with more prominence in the store front and involving the customer.

'Putting the consumer in control' is an increasingly achievable and powerful new market proposition. For example, customers themselves can be given their own, simple hand-held self-scanning devices which they use to scan the bar codes of the products they choose. The current scheme involves them handing over the scanner on the way out to a checkout assistant who then prints off the list and a receipt for the customer to pay. There is no need to unload the shopping basket. A further evolution of this technology is to make an exit channel which automatically reads a radio tag embedded in the product's packaging, computes the cost of the items purchased and prints out the bill – all in about 30 seconds.

Albert Heijn, part of the Ahold supermarket chain headquartered in the Netherlands, has been one of the pioneers of hand-held self-scanners and many of its stores now offer customers this facility. UK supermarkets like Safeway and Tesco have been quick to trial these devices and say they plan to make them more widely available once screen display and image definition improves.

Touch screens

Touch-screen technology is making a significant contribution to the wider consumer acceptance and usage of computers for the purposes of gathering information and shopping. ATMs have already become an accepted way of carrying out basic banking transactions even to the point where the bank branch is, in some instances, being retained but the service staff completely removed. All that's left is a bank of touch-screen machines dispensing cash, taking deposits and enabling customers to transfer money between accounts. For personal advice pick up the white courtesy telephone and speak to a member of staff, possibly located a hundred miles away in a call centre (see also Appendix 2).

Touch-screen formats are fast and can respond to consumers who want to carry out the transaction as quickly as possible. One US retailer, Frank's Nursery, found that touch screens reduced typical transaction times by up to 50% while retaining 100% information accuracy. Touch screens are also attractive because they easily optimise eye–hand co-ordination and can provide a sensory experience to complement what is normally just read on the screen. More sophisticated versions can combine sight and touch with sound as well, beginning to provide a more 3-D virtual reality experience.

This technology is now finding its way into the retail environment in what are called 'multimedia kiosks'. These are often free-standing sites, sometimes enclosed, where people can go to browse through goods displayed on the screen at their leisure and in some degree of privacy and comfort. Banks like Barclays and car manufacturers like Daewoo are but two groups who have persuaded supermarket retailers to provide them with this kind of space. Most kiosks give access to material running on CD-Rom but some are also now linked to a company's internet site enabling consumers to gather more personalised information and place orders. Who needs a bank branch or a car dealer's showroom in the local town if the information and order facility can be provided virtually from a broader-based, one-stop retail environment as found in a large supermarket or still larger shopping centre? As supermarket retailers specifically face their own disintermediation challenges they are ironically facilitating the physical demise of banking and other retail outlets. By providing virtual space for others they are hoping it will prolong their own physical lives!

Touch-screen trials are pushing out the current electronic commerce boundaries. One trial led by Cornell University is called CU See Me. It provides on-line video broadcasts, accessed via a touch screen, to take place between users to give live product demonstrations. Another example comes from British Telecom who have been exploring public touch screen kiosks as the 'new revolution telephone booth'. There have been mixed results so far but the idea is to connect users to travel information, enabling them to book flights or order flowers and send gifts around the world. Eventually the plan would be to provide full internet access. These booths could be located in the street, in shopping areas, inside supermarkets, in hotels, colleges, at motorway service centres. BT plans to trial more than 10,000 terminals in the UK.

*   *   *

These new in-store technologies will be an important aid to retailers in their fight to stay physical and prevent all their custom rushing to a remote virtual shopping environment. It will help them keep their stores fresh and innovative providing new experiences. It will give opportunities to reconfigure store lay out, do away with the rather cumbersome and old-fashioned lines of check-outs and make the in-store environment and service more user-friendly and attractive. They can provide other services in kiosks, put touch screens in the store coffee shops and respond immediately via RF to enquiries about stock or requests for more information. They can embrace the electronic world but do so from their real estate. They can have all the most sophisticated electronic connections that the consumer could ever want, and all under one roof. If they respond positively enough down this path they would certainly have a very strong chance of not just surviving the electronic revolution but coming out the other side all the stronger in their customer franchise.

This potential future world is described in the next few pages showing one particular view as to what an integrated physical plus electronic shopping environment might look like. It's a view that sketches out what could be achieved as technology advances and matures. It's a vision for a retail group that has thought through its options and made a commitment to embrace electronic shopping but from its physical estate. There is no doubt, though, that as the decade unfolds the boundaries of what is possible will extend even further, making today's dreams even more realistic and achievable.

'Best of Both' illustration

As we drive into this 'store of the future' it already looks and feels very different. In this 'Best of Both' option (also see option 9 in the previous chapter), the goal is to retain the essential integrity of the supermarket as distributor and product showcase while embracing the electronic age to provide a more exciting yet comfortable shopping experience. Let's examine a few snapshots:

Frame 1:   The parking lot still contains plenty of room to park the car but there are now a number of customer service options

- Self-Parking
- Valet Parking
- Family Parking – with special assistance for young children
- a route for 'Pick Up & Collection' to drive straight round and pick up orders made electronically.

Walk into the store. There's a substantial revision to what services are available and what products are actually merchandised in front of store. There's an integration of electronic shopping needs with those of the more traditional shopper. The aim is to make shopping fun and enjoyable and still retain the necessary functional elements. Shoppers can wander the store or go straight to the coffee shop. They can order electronically at multiple points in the store or they can pick up a cart or basket and fill up with special foods, new products and the evening meal.

The store is divided into a number of sections and in Figure 9.1 there's an open plan of how it might be laid out:

- Reception Area
- 'Home-Delivery Service Shop'
- Children's Drop-in Centre
- Local Information Area
- Services Arcade
- Ready Meals
- Fresh Foods and Healthy Eating
- 'Electronic Coffee Shop'
- New Products Centre
- Picking Warehouse and Administration.

Frame 2:   Reception Area – the store now offers a range of services and activities so as we walk in there's a hotel-style reception area. There's a general enquiry counter/customer service desk helping us find our way around because it's still new and different and we're still learning what this new store has to offer. There's a lobby area where we can meet friends, wait to pick up the kids or otherwise relax.

Frame 3:   Home-Delivery Shop – just off the Reception area is the Electronic Shopping service counter. It deals with general

Figure 9.1   Plan of the Store of the Future

Electronic
Coffee Shop

Picking and
Admin

Patisserie

Fish and Meat

New Products

Cheese
Counter

Fruit and
Vegetables

'Foods from
around the
world'

Fresh Bread

Services
Arcade

Today's Recipes/
Ready Meals

Juice Bar

Information
Centre

Children's
Drop in Centre

Home-
Delivery
Shop

Check-out
Counters

Reception

Parking

queries and provides information on the home delivery operation. It will set up appointments with in-store representatives for customers to come in and set up their standard shopping order for automatic weekly delivery. Those who want to do it themselves can go to special multimedia booths where they can log on to the store's electronic shopping list.

Frame 4:   Children's Drop-in Centre – this is where the kids can be left under supervised care. It can function as the local community drop-in centre where children can be left all morning or all afternoon while parents are off doing other things. It would have trained staff in a secure environment with learning, education and games facilities. It will help establish the store as a focal point for the community, it can help extend its role from supermarket to one-stop service centre.

Frames 5, 6: Local Information Area and Services Arcade – before walking into the areas where the products are displayed, two other service areas are drawn to our attention. There is a city-county-wide information area staffed by the local residents' associations providing details on local events, school concerts, market days, etc. And beyond the information desk is the Services Arcade. There's a bank of ATMs, a pharmacy, a travel shop offering detailed advice on holiday destinations, also general internet services kiosks where we can access the whole world wide web and carry out any other shopping or information needs we have.

Frame 7: Ready Meals – recognising consumers' busy life-styles and reduced time for preparing meals at home, there's a ready meals section, New York deli-style. There's a chef providing demonstrations of 'recipes of the day', the opportunity to sample some of the prepared foods and a special counter where all the ingredients for the recipes can be obtained.

Just beyond the Ready Meals area we might find a 'Foods from around the World' counter featuring produce and speciality dishes with regional flavours such as Italian, Chinese or Indian. Such areas will be typical of the new store. Instead of going to the frozen foods section to buy the pizza and french fries, it will be merchandised and brought together in more colourful ethnic concepts and ready to 'take away'!

Frame 8: Fresh Foods and Healthy Eating – a large part of the store will be taken up with items that don't come in packages and which more naturally appeal to consumers' instincts of touch, taste and smell. There will be fresh bread counters, cheese sections. There may be a patisserie. There may be fresh meat and fish. Each store will find its own selection which best meets local tastes and interests. Some may add an organics section while others may have 'taste and try' counters where people can test out new things.

Frame 9: New Products Centre – manufacturers will remain especially keen to bring their new products, flavours and variants to consumers' attention. We might find a special section we can walk around with such new products on display and manufacturers 'renting space' from the store for a day to demonstrate their new goods, give away coupons and samples and help establish their new items in the consumer consciousness.

Frame 10: Electronic Coffee Shop – this will be more of a lounge/restaurant than the old-fashioned fast food facility. It will be a place to relax, meet friends as well as get breakfast, lunch or a snack.

What will be special about this coffee shop is that both in the lounge area and in the restaurant there will be tables with computer screens displaying the full range of the store's products. People could order their goods electronically seated comfortably at their table while waiting to be served. They could then either arrange to collect those goods on the way out or have them delivered to their home later in the day. If they already have their standing weekly order set up they could simply enter their password codes and send the order through with a couple of taps on the touch screen. It's shopping while relaxing.

Frame 11: The back of the store is now converted into a large picking area. Many of the items previously laid out in front of the store on shelves are now in boxes in picking slots. A team of staff have responsibility for picking up the orders electronically, packing them and moving them to the Collection Point. Depending on the amount of space available, the picking area might be located on an adjacent site.

*   *   *

Will this store of the future, or something like it, become the reality? Will retailers restructure their physical estate so it does embrace the new technologies? Will they 'wire' consumers up, let them do their own ordering at their leisure, provide instant payment facilities instead of long check-out lines, let the customer pick up their packed order on the way out or have it delivered home later the same day? It will require a retraining of staff. Technical capabilities will have to be upgraded. Communication skills and interactions with customers will need to become even more sophisticated. Front line employees will have to learn the meaning of hassle-free customer service!

Leading retailers are well placed to make these bold moves. They have the financial position, the market clout and as we have discussed a history of making step changes in supply. Timing will be critical, the technology must be user-friendly, fulfilment procedures must be in place, the store must be able to easily deliver what it promises. It is certainly achievable. Experimentation down this path is bound to take place. But, ultimately consumer demand plus competitive pressures will surely force the pace and also the ambition of the services and store facilities retailers set out to provide.

10 Rapidly Improving Technology Meets Growing Consumer Demand

If retailers don't take the initiative, then consumers will. We are seeing the rise of the 'prosumer' – the more experienced and self-reliant consumer who is self-confident and assertive about what they need, is demanding in terms of service and information and is prepared to proactively search out for value and for suppliers who will deliver the services that are required.

As consumers reach out to take more control of their environment so technology will become their key enabler. The growing spread of the internet will help consumers shop around to review competing products, sophisticated search engines will compare prices and point out where the best value will be. Choice will range across the whole world and there will be no constraints from limited shop opening hours or drive times and catchment areas.

This combination of sophisticated consumer demand plus rapidly improving technology are the key forces driving the changes in shopping habits and the arrival of the electronic revolution in retail distribution (Figure 10.1).

These forces have developed an inexorable momentum. Consumers are better educated, have higher expectations and are under increasing stress and time pressure in their lives. They know what's possible and will go after it relentlessly. On the technology side, there are now many organisations across many industry sectors in Computers, Telecommunications, Electronics, Semi-conductors, Software, Publishing and Entertainment who are investing aggressively and are determined to turn electronic commerce into a multi-billion-dollar revenue and profit opportunity. It's a coming together of changing demand with a supply side that's on the move. It's creating the revolution in the world of commerce and this chapter looks at how each will materially drive the electronic shopping market.

Figure 10.1   The Consumer and Technology

On the demand side, we're looking to be more precise as to how many consumers will be imbued with the desire to buy things electronically. Aren't consumers happy enough with today's shopping arrangements? Where there is dissatisfaction, how widespread is it? There's talk of c. 15–20% of consumers – a hard core – who are already impatient for the technology and infrastructure to buy electronically, how ready are they to shop in this way? What's the impact of a 15–20% drop in store traffic on store profitability? Is it going to stay at the 15–20% level?

On the supply side, we're looking at the state of the current technology for electronic commerce. How is it expected to change and what are likely to be the most popular and successful electronic connections? There's talk that current copper telephone wires are limited in their capacity and the cost of replacing them too much for one corporation or consortium. But will that be necessary? Is there technology which can already see past these roadblocks and which will bring data and images at high speed and resolution onto our PC or TV screens and into our homes? How soon will it be available?

Changing Demand

USA Today in a recent article announced the arrival of the 'I want it now' society – an environment where consumers are becoming increasingly impatient and intolerant, where they know what is possible and are unwilling to accept anything less than the best. The article was commenting on a strike at UPS (United Parcel Services) in the USA and the delays that were caused in getting parcels and other mail quickly from one place to the next. One of the reasons for the strike ironically was that UPS employees could not keep up with the pace of demand and that consumer insistence on immediate delivery was exerting too much pressure on them. The strike and the outcry that was caused by the delays was all part of a wider syndrome, *USA Today* suggested, that was sweeping America. Consumers were increasingly demanding: 'I need it now or just don't bother!'

> 'In a society in love with the immediacy of the internet and the speed of the fax machine, overnight delivery services have taken on an overblown importance. We are seeing the emergence of the "overnight society" that is increasing expectations but at the same time adding to the tension and stress in our lives. Technology has been the catalyst that has created this situation. Where companies used to have a week to come up with a big idea now it is expected within an hour over the fax or through the PC.'
>
> *(USA Today)*

As the beginning of the twenty-first century dawns we're moving closer to an environment demanding instant gratification. It's put increasing pressure on all supplier service levels and many have been struggling to keep up with the pace, utilise the improving technologies and meet the underlying consumer need and demand. As a result consumers are often left frustrated and disappointed with late deliveries, long waits, broken promises, insufficient information and inadequate response to queries and complaints.

It's a situation that leaves a large gap in the marketplace – a widespread consumer need that still is not being fulfilled. We've just completed the 'customer service' 1990s, but it seems consistent customer satisfaction is still a long way off in many different industry sectors. No wonder then consumer interest is so high in electronic commerce. Any proposition that looks as though it *can* respond to changing consumer lifestyles and *can* deliver quickly and effectively by exploiting new technologies is likely to have a high take-up rate.

Still a large customer service gap

For retailers the gap between promise and fulfilment remains too high for comfort. They are leaving themselves vulnerable to new, more customer-effective propositions. The American Society for Quality review of Customer Satisfaction, reported in *Fortune* magazine, shows that only one retail chain in the USA made the top 50 companies for consumer satisfaction! That was Nordstrom. But even Nordstrom couldn't make the top ten (Table 10.1).

Table 10.1 Customer Satisfaction Index

	Top 10
1.	Mercedes Benz
2.	H. J. Heinz food processing
3.	Colgate Palmolive
4.	H. J. Heinz pet foods
5.	Mars
6.	Maytag
7.	Quaker Oats
8.	Cadillac
9.	Hershey Foods
10.	Coca-Cola
26.	Nordstrom

Source: NQRC, University of Michigan.

This same survey also calculated average satisfaction scores for industry sectors at large. The retailing community did not come out especially well, not as bad as the IRS (Internal Revenue Service) but still some significant way off the leading pace (Table 10.2). The survey concluded that the service sector generally had the least satisfied customers – mostly because 'down-sizing had reduced the number of front-line workers and made them stressed out'. In contrast consumers were generally 'happier with manufacturers' and certainly many of the top companies in this report are consumer goods manufacturers who are

Table 10.2 Industry Sector: Customer Satisfaction Scores

1.	Beverages
2.	Pet foods
3.	Personal care
4.	Food processing
5.	Parcel delivery
6.	Household appliances
7.	Consumer electronics
8.	Automobiles, trucks
9.	Gasoline
10.	Tobacco
11.	Apparel
12.	Insurance
17.	Department and discount stores
18.	Supermarkets
32.	Internal Revenue Service

Source: NQRC, University of Michigan.

clearly seen as fulfilling their end of the supply chain better than their distributors.

According to a study by Professor Berry at Texas A&M University, 89% of American adults are still 'dissatisfied shoppers'. They can't get what they want when they want it. Many companies, Professor Berry found, just don't do enough to assess and understand what their customers really think, their consumer research is relatively superficial, they struggle to build loyalty and just don't develop the insight and appreciation that would help them retain and build their customer base.

In fact the Technicians' Assistance Research Program (TARP) based in Washington found that consumer complaint was substantially higher than most surveys recorded. In their research they found typically only 4% of dissatisfied customers actually took the time to formally complain – many just changed supplier. For one company they found for every one active voice of dissatisfaction there were in fact 26 more that were never filed or communicated!

Retailers and others must address the service problem as a prerequisite for succeeding in e-commerce

With consumers dissatisfied but more demanding, it is inevitable that the promise of electronic shopping will be seen as especially attractive. That is, if it delivers. If it does it cuts out a large part of the frustration. It eliminates the car journey, the car parking, the crowds, the trolleys, the aisles, the long waits, bored unhelpful staff, inadequate facilities. All this can be avoided while consumers sit comfortably in offices or den searching out at their own pace and leisure what they want.

Yet the various sources of consumer dissatisfaction are *not* outside the retail chains' control. There are areas that retailers could turn to and substantially improve upon. They could still make enormous strides in better understanding their consumers, even within the existing physical environment, isolating the problem areas and fixing them. Right now most retailers still appear to pay lip-service to customer service and it is clear from the (dis)satisfaction studies that few have got it right. Their priorities seem more turned to aggressive new store-opening programmes in domestic or overseas markets (see Appendix 1, p. 303). They are more focused on new space than getting existing space to deliver a totally customer satisfying experience. But as the electronic revolution gathers pace so new space programs will have to come under increasing reappraisal. With that perhaps at last retailers will turn to their existing proposition and begin to pour their efforts into getting that right and maximising its potential so it can stand up and offer such a compelling proposition that it can resist even the finest dedicated electronic service provider.

Significant numbers of consumers see ES as a better alternative

The retailers' task will not be easy. Already consumers are showing high levels of interest in the internet and other forms of virtual shopping and these interest levels do appear to be at the critical mass 15–20% level, even before the technology and infrastructure has been put effectively in place. Research referred to in Chapter 6 by A.C. Nielsen and others has identified how different groups of consumers feel about shopping today, their readiness to explore new things and their desire and need for convenience.

Taking and adapting their research for an electronic environment they found (Figure 10.2) that 17% of the population at large could be categorised as 'frenzied copers' – people who just don't have the time to do what they want and are 'frenziedly' interested in exploring time-saving propositions. Another 16% were categorised as 'mercenaries' – simply out for what they could get switching to whatever offered them the best

Figure 10.2   Consumer ES Interest

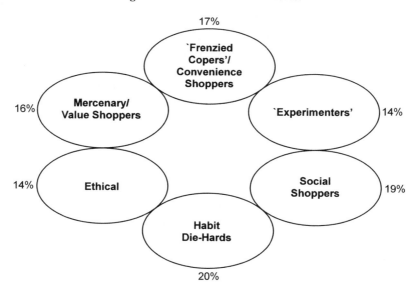

Source: A.C. Nielsen, Mintel, Henley Centre.

value. Another group could be categorised as 'Experimenters', 14% of the population, who also had little loyalty and were among the first to try new things.

This research suggest that there is a core 17% of the population (the 'Frenzied Copers') who will respond without hesitation to electronic shopping in all its forms. Hot on their heels will be sizeable other groups especially 'Experimenters' and 'Mercenaries', who make up another 30% of the population! Does this not suggest there is really a substantial body of people waiting for the revolution to come? Certainly not all will be immediately interested. There is at the same time a large group who in contrast appear relatively comfortable and contented with existing distribution patterns or are 'stuck in their ways'. But like any major social changes, once they reach critical mass they do build an inexorable momentum that can carry even the reluctant before it.

The A.C. Nielsen research also asked consumers the blunt question: 'Would you shop electronically?' They used grocery shopping as their example. The responses were in line with their original categorisations. 19% of all households said they would (Figure 10.3).

This Nielsen research is not unrepresentative. It's not an isolated view of the market place. Another well-respected consumer research group – Mintel – found in a survey that 31% of shoppers did not like visiting the stores to get their shopping (Table 10.3). Such shoppers classed themselves as 'reluctant' or 'obstinate'. They saw no social reason or benefits in visiting the supermarket or other stores. They appeared especially interested in alternative means of getting what they need.

Figure 10.3   Readiness to Shop Electronically

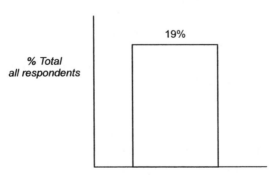

`If there was a grocery shopping and delivery
service in my area, I would use it'

19%

*% Total
all respondents*

Source: A.C. Nielsen.

Table 10.3   Levels of Shopping Enjoyment (%)

– Enjoy shopping and go frequently	15
– Enjoy shopping and go occasionally	19
– Shopping can be enjoyable but only for something I need	35
– Shopping is not enjoyable and go only when have to ('reluctant shoppers')	18
– Hate going shopping ('obstinate shoppers')	13

Source: Mintel/BMRB.

Growing 'kiddie power' fuelling ES interest

While these surveys were all taken among adults, as was pointed out earlier there is also a growing generation of children for whom the computer is as important as the television, who are comfortable in using it, want to use it and readily embrace it as part of their everyday lives. For this generation, while they remain teenagers going out shopping is principally a social occasion that they look forward to and enjoy. But as they reach adulthood, take on jobs and families and begin to experience the time pressures of everyday living, won't their interest in internet shopping and its advantages be even more highly developed? Won't polls among this group in ten years' time show even higher interest and acceptance levels for buying and interacting electronically? Won't this new adult generation provide a further surge of demand for home shopping, pushing it to critical mass volume levels among the population at large?

In 1998, forecasters estimated there were c. 5 million teenagers surfing the net. According to Jupiter Communications that figure will grow to 90 million in 2000. Clinton in the USA, Blair in the UK and Jospin in France have all publicly declared plans to get schools wired up to the internet. The mass middle classes now increasingly feel they should have a home PC and sign up with American On-Line or one of the other access providers to help their kids stay in touch with the new technologies and access the more sophisticated education and information material now widely available.

Suppliers, too, are seeing the emergence of 'Kiddie power' on the internet. They are investing both to meet and to fuel demand. As *Business Week* pointed out 'the kiddie market itself will be a cyber gold mine in a few years time'. Media and web giants are scrambling to offer new kid-friendly sites. Companies like Disney have been the latest to bet that 'net kids' is where the money is and Disney has brought the phenomenon into the spotlight with its Daily Blast site featuring games, stories, comic strips, current news and other services to subscribe to. As they grow up net-literate, won't many surely graduate to doing their shopping in this same way? A recent survey by the Henley Centre suggested 80% of 16–24-year-olds expected to do their banking and food shopping on line in the future. Two-thirds of all under-21-year-olds still in education already claim to be 'regular internet users'.

Whole communities are going electronic

We're already seeing whole cities and towns embarking on a programme to get everyone in their community wired up and inter-connected. We referred earlier to experiments in Palo Alto, in Finland and in the streets of London. But these are just a few examples among many others stretching from Silicon Valley to Malaysia. As the *Wall Street Journal* commented:

'many residents in even the remotest towns react incredulously at first to the prospect of being part of the internet community but these erstwhile computer illiterates quickly learn to log-on to check children's school grades, housewives go on-line to compare prices at local stores and order up things for the home . . . even the town's mayor can be found checking a chatline to hear the latest grumblings about potholes and burned-out street lamps!'

Just a 15% switch can make the difference

It's all adding up to a major challenge for companies in the decade ahead. Few organisations can take the ES Test and conclude that these changes won't in some way affect their business. And we have to remember that it doesn't require the whole population to change their shopping habits for the impact to be significant and far-reaching. For many retail chains it will only require a reduction in store traffic of c. 15% for their stores to be plunged below break-even and into a loss-making situation (Table 10.4). Retail net margins are generally just too thin to sustain substantial shifts in the way consumers buy.

15% of US retail sales would amount to c. $300 billion of commercial activity potentially shifting away from existing physical distribution. In

Table 10.4   Impact of 15% of Consumers Buying Electronically on Store
Profitability

	Current		15% reduction
Store sales		100	85
% cost of goods	75%		76.5%*
Actual cost of goods		75	65
Gross margin		25	20
Fixed costs		20	20
Net operating margin		5	0

Note: *Reduced manufacturer discounts as sales decline.

the UK the figure would be c. £30 billion. This is a substantial slice of
retailers' current business. It may be a big jump from internet shopping
levels today but the consumer interest for this is unquestionable given the
consistent consumer surveys on the subject. Indeed another research
group, Verdict, polled UK consumers and found that around 15% were
so determined to access internet shopping when it became available that
they would be prepared to pay a premium for its services. That response
was especially strong among ABC1 consumers who have already been at
the forefront of bringing PCs and the internet into their homes.

If the demand is firmly in place, then the key question is: can the
technology deliver? What is the range of technology solutions being
pursued, how wide a reach will they achieve and are they able to
overcome roadblocks to meaningfully enable the first 15–20% of the
population – the critical mass – to get on line and become at last the
satisfied consumers they desire to be?

Investing supply side

There is an extraordinary level of investment and activity taking place.
It's involving companies from many different industry sectors from
aerospace through to land-based cable companies. All are jostling for
position looking to drive their technology to the forefront and provide
communication into people's homes (Figure 10.4). It's resulting in a wave
of alliances as companies get together to combine resources, capital and
know-how to accelerate progress and get ahead of competition. For
example, in satellite communication heavyweights like Lockheed Martin,
Hughes Electronics, GE and Motorola are partnering with others to

Figure 10.4   Electronic Convergence

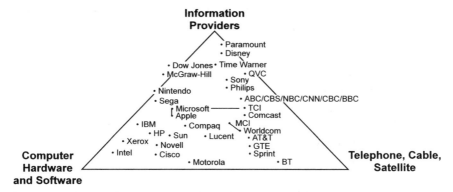

Source: New Paradigm Learning Corporation, McGraw-Hill.

bring universal internet communication across the globe. Among telephone companies we've seen giant mergers in recent times. Vodaphone and WorldCom have both startled the business community with audacious but successful acquisitions. For example the combined MCI WorldCom group not only now controls 25% of the US long-distance telephone market but more importantly for the future it has cornered 57% of the consumer internet access market with UUNET the world's largest carrier of internet traffic, plus MCI's extensive internet 'backbone' systems network.

There are a host of competing technologies exploiting everything from satellite links to old copper telephone wires and even investigating opportunities using ordinary electricity wires and the basic home-electricity grid system. It's not clear which of these routes will become dominant and to some extent that doesn't matter at this stage. They are all contributing to the development of the 'information market place' and each provides unique advantages as well as having its individual set of investment and infrastructure hurdles to overcome. All these companies in the next few years will bombard consumers with services and opportunities, some claiming their communication links to be superior, others packaging up a complementary set of options providing internet, telephone, videophone and TV in an easy-priced, readily accessible formula. They are all making rapid progress expanding reach and improving quality of communication. Each route to market will be commercially viable, functioning and affordable in the next five to ten years at a level that can facilitate the practical and serious development of interactive home shopping.

There are a number of mainstream competing routes for providing electronic commerce. Each by itself offers the breakthrough potential to bring ES to the mass population:

- Copper telephone wires
- Fibre optic cable
- Digital Television
- Web TV set-top box
- Satellite
- Wireless cellular phones
- Electricity grid.

Each of these routes is vying for time, space and attention on the home PC or TV or on a screen phone or via an interactive kiosk. It's a complex set of options and opportunities and we need to examine and understand each in turn.

Copper telephone wires

Telephony offers the most extensive communications network world-wide. It reaches into almost every household among developed nations, people are familiar with it, it's easy to use and inexpensive. In principle it solves the communication challenge in one, but in practice it's had limitations in the amount of information it can transfer each second – its bandwidth. It has reasonable speeds with text but has proved slow for images, video and sound.

Yet in this global race to win the future communications market, telephone companies have been actively searching for ways to improve and maximise the potential of their established network. One way, which will be examined in the next section, is to replace outdated copper wires with high bandwidth fibre optics. Another way is to learn how to transmit more efficiently and more effectively using the existing copper wire network. Some individual software companies have been especially innovative in this respect:

- *Future Wave Software* has developed an ingenious new way of transmitting data. They compress the time required to send it. The company used to send copies of its images but instead now sends instructions along the wires to recreate its images at the other receiving end. The instructions occupy less bandwidth and so take much less time to transmit.

- Software-company *Progressive Networks* wanted to send video pictures over the internet but experienced poor-quality results. Typically video is transmitted at 30 frames per second but existing copper-wire telephone lines cannot cope with that. Rather than wait for all its customers to be recabled with high bandwidth fibre, the company developed a new software technology which enabled it to cram more data through the wires and deliver the same picture with similar quality at 10 frames per second rather than 30.

Aside from individual company initiatives there are three particular recent developments, which are being aggressively pursued by the Telcos that are powering up the capabilities of the existing copper-wire networks.

For reference, as we shall start talking about kilobytes, megabytes and gigabytes, some brief definition of these measures of memory size is required. Typically a megabyte can carry c. 5 seconds of television with a good-quality image and up to 60 seconds with a highly compressed image. The highly compressed image may be acceptable where, for example, there is just a talking head and so it can be used for computer-wide windows that are small in size. 1 megabyte can also carry 500 pages of text, 1 minute of good-quality music or 5 minutes of speech. With an ordinary copper telephone line it can take c. 10 minutes to download 1 megabyte, with fibre optic cable it can take 0.1 seconds!

Copper telephone-line capabilities are being dramatically enhanced now by ATM, ADSL and ISDN developments:

- **ATM (asynchronous transfer mode)** is superfast switching technology that boosts capacity on data links. Originally developed by Bell Laboratories for high-speed voice networks, ATM is now being adapted for internet communications and fast image and data transmission. It's been adopted by the US Defense Department, for example, to relay high-resolution images of Bosnia. The Mayo Clinic in Rochester, USA uses ATM to enable doctors to video conference with other doctors and patients and provide 'telemedicine'. ATM uniquely focuses on switching and routing data at very high speeds known also as 'fast-packet switching'. Its rapid development has been helped because it's been adopted as the world-wide standard and so it allows interoperability of information regardless of the end system or type of information. It's being developed hard by the telecommunications industry because they see it as a way of both exploiting existing copper-wire networks and because ATM allows them to offer not just voice but video and data transmission as well.

- **ADSL (asymmetric digital subscriber lines)** is another new technology, in this case developed by Ameritech. It uses the existing copper-wire networks with an upgrade modem installed in the user's home. It provides a 2 megabit link that allows video and data to be transmitted quickly and at good-quality levels. It significantly improves existing bandwidth capability using digital compression to cram more images and data and transmit them at higher speeds. ADSL increases speed from c. 64 kbps to c. 1.5 to 2 Mbps and latest developments show that might get up to 9Mbps.

  'This represents another boost for Telcos – it's a copper renaissance' the President of US West has commented. A consortium of companies including Intel, Compaq and Microsoft have got behind ADSL technology to agree operating standards and the modem equipment. ADSL is being heavily backed but it does require local telephone exchanges to be rewired and modems installed.

  However there is yet further technology in the pipeline – this time being developed by Rockwell and Nortel – which allows ADSL to work using only existing equipment. Known informally as 'ADSL Lite', a stripped-down version of ADSL is soon to be available for the consumer market. It will involve a much simpler modem connection at the home end which can be retailed easily and plugged in without needing a visit by a specialist technician. While operating at a lower speed than full ADSL, it will still power superfast internet connections.

- **ISDN (Integrated services digital network)** is already old-fashioned technology – it's been around for nearly five years! It was designed to utilise the existing copper-wire network running between telephone exchanges and the customer's premises. It adds a special component to the end of the telephone line that increases capacity. The component digitises voice or data. ISDN can operate at between 64 and 128 kbps and can be combined to achieve speeds up to 1.5 Mbps (see Table 10.5 for comparisons).

  Because ISDN has been around a little longer than ATM and ADSL its commercial applications have been more developed and the 'special component' links can now be installed in the home or in the office for a relatively small fee (c. $100). ISDN can now also be made available over fibre optic cable ('broadband' ISDN or B-ISDN) and in that environment operating speeds could eventually get up to more than 2 gigabits per second.

  B-ISDN and ATM are now combining to not only maximise bandwidth opportunities but also to ensure the data is routed and switched at fastest speeds.

Table 10.5 Types of Connection Possible to the Internet

Connection	Speed (000 bits per second)	Time to download a megabyte
Telephone line	14–28	4–10 minutes
ISDN	64–128	1–2 minutes
Cable TV modem	1,400	5.5 secs
ADSL	2,000–9,000	1–5 secs
Advanced Cable TV modem	40,000	0.2 secs
Optical fibre	80,000+	0.1 secs

The goal of these various innovations is to provide broadband capacity that is fully interactive. The aim is not just to send data and images fast and with high quality but allow the consumer to send information back with the same efficiency and satisfaction. The technology is getting there but many of the developments are barely out of the lab and have not yet been fully commercialised. Even so, it's extraordinary to witness the rate and progress of the innovations that have already taken place in just the few years since the internet went commercial. If ATM, ADSL and other technologies can achieve the communication goals without the high costs of replacing existing wires with fibre or ringing the earth with satellites, then of course the race to bring the internet to a mass audience will gather even greater pace and critical mass will dawn even earlier.

Fibre optic cable

Fibre optic cable must be distinguished first from coaxial TV cable. TV cable has high penetration already in place, especially in the USA where it reaches c. 90% of all households, with c. 65% of those signed up and using it. However elsewhere in the world, TV cable's development is much lower reaching an average of only 27% of households in Europe. In the UK some 20% of households have cable laid in the streets outside, but only 8% are connected up to the networks.

TV cable does have higher bandwidth than the telephone line because it can move video but it does not have the same capacity or potential as fibre optic technology. As a result it has to be adapted to enable it to provide fast and satisfactory internet communication. This is principally achieved by digital compression which can achieve significant improvements in capacity. For example up to 16 video channels could go into the space that had previously carried 1 analog channel. Users, however, need a cable modem or set-top box to enable the decompression and receive and process the text and pictures.

Because TV cable has 40–80 times the bandwidth of the ordinary telephone line and especially in the USA already has a considerable infrastructure, there is a substantial amount of investment and activity looking to exploit that and make it internet friendly and attractive. Intel, Zenith, General Instruments, Telewest, Nynex and others are all developing cable modems with capacity to transfer internet data at up to 4 Mbps. Current tests show this could be pushed up to 40 Mbps.

As for fibre optic cable, it can send its signals with significantly less signal degradation than coaxial TV cable. It has higher bandwidth capacity and can send more channels into a subscriber's home. A typical fibre optic cable contains 40 strands, each the size of a human hair and is capable of carrying 1.3 million phone conversations or c. 2000 TV channels. A two-hour movie can be sent through a glass fibre in a few seconds. It would take a month over an ordinary phone line.

Up till now fibre optic technology has principally been the domain of the telephone companies, again especially in the USA. They have been weaving high-capacity fibre throughout their networks to facilitate long-distance calls at lower prices. Local telephone companies then used fibre to connect to the long distance carrier's network. As a result in the USA much of the backbone infrastructure is fibre. However local loops into businesses and homes are still the old copper wire with its capacity limitations. Frustratingly, it means that bandwidth available to residential subscribers is constrained by the limited local connections.

Replacing this 'last mile' of copper wire would still require a massive investment. This is true not just in the USA but in other countries many of which don't even have any significant fibre optic backbone infrastructure. For example, a consortium in Malaysia has announced its plans to invest nearly $30 billion in its country (population just 15 million) over the next few years to establish a fast fibre optic information highway.

Not surprisingly therefore telephone companies are turning back to existing infrastructures and exploring what technologies like ATM and ADSL can achieve. Equally cable companies, rather than digging up all the streets with again the massive cost and disruption, are putting significant effort into using digital compression for example to achieve satisfactory internet communications.

To compare the capacity and potential of each of these developing technologies, see again Table 10.5 for a brief summary of speeds and times. It demonstrates the dramatic gains that will be increasingly available to consumers as these various improvements in capacity become more widely available and accessible.

Digital television (also see Chapter 17)

While telephone lines and cable look set to be the main foundations of the information superhighway, many companies especially in consumer electricals and in the media are focusing their efforts on getting digital television established and developed for mass consumer appeal. Digital TV broadcasts digital signals by satellite, cable or over the terrestrial transmission network. Digital transmission is attractive because it compresses the amount of bandwidth space the data or image takes up. For example, not every line and frame of a picture is transmitted, only those that change from one frame to the next. Sound and picture quality improve significantly vs analog and many companies have as a result been investigating how they can exploit the technology to bring digital broadcasts and digital shopping to the TV screen rather than through the PC. Their goal is to make surfing the internet more like watching TV and so make electronic commerce generally and the whole internet experience immediately more user-friendly and accessible.

Prospects for digital TV have advanced quickly, especially in Europe where there is an open standard known as DVB for digital video broadcasting. This has enabled leading TV broadcasters such as British Sky Broadcasting (BSB) to broadcast digitally in the UK. Starting in 1998, it's already looking at its next wave developments (see page 292). In the USA, on the other hand, digital TV has a range of proprietary standards and that is slowing down the market, though Microsoft has recently been leading efforts to change this and establish a common approach.

In the UK, BSB is very aggressively building its digital subscriber base for the digital TV broadcasts. It's also just bought out its consortium partners British Telecom, HongKong & Shanghai Bank and Matsushita Electric. It delivers 300 channels and brings the cost of owning a channel down to < $60,000. At that price many organisations have enquired about setting up their own TV operation and leading UK retailers such as Kingfisher, HMV, Thomas Cook and Great Universal Stores are already involved with BSB in interactive TV shopping.

This digital operation requires consumers to obtain a set-top box as a digital decoder and a keypad that links to both their TV and their telephone line. The telephone link is to make the service interactive, enabling subscribers to the service to respond back to the digital TV broadcaster. Set-top boxes were set to initially retail in the UK for less than £300 but are being given away free! Advanced decoder boxes will permit access to both digital TV broadcasts as well as digital data transmissions on the internet. TV broadcasts may be by satellite or existing terrestrial network of TV transmission masts.

Microsoft has not confined its own digital interests to the US market. It plans to offer in the UK free or low-cost interactive digital TV services to users of its latest version of its Windows operating system – Windows 2000. Users will need a PC that is also equipped with a TV tuner, though at this time few UK PCs in the home yet have that level of sophistication.

Digital TV is expected to develop over the next few years and is forecast to reach c. 20% of all television households in Europe by the middle of the decade through cable and satellite connections. In addition, pressure to switch off analog transmissions is expected to build, pushing total digital TV penetration to well over 50% by 2010. Like many of these initiatives, success will depend on how effectively the service is marketed, the price of the decoder boxes for the TV and how well it beats rival technologies. One thing in its favour is the involvement of British Sky Broadcasting who have demonstrated their marketing prowess in the UK with their single-minded hard-hitting conversion of UK TV audiences from a four-channel to a multi-channel satellite TV environment in just five years.

Many of those initially involved with digital TV saw its potential mainly lying with bringing 'video on demand' into the home. But that service has been trialled with only mixed results. The greater opportunity lies in its ability to bring electronic shopping to a mass TV audience who can pick up the signals at a relatively low on-cost. Customers will be in a position to order their wares using just a keypad which could be little more than a standard remote control service with a click facility. Their signal will then go out through the set-top box up the telephone line.

BSB's plans are to offer the broadest possible range of shopping and other services. They are actively encouraging the involvement of banks and retail groups in an effort to create one of the first mass audience 'electronic shopping centres'. Internet services and games will also be made available. BSB itself forecasts 5 million customers by 2002. The reach of the TV may prove at least as attractive as rival PC-based initiatives.

Web TV set-top box

Web TV (see colour plate) is intended to be a simple internet connection to the TV screen. It's marketed by the likes of Sony and Philips and utilises the existing TV and phone line providing internet access through a slimline receiver. Surfing is carried out through an adapted remote control. The main difference from Digital TV right now is that the connection is mainly made over the telephone wire rather than by a TV broadcast. By 2003 the set-top box could alternatively receive signals by satellite or terrestrial broadcast. Eventually the decoder box will be incorporated into the digital television itself.

But over the next few years Web TV represents an immediate user-friendly opportunity to get consumers wired into the internet. Early investors have included Citicorp and not surprisingly Microsoft hedging its bets with involvement in yet another one of the communication technology options. After slow sales on launch, Sony and Philips plan to ramp up their own marketing with an estimated $60 million annual spend and a push to lower the price well below the initial $300 ticket.

Satellite

Satellite communication promises universal access for the internet around the globe. It has no need for expensive wire or cable infrastructure. It can reach the remotest island or hilltop. All that's required is to ring the earth with enough satellites to enable this communication through the skies to take place!

Yet this dream is fast becoming reality with as many as 15 different American-based consortia developing plans and looking to invest as much as $40 billion on their systems over the next few years. They will be operating in a newly opened part of the radio spectrum called the 'Ka-band' which purports to offer high bandwidth communication and do that relatively inexpensively between any two or more customers on earth. It promises to transmit data up to 800 times faster than current analog phone systems, for example transmitting an entire 64-page edition of the *Wall Street* Journal in under two minutes vs the hours it would take on existing phone lines!

The leading satellite consortium so far is Teledisc which has the backing of Bill Gates – again – but this time in his personal capacity. Teledisc's plan is to ring the planet with 840 satellites at low altitude. They are in competition with a second consortium led by Motorola and Loral Aerospace but they will use a different number of satellites and different frequencies. Both teams expect to be operational by 2002–2003, but they still have a long way to go – not least of which is launching the satellites!

The pioneer at Teledisc is Craig McCaw, who is almost evangelical in the benefits he foresees:

> '... here's a poor village in Guatemala . . . they have electricity, they have TV, they see the wealth of developed nations but they can't afford them. They don't have the communications in place yet they are rich in agriculture and local produce. They could become part of the world market if they could more easily join in the global communications network.'

But McCaw does not only have to manage both the financing and logistics. The other satellite consortia include such heavyweight partnerships as Hughes Electronics, AT&T, GE and Lockheed Martin. They plan, in contrast to Teledisc, to use fewer satellites and instead have a handful of giant geosynchronous satellites thousands of kilometres above the earth rotating in a fixed orbit. Yet they all face perplexing technical problems and will have to watch while other terrestrial-based internet and communication operations continue to build their own networks and momentum. An extraordinary race between the different technologies is taking place, with huge bets being made that one will ultimately triumph as a dominant mass-volume communicator.

Wireless cellular phones

In the James Bond movie *Tomorrow Never Dies*, Bond swaps his gun for a mobile phone. The special phone not only makes calls but can drive a car, crack open a safe and even take photographs. While it will be a long time till that type of phone can be purchased at the local store, the mobile phone is fast evolving, as articles in journals like *Banking Technology* are pointing out, from just a device to make and receive voice calls. There's now a new generation of small portable electronic hand-held phones emerging which can also plug into the internet and receive a whole stream of data services.

The term 'mobile commerce' has been coined to describe the delivery of electronic commerce capabilities directly into the hands of the user via wireless technology. It's predicted that the new phone will act as yet another catalyst encouraging consumers to shop electronically and its particular advantages are its easy portability and familiarity.

By 1998 almost a dozen companies had begun trials building off GSM – the global system for mobile communication. It is the European standard for digital cellular telephone systems in operation since 1992 and offering teleservices and wireless data services internationally. These trials include elements of electronic commerce collaborating with banks and retailers to provide information, shopping, share-buying and retail banking at the touch of a few buttons.

One of the trials was set up by Nokia, giving 100 users in the Netherlands access to banking and commerce via the internet using the Nokia 9000 Communicator. It's a portable phone and personal organiser equipped with the software to browse the internet and send and receive e-mail. The early price was £1,500 but it's an early prototype and like many such items can be expected to come down rapidly once the technology is fully commercialised for volume sales. Transactions are carried out using a smartcard reader to send and spend electronic cash. Nokia's new 2000 WAP product retails for c. $150, is easier to use and has a much sharper screen.

Nokia is not the only heavyweight investigating this medium. AT&T also launched its Pocket Net Phone recently. This sells for less than $200 and is intended to act as a cellphone, e-mail reader and web browser. The phone can be 'purchased' for free if the customer signs up for the basic services at a flat $30 monthly fee. The Pocket Net Phone uses digital technology though sharing the analog cellular network with voice calls. Early users praise its pocketability but have found the screen and keyboard doesn't yet provide clear enough resolution for typing in messages.

Yet another new screen phone product comes from CIDCO Inc. out of California whose product is the iPhone. This is a $400 phone that can also surf the internet but it's larger and has a c. 7.4 inch lap-top like screen and mini-keyboard. It rivals the fastest PC modems. Among other interested parties Smith Barney was expected to announce plans to provide iPhones to all its retail brokerage customers. CIDCO executives see their target market as the 50% of US households that don't own PCs, providing an easier route to the web. 'Our vision is to own the kitchen countertop,' claims CIDCO's marketing chief. 'We believe Web Phones have a much better chance in cyberspace than gizmos like Microsoft's Web TV'.

Meantime other companies are seeing the opportunities and jumping into this arena. Philips and Northern Telecom have set up a joint venture and Alcatel is busy in Europe putting together what it calls its 'Screen Phone' which will be a touch-sensitive screen and pop-out keyboard connected to either a fixed or mobile phone.

'Mobile commerce' may be in its infancy but as it develops, and especially once third generation (3G) wireless technology becomes available in 2002/3, and the equipment and technology mature it will doubtless encourage yet more groups of consumers to try out what it can do. Even the most technophobic may find it hard to resist its simple charms!

Electricity Grid

An unexpected alternative technology emerged toward the end of the 1990s. UK-based Norweb Communications together with Nortel, the Canadian Electronics Group that specialises in telecommunications equipment, announced they had discovered a way to deliver internet services to the home, tapping into the electricity grid system.

The new technology prevents the electrical current distorting internet signals and other computer data and has been developed so that electricity companies could offer their customers internet access at speeds 30 times greater than today's high-speed modem links. Customers would simply have to plug their PCs into their nearest household electricity point to link up to the internet. The only set-up cost would be c. $250 to put in an appropriate PC card.

Is this the Holy Grail of mass internet communication? It would appear the technology provides immediate internet access to every household in the land and the technology is undergoing a series of tests and trials. Norweb and Nortel believe they will eventually be ready to build this into a 'serious volume business'.

*   *   *

With so much supply-side investing going on and such a range of technologies being developed there is no question that the latent consumer demand for convenience will be easily met in just a few short years. Even if consumers wanted to, how could they resist? They will be marketed to from all sides by TV broadcasters, telecommunications companies, software houses, computer hardware manufacturers and even by their local utility offering a packaged electricity supply plus internet service. The investment taking place is enormous and the commitment to build the new electronic age growing with each new product advance. The coupling between these new improving technologies and time-pressured, demanding consumers is still in its early days but it looks set for a long marriage and commercial prosperity!

11 The World is Changing: Assets to Knowledge

The advent of electronic commerce is heralding a new world order for business. The traditional rules of competition that generations have become familiar with are having less and less relevance. A tide of technological, regulatory, geographic and political change has come about since the early 1990s. Scale can no longer be relied on to provide competitive advantage, many products and services are seen as commodities, new competitors are emerging from surprising places and with dedicated efforts are quickly winning market share, formal borders and barriers are being swept aside, customers have gone truly global in their aspirations, technology now makes possible what once was only dreams and there's a virtual environment fast becoming reality.

The commercial world is changing from an industrial economy based on physical assets, factories, roads and heavy equipment to a new economy built on silicon and computers. A transformation in our lives is taking place that's as revolutionary as the eighteenth-century shift from agriculture to industry. It's bringing with it new dynamics and new drivers for success (Figure 11.1).

This chapter looks to provide some perspective around this fast-changing commercial scene. For a moment let's stand back from the helter skelter of week-by-week ES initiatives and announcements. Instead it's helpful to recognise the historical context and consider the underlying trends and dynamics fuelling these changes. What's the impact for business at large of operating in a digital economy, what does it take to become 'knowledge-based' rather than 'asset-based' and what are the implications? Finally what new economic and financial levers emerge

Figure 11.1 The Changing Commercial World

Agrarian	Industrial	Electronic
→1750	1750–1990	1990 →

with which business must now come to terms and aim to take advantage of?

Electronic technology generally is moving at a remarkable pace with remarkable advances in just a few short years. The major breakthroughs have come from developments in solid-state electronics and the microprocessor. The number of transistors per chip is doubling approximately every eighteen months (Table 11.1). It represent an enormous increase in the power available to drive information technology applications in all dimensions. In 1998, the world's chip population had risen to 350 billion, including 15 billion microprocessors. That's more than two silicon 'brains' for every person on earth!

There appears no limit to these technical advances. Andy Grove, CEO of Intel, predicts continued progress for at least the next ten years. By 2010 he envisions microprocessors with a billion transistors chewing through 100,000 MIPS (millions of instructions per second). That compares with today's fastest Pentium Pro Chip with 5.5 million transistors and speeds of 'just' 300–400 MIPS.

For retailers these digital developments pose particular challenges. Their industry sector especially is built on physical foundations. It's asset-based. It's all about 'location, location, location' – about land and buildings and physical logistics involving warehouses and fleets of trucks. But such assets become largely redundant in the electronic world. Intangibles like knowledge capture, information management and brand equities become the new core competencies and drivers of value. It's a sea

Table 11.1 March of the Microprocessor, 1971–2010

Chip	Debut	No. of transistors	Initial MIPS
4004	1971	2,300	0.06
8008	1972	3,500	0.06
8080	1974	6,000	0.6
8086	1978	29,000	0.3
8088	1979	29,000	0.3
I286	1982	134,000	0.9
I386	1985	275,000	5
I486	1989	1.2 million	20
Pentium	1993	3.1 million	100
Pentium Pro	1995	5.5 million	300
886 (Forecast)	2000	15 million	1000
1286 (Forecast)	2010	1 billion	100,000

* MIPS = millions of instructions per second.
Source: *Business Week*; Intel.

change in the fundamentals of their business. If a new company were starting out today to distribute food, clothing or financial services to the consumer, would it be planning to build expensive real estate? Would it not set its sights very differently? Looking to the future, wouldn't it more likely focus its investment on communication technology providing immediate reach to a total universe of customers at a lower cost of entry? It would surely find it more attractive to develop a virtual rather than physical infrastructure.

The future business model will be built around these very different success factors:

'The traditional factors of production – land, labour and capital have not disappeared. But they have become secondary. They can be obtained and obtained easily provided there is knowledge. Knowledge is a utility, the new means to obtain social and economic results. Knowledge is becoming the only meaningful resource.'

(Peter Drucker)

Knowledge has become power, and it is estimated by Drucker that more than 1 trillion dollars per year world-wide is being invested in developing new information and communication technologies, software and hardware to exploit knowledge as a driving source of competitive advantage. Drucker also estimates that one-third of all capital investment in developed countries in the last thirty years has gone into data, information and communications equipment. Nowadays three-quarters of the labour force in most developed countries can be categorised as primarily involved in knowledge work or service. Forty years ago it was less than one-third:

'Leveraged intellect and its prime facilitator, service technology are reshaping not only service industries but also manufacturing. Overall growth patterns, national and regional job structures and the nature of international competition are all being affected.'

(Peter Drucker)

The twenty-first century corporation will gradually take on a very different shape. A significant part of its activities will take place in a virtual realm. Physical constraints will be limited. Compaq, for example, can close all its sales offices and instruct its salesforce to work from their homes instead, with computers linked to comprehensive databases. Ford can build its new world car with a virtual team of designers, engineers and

others remaining in their different locations scattered across the globe
but linked together electronically in a high-tech CAD/CAM video-
conferencing virtual environment. Goodyear can check the quality of its
raw rubber materials at source and immediately transmit changes in
quality or specification directly into centralised flexible automated
manufacturing plant. Toyota can outsource even more aggressively and
confidently, farming out critical parts of its design and components
supply to third parties but with the ability to easily track and check and
audit exactly what's going on, on a real-time basis even if the third party
is thousands of miles away. Distance will be no object. Corporations need
have no boundaries as they reach out to access and integrate allied skills
and competencies.

Forward-thinking companies are abandoning old organisation structures and are already aggressively building their virtual world, looking to
establish new sources of market opportunity and competitiveness (see
more in Chapter 16). But as they evaluate their options, the economic
model they consider has fundamental differences. If the value-added
levers are virtual rather than physical, are about knowledge rather than
assets, then why establish high levels of fixed-asset costs? The virtual
environment helps keep costs variable. If fixed assets are required, then
they can more readily be outsourced. They can be left with a third party.
The company itself can stay flexible and virtual. It can focus, without
physical distraction, on leveraging the electronic interactions with its
customers. Let fixed assets, mostly in manufacturing and warehousing, be
managed by fixed asset specialists. Free up other corporations to
establish their value networks (Chapter 7) and find their own key
leverage points.

Retailers, for example, who wish to take advantage of the ES potential
and gradually transition more of their business down that road will be
looking at a very different P&L (profit and loss account) (Table 11.2).
Key cost drivers will change and there will be more operating margin
flexibility.

A significant area of fixed costs in the Stores is removed. A far greater
proportion of the costs is in making each customer interaction more
successful. Cost items such as Delivery and Customer Service become
significant (though these can be made to be largely variable driven by the
number of those customer interactions). Branding becomes a more
critical lever. In effect, the brand value is replacing a large part of the
asset value. Where previously it was the location that attracted custom
now it's the awareness, reputation and emotional values that the seller
builds up, communicates and exploits.

Table 11.2 Changes in Retail P&L – illustrative only

Annual P&L items	Conventional retail store ($000)	As %	Electronic 'retail' operation ($000)	As %
Revenue	20,000	100	20,000	100
Gross margin	6,400	32	6,400	32
Warehouse costs	(600)	3.0	(200)	1.0
Store costs	(4,200)	21	(1,502)	7.5
Delivery	0	–	(1,185)	5.9
Customer service	0	–	(200)	1.0
Brand advertising	(160)	0.8	(500)	2.5
Contribution	1,440	7.2	2,813	14.1
Overhead	(600)	3	(400)	2.0
EBIT	840	4.2	2,413	12.1

Source: CSC Kalchas.

This virtual world will certainly put a premium on brands. It will be intangibles like brands, designs, patents and trademarks that will become the financial bedrock of the future corporation. They will replace the pivotal role of fixed assets on the balance sheet. They will become the capital employed that investors seek to leverage. In a world going increasingly electronic it is surely these items and their balance sheet value that will provide a better guide to the company's market valuation and potential.

US accounting rules still prevent this kind of intangible asset valuation but some commentators are already calculating and quantifying their view as to what US brand assets might be worth if they were translated onto the balance sheet. A study, for example, by Interbrand and *Financial World* identified how much the top ten US brands would be valued at (Table 11.3).

Some of these brand values are truly massive and even without being incorporated into a balance sheet they offer a compelling view of the value of the company and the power the brands can play. For example Coca-Cola's fixed asset base in 1998 was $4.8 billion, but that bears little relationship to the underlying value of that company: it all resides in the Brand. As former CEO, Goizueta commented:

'If all our fixed assets and buildings burned down tomorrow we'd have no trouble rebuilding Coca-Cola based on the strengths of our brands and trademarks alone.'

Table 11.3   Top Ten US Brands

Brand	Value $m
Marlboro	44,614
Coca-Cola	43,427
McDonalds	18,920
IBM	18,491
Disney	15,358
Kodak	13,267
Kellogg's	11,409
Budweiser	11,026
Intel	10,491
Gillette	10,292

UK accounting rules have already moved to recognise these intangibles, acknowledging their value rather than treating it, for example, in an acquisition context as purely goodwill to be written off. While there remains some dispute about the valuation rules, nevertheless a number of UK leading consumer goods companies such as Grand Metropolitan, Guinness (now both merged in Diageo), Cadbury Schweppes, Reckitt & Colman and United Biscuits have all calculated brand values and incorporated them as part of their net financial worth.

Should companies resist this opportunity to recognise and acknowledge intangible values? Should US accounting rules prevail? Or should the business community rather accept this as one of the shifting realities of the late twentieth/early twenty-first century? Are UK accountants for once in fact more prescient than some of their supposedly more commercially-minded US colleagues? Is the current uncertainly about whether to allow brand valuations simply a symptom of an era transitioning between one economic order and the next, waiting for the new rules to be established? Why should Amazon.com, 1-800-FLOWERS and others be penalised for having lower net worth than their physical asset rivals? Why should tangible assets be counted and intangibles overlooked? Why value the custom-pulling power of the real estate and not the same power of the brand equity?

As the electronic age matures so these issues and questions will necessarily be resolved. As companies are forced to put more of their investment into systems, knowledge capture and dissemination so the pressure will mount to have that capitalised value recognised. As companies move out of real estate into virtual economics so they and their investors will be keen to see the net worth of the corporation maintained and hence *all* assets counted.

The future world of commerce will be very different from today. Business will develop a totally different view about how to reach customers, how to transact with them and the infrastructure required to do that. The P&L will have a different emphasis, the balance sheet will recognise the currently unrecognisable and investors will develop a different set of tests for measuring the future potential of a corporation. The external market place changes will not only drive the economics but also impact the very shape of the organisation itself, changing the way things are structured, the skills that are required and the processes that need to be developed to interact efficiently with the customer. While the transition is taking place to the new electronic order, the environment for doing business will be more uncertain than it's ever been, employees will need to become even more flexible and ready to embrace change and a company's senior management will have to be ever more adept at planning their way through these changes and demonstrating leadership and clarity of vision in so far as it's possible. It's a changing world and the winners will be the ones who are in the vanguard of changing with it.

12 Structural Difficulties with the Internet will be Overcome

On the demand side, significant numbers of consumers are ready and waiting. On the supply side, technology and communication links are rapidly improving. All that is now required is a satisfactory infrastructure that can reassure consumers that their privacy will still be protected, their payment methods secure, that shopping in cyberspace will be as safe as anywhere else. This necessary reassurance is the final piece in the jigsaw. It will be the coming together and maturing of all the three elements – demand, supply and enabling infrastructure – that will trigger the surges of growth that are predicted for electronic shopping. The fusion of consumer interest plus accessible technology is perhaps the most critical. But underpinning that 'marriage' there needs to be a transaction infrastructure that is secure (Figure 12.1).

In this chapter the key security issues are investigated. It is a matter of particular concern to the growth of internet commerce as that is of course the least mature of the electronic shopping options. The key question is whether that medium especially can be made safe enough to give consumers sufficient confidence to shop. Can a satisfactory environment

Figure 12.1 Demand, Supply and Enabling Infrastructure

be created? What progress has been made to date, how far away are we till the necessary controls and reassurances are firmly in place?

Some argue that the internet will never succeed as a commercial medium. They claim that credit card protection will never be totally secure, that messages can be easily hacked into and subverted. But since the mid-1990s there has been extraordinary progress on many fronts. There have been rapid advances in the use of encryption and data protection, for example, and suppliers and banks have worked hard to establish common standards and protocols to better manage and prevent payment or credit card fraud. We will examine this in more detail but the bottom line is that shopping on the internet looks likely soon to be as safe as any other method of buying goods and services – if not more so.

The security infrastructure issues break down into four key areas and it will be important to examine just how effective the various new technologies and initiatives will be. Which of the many different security systems being developed will be most widely adopted? Will there be common standards that all banks, providers and suppliers can subscribe to? How user-friendly will the security options be and can they actually be developed so they make shopping and payment actually easier and more fun?

The four areas to examine are:

- Personal Privacy
- Message Security
- Payment Security
- General Regulation and Control.

As each of these areas is explored we should bear in mind that these issues are more executional than strategic in nature. In other words they relate specifically to how shopping will get done, they don't by themselves negate the underlying market demand and strategic opportunity. If it's clear that these security hurdles can be overcome then it would appear there is nothing left in the way of realising electronic commerce's full market potential.

Personal Privacy

Even without the internet, we already live in an age where information about individuals is kept on any number of databases. When we take out insurance, set up bank accounts, register with a doctor, apply for credit cards, subscribe to monthly information services, join clubs, join air miles or other reward schemes we are listing out information about ourselves. Yes, we can tick the data protection box insisting we want that information kept confidential and not communicated to third parties or sold onto others for direct promotional mailing. Most times when we tick the box we are dealing with a trusted provider whom we can be sure will respect our rights – but we can never be 100% sure. Also we can't be totally safe from determined expert hackers who have set their sights on breaking into information databases to check out or extract information.

Our world is full of information and despite reassurances and regulation we have to make the trade off. We have to decide whether we want the services or products on offer, can vest sufficient trust in the provider to do all that's possible to protect the information we provide and at the same time accept the very small risk that that information might be abused.

Privacy of information on the internet must be set in this context. It's potentially a medium with no greater or less risk in information management than any other. Furthermore because of the investment attention the internet is getting, there are mechanisms being put in place to provide additional forms of protection which are over and above the norm. Providers of goods and services are especially keen to address this situation because they are determined to remove any roadblocks in the way of electronic commerce. But we are unlikely ever to arrive at a state of perfect protection either on the internet or with any other communication/information environment.

Governments have long been concerned about the privacy of the individual and tried both legislative and voluntary routes to try to control how information about people is held and on what basis it can be communicated. As far back as 1980, the OECD (Organisation for Economic Co-operation and Development) established a set of guidelines to assist in the protection of personal data. The principles contained in these guidelines are commonly referred to as the Code of Fair Information Practices and have formed the basis of all privacy legislation world-wide. They include goals of:

'collecting only the information that is needed, inform the person of the purpose of collection, use the information only for the purpose intended, keep the individual informed and give people the opportunity to access the information and get it corrected.'

Building on that 1980 code most western governments have passed some basic privacy legislation. For example, the UK has a charter of data protection rights, in Germany it is unlawful among other things to sell information lists with people's names and addresses without their consent and it's also unlawful to mail people unsolicited material. In the USA in 1986, the Electronic Communications Privacy Act was passed, designed to protect access and misuse of electronic information, reinforcing common law personal data privacy rights protecting individuals. More recently Germany became the first nation to establish a multi-media law specifically aimed at regulating privacy on the internet, requiring disclosure as to how any collected information will be used and certification that a company's use of personal data does adhere to set standards.

However the world of electronic information has moved on so rapidly that governments are generally struggling to keep up and typically don't have the resources to adequately police how specific companies use and control personal information themselves. Fortunately, though, there are new initiatives coming along which can supplement government attempts at regulations and provide some further reassurance that personal information can be managed effectively and kept private.

One initiative is a kind of self-help device which comes out of responsible people and businesses wanting to act to create the right environment. It's something that can probably only be done easily on the internet and is an example of how the flexibility of that mechanism can also work to help protect the individuals. What's developed has been self-help pages like the web home page: 'Blacklist of inappropriate advertisers.' That website lists out all those companies who have offended the voluntary code of fair information practices. It details what they have done and actively encourages consumers not to deal with them. In addition, the US Federal Trade Commission is vigorously encouraging self-regulation. A recent spot check on the top 100 US companies found that 43 of them did display privacy policy notices. But federal regulators want all organisations to voluntarily adopt this sort of code of practice. Otherwise more legislation is threatened and there are currently 32 bills in US Congress all looking to centrally control internet information and communication.

The second initiative comes with the development of new software that protects the individual from being information-abused. For example 'Net Nanny' catches certain words or phrases such as 'where do you live', 'what is your telephone number' and shuts down the computer, preventing the internet user from accidentally or mistakenly providing information they subsequently wish they hadn't.

The third and most powerful development came from the original big two makers of software for browsing the web – Netscape and Microsoft. Unusually these two joined forces specifically to protect the privacy of consumers who visit world-wide web sites. The aim, originally put forward by Netscape in conjunction with two of its software partners, Firefly and Verisign, is for both the big two companies to adopt an open profiling standard that lets users of personal computers manage the information they want disclosed to or withheld from a particular website. The new technology ensures that any information which might have been automatically exchanged between different websites is restricted. Only that which the user specifically authorises can be communicated. Industry observers believe alliances on this technology will make it possible to provide significantly better data protection. 'These are the sort of initiatives that are needed out there', the Forrester Research group has commented, 'it's going to be the starting point that will transform individual privacy on the net'.

In addition to these developments there is a host of other improvements as we shall see in encryption, use of passwords and methods to protect credit card data and credit payments that are all moving forward with the same intent and the same rapid pace. They will evolve to establish a series of mechanisms that will provide measures of personal reassurance and security on the internet that will be at least as effective as those found elsewhere.

Message security

On top of the protections being put in generally around information and personal privacy must be added specific measures to manage message security – that is, who can access the information or communications being made. There are three particular initiatives – (1) encryption, (2) biometry and (3) firewalls.

Encryption

Encryption is simply a system for translating message data into code that cannot be read by anyone without the 'decryption' key. It's an idea that's as old as history and now IBM has established a world-wide standard – the Data Encryption Standard (DES). The software for it is readily available at no cost to anyone with access to the internet. Browsers indicate that they are in secure encrypted mode by displaying a lock icon, in the lower left corner in Netscape and lower right corner in Microsoft. Early versions of DES were available as early as 1975 and it is now the most well known and widely used cryptosystem in the world. It is especially reassuring that this system is still recognised and has withstood the test of time. More recently it has been enhanced with what is called 'triple DES' which encrypts each message using three different keys in succession. It will basically stop anyone trying to hack in. They would now require not only extraordinary determination but also massive computing power.

Encryption is increasingly used to protect credit card data. It is often linked with additional security measures such as verification procedures to check signatures or passwords that are unique to the consumer. Of course encryption and verification procedures can slow things down – behavioural psychologists estimate that consumers will tolerate a wait of around 20 seconds before impatience and irritation set in – but software is improving and the connecting servers on the internet are increasing capacity to meet demand.

No one is yet suggesting the perfect solution is in place, but many banks like Citicorp and Barclays as well as credit card transaction-processing businesses such as First Data have vested interest in building effective data and message protection systems that can provide as least as much reassurance in the virtual world as they do in the physical.

Biometry

Biometry is potentially the most secure level of message security. It involves using some unique aspect of the human body such as fingerprints, voice recognition or verification of retinal patterns. Special biometric software has been developed that would come up on line during the ordering process. Customers, for example, would sign the screen in their normal signature using a digitising pen. The software would assess the speed of writing and stroke order among other keys to verify the signature.

Biometry is still in its relatively early days. There is no accepted global standard and a number of software companies like Peripheral Vision in the UK are developing their own unique approaches. As a result, adoption is still expensive and few commercial companies to date see this approach as their key. But again in the coming years software is predicted to improve, costs will come down and for sure biometry because of its ultimate simplicity and user-friendliness will find a place in the electronic commercial world.

Firewalls

Firewalls is the last of the main message-protection devices to discuss. The idea is that a core network should not be connected to the public internet without some form of protection. In other words it should be possible to put a 'wall' between the public internet and private access. A firewall itself is a term to describe the computer or router that's specifically installed to filter messages and not allow them to pass from public to private access or back without verification or authorisation. Typically it allows insiders to have full access to the outside while controlling access from the outside in.

There are many computer companies now offering firewall services and it's quickly become a very sophisticated means of protecting message security and keeping hackers out. It's endorsed by the National Computer Security Association as currently the most effective way to protect data and message. The equipment can be quickly installed and the time delays in data transmission through the firewall filter are now negligible. Firewall systems are now commonly put in together with encryption providing particularly secure environments. Indeed a British company, Janus Software, claims to have now developed a totally hacker-proof security system. It recently put up a £10,000 reward to any hacker who could break in. The challenge attracted 80,000 hackers from all over the world. Its challenge ended in March 1998 and none had succeeded!

Payment security

In addition to the various initiatives in personal privacy and message protection there has been significant progress in providing payment security, especially with reference to credit cards.

IBM have pioneered a global standard called SET (Secure Electronic Transactions) which after a few early hitches is now becoming more widely adopted. In Europe a consortium of 38 banks is encouraging its use. They are led especially by Commerzbank with Kardstadt the German department store retailer, both of whom are far advanced in their trials around electronic commerce. The consortium is working closely with Visa and Mastercard and together they are promoting the service to all their members.

SET, like a rival approach called SSL (Secure Socket Layer) uses 128-key encryption to scramble the credit card data. It creates a secure channel to prevent third parties on the network from being able to tamper with payment information passed between the customer, the bank and the merchant. SET and SSL are now fully 'debugged' and operational. Microsoft seems to be moving to build in either SSL or SET into its browsers and many commercial websites have expressed an interest in linking up.

The disadvantage of this approach is that 128-key encryption, while legal in the USA, is discouraged in a number of other countries including the UK, where government fears its own systems couldn't break into and therefore control that degree of sophisticated encryption. Nevertheless Barclays Bank, for example, in the UK is trialling SSL on its website Barclay Square to provide its customers with a secure method of paying by credit card over the internet. Since its launch Barclays claims 'it has had no fraud whatsoever'.

Payment security had been shown in the early days of internet commerce to be a major concern for consumers and there is research to show that it has been an inhibiting factor discouraging shopping on the internet. However, what is emerging is that technologies like SET and SSL, combined with initiatives in areas of data privacy and message protection, are creating safe and secure environments. If anything there will be more security shopping on the web than with traditional shopping methods. The *Financial Times* has predicted, 'the internet will soon be completely safe for commerce'. *Business Week,* in its regular surveys of what is happening on the internet, endorses this view but points out that as with many security systems, 'self-help' is also important and there are steps it also advises would-be electronic shoppers to take. These include some common sense items as 'keep security software current and download browser security updates when offered', 'don't lend your password to someone else to use', 'choose a bank like Wells Fargo that will cover losses from any cyber break-ins' or 'choose providers like AT&T that guarantees to cover any fraud for users of its services'.

If a consumer is still not comfortable then there are yet further alternative means of payment being developed which provide their own security and safety reassurances.

One of these is 'digital cash' or 'electronic cash'. It's intended to be a new form of tender that can be passed from buyer to seller almost like real cash. The electronic cash company is either linked to a bank or is part of one and it provides the consumer in effect with a digital current checking account converting the cash in the account into digital information and creating a kind of electronic purse for shoppers to use to buy goods and services. The consumer then purchases using an assigned digital account number which is suitably encrypted.

'Digi cash' or 'e-cash' providers claim it will especially interest consumers because all transactions can be anonymous: 'Without the spender's consent, no one should be able to trace who paid whom for what, the spender is the only one with the digital account number.' Some 30 pilot schemes have been tested from sophisticated environments in the USA through to places as far-flung as China and Zambia.

One particular advantage for digi cash or e-cash is that it lends itself more easily for 'micropayments', enabling consumers to pay for small items easily without the complexities of credit card data management and the processing overheads attached to it. For example, people may want to download one song from an album or access a new food recipe or a page of information on a tourist resort. The price might be cents not even dollars and electronic commerce requires a simple payment system to facilitate that.

Yet another approach is the smart card. This is a plastic card which can also act like a debit card. It can be loaded up with money. It can be inserted into the ATM and charged up with, say, $500 from the bank account. When consumers then want to place a shopping order electronically they can insert the smart card into a reader in the computer which together with a password or PIN authenticates the card and at the same time confirms to the 'cybershop' that the Bank will honour the amount to be paid.

SmartGATE is one software company now promoting the use of Smart cards. They work with retailers to provide customers and employees with personalised PIN smart cards which operate with software installed on the home or office PC. There are a series of verification and authentication steps built into the software, all the data that is transmitted is encrypted and there is a firewall that can be additionally installed to provide further protection.

Smart cards are widely used in France today where they function mostly as credit cards with some 20 million cards in service. In Germany, Siemens is testing out a 'super smart card' that in addition provides biometric fingerprint recognition. When the card is held with the thumb covering the lower right corner the card reads the actual fingerprint, compares it to the print stored digitally in the card and then clears whatever transaction is planned, whether withdrawing money, charging a purchase or even opening the door to your home!

No doubt some of these developments will stay in the lab but others for sure will become widely commercialised. There will be a number of payment methods available for internet transactions, each offering different levels of reassurance and comfort to first-time or nervous shoppers. Certainly technologies are improving so rapidly that a secure commercial environment will be created and the *Financial Times* prediction at the time of writing looks readily achievable.

General regulation and control

At the moment there is uncertainty about legal jurisdiction in cyberspace. The legal status of electronic copyright, for example, is vague, as are the legal and practical issues surrounding on-line exchange and electronic cash. There is also no global authority to enforce rules on the internet or possible sanctions for those who break the codes of practice. Yet these are issues which national governments, the United Nations, the OECD and trade associations are all acutely aware of and they are actively developing plans to manage electronic commerce more effectively either by regulation or voluntary code.

While suppliers of internet services are very aware of these executional problems they have nevertheless spent time and funds focusing on getting themselves wired, establishing their websites and exploring the market potential the internet can bring. As the market grows and supplier experimentation matures so they will inevitably also turn their attention to the rules and laws of commerce and set about promoting more effective control and regulation.

In the meantime the US government has been setting the pace in investigating ways of developing the new rules and regulatory regime. For example it established the Information Infrastructure Task Force which among other things has made recommendations on amending copyright laws to specifically cover electronic transmissions. In addition the WTO (World Trade Organisation) has set up working parties to make recommendations on commercial rules including reviewing the extension of individual governments' rights of jurisdiction from the physical into the virtual world. The French government has also tried to attack this problem by devising a central registration system for all who want to supply or use the internet. As a more hard-hitting mechanism the FBI has put together its own task forces to track down hackers, on-line pornographers or suppliers who try to avoid taxation. Their goal is to ensure such individuals or companies get charged with criminal offences.

Another approach to improving regulation and control is the development of on-line communities that provide their own rules and securities. Companies with common interests could cluster themselves together. For example, auto parts suppliers might band together in an exclusive network serving the auto industry. Investment management firms may decide to sell their services only through distributors who have signed up to the same rules of commerce. Universities could choose to distribute course details only within their own selected network and effectively establish an extended intranet to groups of dedicated linked users. Banks, insurance companies, computer manufacturers could all set about doing the same thing.

Where common or mutual interest is insufficient, individual companies could turn to third parties who could choose to develop the on-line community and put in place a satisfactory framework for doing business. For example AOL currently sells access to the internet and provides a forum in which to advertise, buy and sell or supply information. In effect AOL has already established a well-regulated and well-maintained environment which does have a set of rules and creates a secure regime where basic laws of commerce are expected to be adhered to.

AOL and others like Microsoft Network may not see their role as law enforcers but they do in effect provide that value-added service. That need for control and regulation may well become a key growth driver for AOL and others as providers and shoppers are likely to become increasingly comfortable shopping in what is presented as a reputable and familiar environment. As this value-added role becomes more widely recognised we can expect others, especially the telecommunication companies, to step up their profile in managing access and offering secure 'community services' on the net.

*   *   *

Business has moved a long way since the internet first went commercial. Since the early days when surveys showed significant numbers of executives weren't even sure if the internet had any application to their organisation, companies have rapidly got more aware and sophisticated. Many can now see the market potential and want to exploit it. In chasing that goal they are themselves putting pressure on software and hardware operators to help make commerce on the internet as smooth and as efficient as possible. Investment and trial in developing the infrastructure is moving at a fast pace and many more enlightened commentators now recognise that security will quickly cease to be an issue. 'Lack of security is no longer a barrier,' conclude US researchers Aberdeen Group, 'the debate is now quickly moving on to focus on improved bandwidths and delivery logistics. There is now sufficient security protection in place that especially where the provider is a recognised brand name there is now little perceived risk.'

Only the most reluctant electronic shoppers may still be concerned. But even now there are plenty of 'frenzied copers' and 'experimenters' out there wanting the convenience and the new forms of service. Their motivation is such that they will make the trade off between the new shopping advantage vs any lingering questions of payment security and will likely be quickly reassured there is sufficient protection and assurance built in.

13 How Can Manufacturers Respond?

In previous chapters we considered the retailer's dilemmas in facing up to the electronic shopping challenge. Now we turn the spotlight on manufacturers and suppliers. What will be the impact on their established ways of doing business, what are the threats and risks, is there an upside and what strategic options do they have moving forward?

In fact, they have a unique window of opportunity. They have a once-in-a-generation chance to truly connect with their end-user customer base. They can look to break their dependence on their retail customers. They can exploit the new technology and consumer interest by dealing direct – themselves. They can establish their own sales, marketing and home delivery contacts. They can disintermediate those who have for the last 25 years dominated them and the supply chain.

For the first time, manufacturers have a choice in how they distribute. They can decide that their future business *does* still lie with their existing retail customers. Or, they can decide to develop their *own* consumer supply lines. Electronic commerce creates this strategic crossroads (Figure 13.1). Down the first path may lie continued dependency but existing custom and business is preserved – at least in the short term. Down the alternative route lies adventure, new revenue potential, a platform for the future but also risk – risk that the retailers will see the manufacturers' ES activity as a direct competitive threat and cut off distribution. While electronic commerce is in its early phases, manufacturers can duck this issue. But as it develops it will come to confront them head-on and tough decisions will need to be made.

In addressing this challenge, all manufacturers will be acutely aware of the history of their relationships with their customer base. They will have seen their early dominance in the 1970s continuously undermined by their more sophisticated, larger, demanding distributors. They will be frustrated by relationships which are often confrontational and aggressive and despite sometimes warm words rarely move beyond periodic fights over price and discounts and rebates. They will wonder how they got themselves into this position where the retailer customer has

Figure 13.1   Manufacturers at a Crossroads

The manufacturer's dilemma

	Preserve existing retail relationship	Exploit ES
Advantage:	– Keep existing business intact, for now	– Distribution under own control
Risks:	– Remain dependent	– New revenue potential
	– As demand for ES grows manufacturer not in position to exploit it	– Existing retailer customers may cut off distribution

so clearly wrestled the balance of power from them. They will want to challenge whether they do have a profitable future continuing with these relationships. They will want to explore just how much flexibility they do have in pursuing alternative options. Do they have the competencies and the strength of purpose to develop their own direct operations? Do they have or can they acquire sufficient market clout that they can be sure consumers will continue to clamour for their products – wherever they are distributed or located? Do they seize this opportunity now, do they wait and see or do they conclude that the risk of losing existing business is too great?

To understand how manufacturers can best respond to these issues we must first review in more detail the historic baggage they are bringing into this debate. In the early days, in the 1970s (Figure 13.2), when manufacturers' brands were generally dominant, they could virtually dictate terms to their distributors. In the supermarket sector, for example, which has been a hothouse environment for the supply relationship, companies like Heinz, Campbells, Procter & Gamble all had well known household brands that had strong franchises. Their technologies were still relatively immature so they could establish a stream of innovative new products which continued to keep their proposition to the market fresh and stimulating. In some countries and sectors there was even a system of 'retail price maintenance' where the manufacturers could print on the pack or otherwise control the price the product was sold at, thereby

Figure 13.2 Retailer–Manufacturer Relationships

→ 1970s	1980s	1990s	2000 →
'Manufacturers Dominant'	**'Retailers Consolidate'**	**'Retailer Sophistication'**	**'New Equilibrium?'**
– Manufacturers bigger/more sophisticated	– Retailers grew larger	– Seized initiatives in logistics and supply chain	– Manufacturer resurgence on back of ES?
– Back Brands with heavy advertising	– Learnt to leverage their direct relationship with consumer	– Manufacturers found in defensive reactive mode	
– New product technologies led by manufacturers	– Development of private label competition		

Growing Retail Power

guaranteeing their profit margins and locking them in at attractive levels. In contrast, their then distributors were relatively small, fragmented and lacking the know-how to exploit their contact with the end-consumer.

Through the 1980s all that began to change. Demand in most developed economies was buoyant. Retailers began to expand rapidly building new stores and adding space with a frenzy. Part of that expansion also brought with it the inevitable wave of mergers and consolidation as some tried to achieve winning positions more quickly. As these developments bore fruit so retailers also began to stand up to their manufacturer suppliers. Suddenly they realised that they often accounted for c. 10% of a manufacturer's business and they found their threats to clients were usually accompanied by a gradual giving-in to whatever demands the retailer was trying to impose. Power changed hands. Within a few short years a handful of 'super retailers' began to emerge. They backed up their new-found clout by investing in systems like EPOS that gave them greater knowledge about their customers' buying habits, which product lines were selling especially well and which were below target, and linked to DPP they could tell which were adding profit on a net profit per square foot basis and which weren't. New-found IT power, new market awareness, increasing breadth of range and choice

Figure 13.3   Private-Label Grocery Penetration (%)

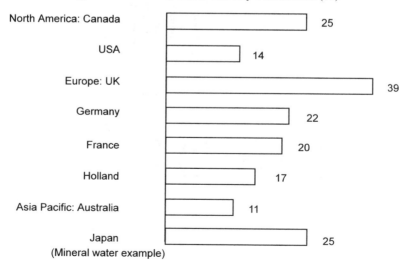

Source: Wileman and Jary, *Retailer Power Plays.*

in store, smarter environments all combined to put them in the driving seat topped now by their own brands. Why be dependent on Coca-Cola or General Mills or Kraft when they could provide similar quality at lower prices to what had now become 'their' consumers? By the mid-1990s retailers' brands had taken over from manufacturers in many sectors in many countries (Figure 13.3).

As we now start the new century, retailers are as strong as ever. They are the power base. Manufacturers remain on the back foot. Observers must feel they're at a boxing match watching two heavyweights slugging it out. As the contest has gone on it's become a wretched spectacle. The result looks a foregone conclusion. The weaker fighter is punch-drunk, lurching around the ring looking dazed, struggling to stay on his feet, hoping for some miracle intervention. The stronger fighter is dancing, cock-a-hoop, throwing punches at random – some looking suspiciously below the belt. Let's look at some of the photos from the fight so far:

- 'Sainsbury has humiliated Coca-Cola, the biggest and most heavily hyped brand ever, by grabbing 60 per cent of in-store cola sales with its own private label brand. Sainsbury is now launching its own brand of luxury ice cream to rival Häagen-Dazs and Ben & Jerry's. It was not more than a year ago that Sainsbury's own washing powder brand Novon stole market leadership out-manoeuvring mighty Procter & Gamble and Unilever.'

(Times report)

- 'The war is still on between retail-owned products and manufacturers' products in Japan. Japanese manufacturers have been facing the onslaught of private retail brands prompted by sluggish domestic demand. The easing of retail laws has increased the number of large scale stores and retailers with extensive networks have taken advantage of their distributor power.'

(FT article)

- 'Unilever used its AGM to vent its irritation at the emergence of so-called retailer copy cat brands which closely imitate manufacturer brand names and packaging but undercut on price. Unilever has joined with other industrial groups such as Coca-Cola in an attempt to persuade the UK government to prohibit what they regard as unfair competition.'

(FT)

- 'The trade philosophy in France is a hard discount mentality. It is antagonistic to the manufacturer. Margins are being pared to the bone and there is no sign of a let-up.'

  (*McKinsey report*)

- 'If any supplier opens up a direct Internet sales link with the consumer we will stop selling their products.'

  (*Target Corporation, 1999*)

Not surprisingly, against this background, manufacturers generally are extraordinarily nervous at doing anything that might make their adversary fight even harder. They're very aware that developing their own direct links might be taken as a red rag to a bull. Yet they see the enormous opportunity ES can present. Is there a way out of this dilemma? Can they find the inner resourcefulness, as the bell rings for round 12 in the boxing match, to get back into the contest, work out a way that lets them pursue their own tactics and at least get themselves back to all square. They don't need to find the knock-out blow – win:win would do.

More prosaically, can they manage the conflict of distributing through retailers and direct to consumers at the same time? Aren't there any success models out there to draw on? Some manufacturers must have managed this already, if not yet in an electronic context then nevertheless dealing with similar market pressures? And indeed, thankfully for our hapless pugilist, there are some pointers and lessons learned. Companies like Procter & Gamble, Sony, Nike, Mars, Gillette, Seagram, IBM, Kellogg's, Mattel, Unilever and others – companies operating in many different retail sectors – have demonstrated that it is possible to manage retail customers successfully. They have shown there are ways to pursue their own goals and initiatives while still building and sustaining a successful business with retail distributors.

Coca-Cola provides one immediate illustration of a manufacturing company that sells simultaneously through different channels and has learnt to live successfully with any channel conflict that might result. As the company has grown, Coca-Cola has developed business through grocery multiples, discount stores, small neighbourhood convenience stores, bars, restaurants, delis, theatres, take-home fast-food outlets, vending machines as well as even having some showcase stores of its own. Yet Coca-Cola has persisted with its competing channel customers and over time has persuaded them to largely accept this. It's acknowledged as an inevitable condition of the marketplace.

What have Coca-Cola and other successes done? How have they managed the inevitable friction when they do open up a new channel of distribution? How they have dealt with the possibility that one channel's sales will cannibalise the others? How have they responded to existing distributor's initial threats to delist the product and stop distribution?

Researching and interviewing with these companies it becomes clear that their key lies in segmentation. Their route forward is to clearly differentiate between the channels and establish different value propositions. The learning is that separate channels exist because by definition they are responding to customers who have different needs. One wants to buy a multi-pack of Coca-Cola as part of the weekly supermarket shop, the other wants the convenience of a single can purchased on impulse at a vending machine on a street corner. The answer is to understand those different customer needs – profoundly, develop the differentiated propositions and market them in that way. Do this persistently, accepting some initial kickbacks until the market place accepts it as a necessary and integral part of the market scene.

There are in fact three segmentation options, each is illustrated with brief case examples:

1. Product Segmentation
2. Territorial Segmentation
3. Complementary Segmentation.

1. Product Segmentation

- Black & Decker has developed three distinct product ranges each targeted and tailored to different channels and set up to provide a differentiated proposition. Black & Decker uses its Quantum brand at the heavy DIY end, the Black & Decker brand for the major multiples and De Walt aimed at trade buyers and contractors. While this does create significant product-line complexity for Black & Decker it has helped manage potential conflicts. For example, different promotions and incentives are made available but because they're on different brands the scope for comparison or conflict between channels is much reduced.
- In a similar way, Levi's established Britannia jeans and the Levi's brand in major multiple outlets, Dockers through department stores and speciality retailers and Slates for upmarket stores. To strengthen the product segmentation Britannia was targeted at the lower price end of the market, Dockers is mid-range but its image is young and fashionable, while Slates is targeted more to the 30+ age group.

2. Territorial Segmentation

- Nationwide Insurance in the USA has long relied on its network of agents to build its business. However it has seen the potential of direct consumer links. It has evaluated how to build its own direct channel while preserving the integrity of its agency network and their business potential. Nationwide's solution has been to split the USA geographically. In a number of states the agency network was especially strong and rather than risk cannibalisation, Nationwide has kept those as 'agency states' and is working to reinforce the business there. However in other states, Nationwide either had no or limited agency coverage. It is in these states where it is building its direct network, learning what can be achieved, whether the two approaches to market can work in harmony and what is their long-term potential.
- Kodak, when it was in the photocopier business, had a long history of selling through distributors. But relationships were often unsatisfactory. In many regions there were several rival distributors covering the same territory. Each demanded more favourable business deals and invariably assumed, even without evidence, that Kodak must be treating one more favourably than the other. There was continued conflict and sales were being jeopardised. Kodak determined to resolve this. Its solution was to select the best distributor for target groups of customers. It picked one target distributor per region. While there was some initial sales fall-off from disappointed distributors, Kodak gritted its teeth and by persistent application gradually built its chosen distributors into dominant but differentiated sales channels.
- Now ASDA, the UK supermarket chain, has announced plans to set up its own electronic ordering and delivery service *but* it plans to establish this in territories where it has few if any stores. In doing this it minimises cannibalisation, reaches new customers it could never normally reach and attacks the home bases of its competitors!

3. Complementary Segmentation

- Coca-Cola did have significant problems from its established retailer outlets when it started installing vending machines on a wide basis. But Coca-Cola had also conducted detailed consumer research that showed that vending machines sales could actually *add* to the total Coca-Cola brand and market. Sales could be incremental rather that cannibalising existing outlets. The vending machines did serve the same consumers, but did so on different occasions. Tests had shown the vending operation could actually benefit all parties. It was a classic win:win.

- Similarly, Nike ran into problems when first opening its own Nike Town stores. But it too had carried out detailed consumer surveys that clearly demonstrated the role the stores could play. They were perceived as reinforcing the brand name, as showcases that could also generate increased demand and sales in the established channels. Again the case was put forward that this could complement not cannibalise. Subsequent market success proved the point.

- The major pharmaceutical companies can also provide a lesson. They have been switching sales and marketing effort from traditional independent pharmacies toward the large health management organisations (HMOs) and mail-order drug operations. But they have taken the view that both channels need to and can coexist as complementary sales operations. With that goal they have developed distinct but separate marketing support packages which do recognise where the future volume sales will lie but do also provide specific support at a local level specific to what the independent pharmacies need. While initial coexistence was not easy, the independents – who stood to lose the most – have come to appreciate the pharmaceutical companies remain committed to them and are backing that up with sales and marketing action.

- Other examples come from Sears, who continued to provide discounts, rebates and business support to its distributors in small towns even though its business had begun to shift toward the major malls and outlets. GE, too, had originally depended for its business on a vast number of small independent dealers and even as its business shifted away to larger outlets it continued to provide sufficient support in financial deals but also through its salesforce. The same dedicated and complementary approach to different channels has been taken by pet food suppliers as their business develops away from independents to the larger outlets like PetsMart and also by Avon who continue to base their business on their large number of sales representatives while targeting new and different types of consumers via their internet operation.

Channel conflict can be managed. It's not easy. It takes time and persistence. It requires a clear value proposition that reflects a deep-rooted understanding of customers and their differing needs. It involves a focused segmentation and a differentiated sales and marketing approach. The channels may be naturally complementary so that all will gain or they may be more directly in conflict. Whatever the situation, the onus rests on the manufacturer supplier to find the win:win where all parties can ultimately benefit. It's an education and acclimatisation process in which manufacturers and their distributors can get used to a new set of market variables, readjust expectations and learn to operate effectively with the different challenges.

Which manufacturers are best placed to succeed in a channel conflict situation? What steps can be taken to ensure the segmentations that get identified can be effectively marketed? How can they ensure that existing customers do gradually adjust and accept the new market conditions? The research has shown that there are some ten key criteria a manufacturer must aim to score well against. Each criterion represents an organisation and market state that manufacturers must aspire to if they dare to succeed in the channel conflict game. The stronger the position the company can establish in the market the more able it will be to arrive at a satisfactory end game.

The ten key criteria are set out as questions in Table 13.1. Current market strength and flexibility to manage the ES challenge can be measured by scoring each question 0–10. A strong Yes answer scores 10, a strong No 0. A high positive score > 70 would indicate high chances of success. Lower scores would raise a cautionary note and suggest that *before* embarking on a potential channel conflict, the company has work to do to get its products, customer understanding and market position up to strong enough levels that it can take on the challenge. That break point $< > 70$ is critical. If a company does set up its own direct consumer links and takes on a channel challenge without sufficient market clout it will likely fail. If it recognises its weaknesses beforehand then it still has time to build a sufficient platform so it can succeed. In this regard, electronic commerce may be the trigger that gets the manufacturer to finally deal with some of its sales and marketing issues that have bedevilled it but have been allowed to continue. It may have too many products or brands to support, it may need alliances in order to access more marketing funds, or improvements in its product technology, it may never have adequately segmented its customers and neglected to respond sufficiently to their underlying needs. Most companies will be able to intuitively score the ten questions set out and know immediately for themselves what are the key issues they need to address.

Leading manufacturers have driven hard in recent years to reach a position where they could score highly, where they have got the market clout. For example, Philip Morris, Campbells and Unilever have been aggressively rationalising their product portfolios to focus down on their

Table 13.1 'The Manufacturer's Test' – has the manufacturer the strength and flexibility to manage channel conflicts?

1. Does the company currently sell successfully through different channels with significant sales in each?   _____
2. Is there a rigorous process institutionalised in the company for researching customers and precisely understanding their different needs?   _____
3. Is that knowledge effectively exploited so that there are truly differentiated value propositions for each channel?   _____
4. Is that differentiation also translated into different and targeted sales and marketing programmes responding to segment needs?   _____
5. Has the company been able to establish strong collaborative partnerships with its customers vs a relationship of confrontation and mistrust?   _____
6. Does the company have a strong brand portfolio where most products are No. 1 or No. 2 in their sector?   _____
7. Would industry observers rate the company's sales, marketing and channel management skills as core competences?   _____
8. Is the company building off a relatively solid platform of rising sales and stable margins?   _____
9. Does the company have a history of ring-fencing sufficient sales and marketing funds and investing consistently and persistently?   _____
10. Does the company have the leadership at senior management to take bold marketplace decisions and see them through?   _____

major brands and give those the attention and investment that can get them to No. 1 or No. 2 market positions, and keep them there. If consumer demand is strong enough then of course they have much greater flexibility to explore new distribution routes to the end-user. As another example, computer hardware manufacturers such as Hewlett Packard, Compaq and IBM have put substantial efforts into improving their supply-chain capabilities. They have put themselves in a position where retail distributors *want* to deal with them, not just because of their brand but because they can more or less guarantee stock availability, consistent supply and product reliability. Other companies like P&G, Johnson & Johnson or Levi's have focused on the pull-through effect of their brands making them a 'must stock'.

There is no doubt, then, that a number of manufacturers in different sectors arrive at the electronic shopping starting post with all the right qualifications, competencies and experiences. Of course e-commerce itself is new and different, it will pose its own unique challenges but the underlying market and channel issues are at the end of the day the same. It will all come down to being able to pass the Manufacturer's Test with a high enough score, establishing the 'channel conflict-management confidence' and then rigorously pursuing an effective segmentation strategy that is set up to meet different consumer needs with demonstrably different value propositions.

To date, only a few manufacturers have raised their heads above the parapet and made any public pronouncements about their ES plans and their preparedness to manage any channel conflicts that arise. But as the electronic channel to market grows and matures, as is predicted, then expect more of the leaders to come forward with strong market propositions ready to see them through. Unilever has already declared its interest and this excerpt from a recent interview with its Chairman provides a suitable resumé of not only the manufacturer's dilemma but also its need to come to grips with it and move its business on:

'Unilever is one of the few multinationals to go public and be proactive about its on-line intentions. It has announced a radical diversification into new service-related methods of channelling its foods and personal products to the consumer . . . areas being examined include home selling on the personal care side where products include Elizabeth Arden cosmetics.

Niall FitzGerald, Unilever's head, said such arrangements needed to be studied: "in both food and personal products we are seeing the emergence of alternative channels to the consumer . . . unless we are careful we will find ourselves boxed in to what is sold through a consolidating block of retailers. So we need to consider ways to broaden the channels through which we can reach the consumer."'

(Times)

14 Ten Strategic Options for Manufacturers

As manufacturers reflect on the new electronic shopping challenges, must they inevitably transition their business to embrace it? Can they sensibly resist it, eschew building up their own direct operation and stick with their existing distribution arrangements? Is there a half-way house that keeps a foot in both camps and gives the flexibility to move one way or the other as the market develops? What are the basic strategies that a manufacturer can choose, what are the options?

The testing and research have identified ten strategic options (Table 14.1) that a manufacturer could pick from. They fall into different categories. The first two are 'partnership-based' and assume future success can be derived from getting even closer to existing physical retail customers. The second two are 'pull-based' and care less about channels of distribution, simply focusing on making the products so attractive that they will be demanded and sell through any and every route to market. The next two take the first steps down the ES path. The final four strategic options involve a more significant electronic commitment all the way through to a 'fully direct' transition.

Table 14.1 Manufacturers' Ten Strategic Options

'Partnership-based'	1.	Woo the retailer
	2.	Move to private label
'Pull'	3.	Technology-led
	4.	Brand-driven
Electronic Information-based	5.	Information only
	6.	Forming a club
'Own Direct'	7.	Treat as another channel
	8.	Set up as separate business
	9.	Band together
	10.	Go fully direct

Determining which is most attractive is going to be something for each manufacturer to evaluate and decide on an individual basis. The decision making can be guided using the two tests that have been described in Chapters 6 and 13:

- The 'ES Test' will provide a clear indication of the product's attributes, its susceptibility to the forces of electronic shopping and the degree to which target consumer groups are likely to be responsive to ES initiatives and demanding of that means of selling and distribution.
- The 'Manufacturer's Test' will help determine what market strength and flexibility the company has. The greater the market clout the greater the choice and the more likelihood routes that break dependence on existing partnerships could be made to work.

Figure 14.1   Picking from the Ten Options

Decision Drivers		Strategic Choices	
Low ES potential	Low flexibility	Woo the retailer	1. 'Partnership-based'
		Move to private label	2.
		Technology-led	3. 'Pull'
ES Test – product/ consumer responsiveness	Manufacturer's Test – degree of market clout	Brand-driven	4.
		Information only	5. Electronic information-based
		Forming a club	6.
		Treat as another channel	7. 'Own direct'
		Set up as separate business	8.
High ES potential	High flexibility	Band together	9.
		Go fully direct	10.

Scores on these two tests will influence choice of strategy. They will help identify which of the ten options give individual manufacturers the best chance of success (Figure 14.1). If there's high ES potential, then only a high 'Manufacturer's Test' score, for example, will make the full range of options available for the manufacturer/supplier in the market place.

Before going further in comparing the attractiveness of the different options, each can be illustrated and described in more detail to provide a clearer definition of what the different choices entail.

1. 'Woo the Retailer'

The benchmark here is the Procter & Gamble Wal-Mart relationship. These two organisations don't just talk about partnership. They've gone beyond co-operative marketing or 'joint action teams'. In many respects they have locked together into one business system (Figure 14.2).

Figure 14.2 Sharing Responsibility

P&G and Wal-Mart now share responsibility for the supply chain, second staff to each other's operation (Wal-Mart has some 50 P&G people permanently located at its facilities) and decide which is best placed of the two to take the lead and accountability for different supply initiatives. For example, P&G is 'trusted' to do the store re-ordering of its products and a process has been set up to agreed parameters which instantly replenishes shelves and warehouse stock levels, triggers the invoice and causes funds to be transferred – all automatically. Costs are reduced, errors minimised, stock-outs unheard of, the relationship is vigorous and each is responsive to the other's needs. They already deal electronically and it is easy to imagine the two partners now jointly investigating and exploring how to best reach the new electronic consumer in a way that is to their mutual advantage.

The benefits of collaboration can be considerable for both parties. Recent research by Professor Kumar showed that where retailers and manufacturers operated with a high level of trust sales generated were anything from 11% to as much as 78% higher, compared to situations where there was confrontation and antagonism. As Kumar points out:

'Trust creates a reservoir of goodwill that helps both parties fulfil their potential . . . sharing information, investing in each other's business, customising systems, dedicating people and resources . . . and capturing economies of scale and efficiency in working together.'

In P&G's case its 'wooing' of Wal-Mart has lead to it generating more than $3 billion in annual sales together, which is about 10% of its total revenues. The profitability of those sales has been 'significantly enhanced'.

The automotive industry offers another illustration of how partnerships generally can operate to mutual benefit. Unlike the P&G/Wal-Mart situation, examples from the automotive sector typically deal with smaller manufacturers and show that even if there is an imbalance in size between the parties nevertheless a meaningful partnership can be forged that works to each other's advantage.

Pressac is good example of a small electronics manufacturer based in the UK with a turnover of c. $100 million yet successfully supplying leading automotive manufacturers like Ford and GM around the world. Pressac specialises in electrical components such as lampholders and wing mirror heater elements and has dedicated itself to achieving excellence not just in product quality but in its commitment to making its key customer relationships work. Pressac has the advantage of supplying to a sector which is very supplier-oriented and which has long recognised for itself the value of close relationships. For example, Nissan's stated strategy is

> 'to achieve our objective through long term close working relationships with a limited number of suppliers and to develop that supplier base so that together we are capable of achieving Nissan's development plans world-wide.'

Retailers of fast-moving consumer goods are generally some way behind the automotive companies in cementing this level of partnership and realising its benefits, but there are a few pointing the way. One such company is Marks & Spencer, who not only have sophisticated manufacturer partnering arrangements but show that success can be achieved by small manufacturers as well as large. For those manufacturers who commit to them and demonstrate their product excellence, M&S can be a supportive and caring distributor partner, keen to ensure its manufacturers make a decent enough margin and are not so squeezed that they cannot sustain their own business and continue to build it. Successful suppliers to M&S find they are invited to join a club which involves among other things being given a key card to enter M&S's head office encouraging them to drop in to discuss any small issues. There is also joint product development and joint investigation of original source materials, participation in internal store operation meetings and guaranteed access to the 'boss' if things aren't working well.

Achieving this mutually beneficial state is not easy, of course, and requires years of proactive investment and effort especially now from the manufacturer to overcome initial scepticism and show that previous adversarial dealings are decidedly a thing of the past. Manufacturers who choose the partnering approach and select this strategic option to deal with the ES challenge will have to be persistent and dedicated if they are to reap the benefits. They'll need to work hard to get to the level of trust and collaboration so that future market developments are faced together and not with self-interest at the other's expense.

JE Ekornes, a Norwegian home furniture manufacturer, represents a good illustration of the effort and change required to get the benefits of this approach. In the mid-1990s it decided to review its European sales operation and was disturbed by a singular lack of progress especially in its French retail market. It sold in France through 450 distributors and quickly realised that its relationships with them were very poor and this was proving the major roadblock. Neither side shared information or trusted in the other's commitments and the brand and sales were suffering.

Ekornes decided to focus on a core group of distributors and turn that relationship with them into a true partnership. This meant changing the economics so that these distributors could make a satisfactory margin. To achieve this, Ekornes set about restructuring its position in the market. It awarded chosen distributors exclusive territories to remove the previous conflicts. It set up long-term contracts and guarantees of on-time supply. It established a jointly led process for improving the supply chain between the two. It involved the distributors much more heavily in its own business, getting them over to the Norwegian head office and factory, for example, to spend time there and understand their manufacturing operations. It also put in place joint system links so each could track order and sales progress. As a result of these changes, roles and expectations changed. For example, Ekornes redefined the role of its salesforce. Instead of just selling it gave them a stronger responsibility for relationship management and providing a more general level of business support. These changes and restructurings paid off. Sales tripled over three years.

There are other examples that can be drawn from Compaq, Goodyear, Sherwin Williams, Sara Lee and Philip Morris – all of whom have in the last few years made major strides, which have been well publicised, in achieving the benefits of partnership. Successful 'wooing' means breaking down the old relationship barriers, changing ways of operating and interacting and persistently signalling win:win intentions. Once major distributors and customers recognise that there is a long-term commitment to behave in this way, then enormous advantages can come from sharing the future together.

For the manufacturer who remains uncertain, even after the ES and other tests and checks, partnership is the most natural evolutionary step. It is most likely to maintain the status quo and is no doubt exactly the sort of strategic response any retailer wants to hear. The only risk, of course, is that if the retailer itself is either slow to respond to the specific ES challenges or otherwise finds itself disintermediated by more aggressive competition then the manufacturer, too, can find itself left high and dry and outmanoeuvred.

2. 'Move to Private Label'

The partnership route assumes that manufacturers retain the integrity of their product and brand proposition and even while collaborating on parts of the supply chain they nevertheless retain their independence and ability to determine their own future. However, when a manufacturer moves down the private-label path much of that independence and flexibility is surrendered. The manufacturer is now firmly locking its future in with its retail customers.

The principal benefit is the greater sharing in their retailer customers' success. Provided the retailers do well the manufacturer's sales and profits will prosper. But if the retailers do poorly the manufacturer, of course, has limited options and possibly few alternative sources of distribution.

What is the appeal, then, of this strategy? Why choose it if it involves limited long-term flexibility and has a high dependency level of risk attached to it? Those manufacturers most interested will likely be today's small–medium-sized companies who find their current brand product portfolio relatively weak vs the competition. Such companies will also typically find themselves in market sectors where the technology is mature, consumers see products as largely 'me too' and commodity-like, the sector is dominated by one or two large long-established competitor brands and retailers themselves have likely already introduced their own store label.

In such circumstances, smaller manufacturers are sub-scale and struggling to find the investments and other resources to stay in touch or attempt some meaningful differentiation. In these situations the arrival of yet another major new market place challenge such as electronic commerce may be one challenge too many to fight on their own. Just in the past ten years they will have already experienced the turmoil of globalisation, the arrival of new low-cost, low-price competitors from overseas, new technology raising the hurdle on supply-chain activities and efficiencies, pressure on margins as the lid is kept on inflation and consumers search for everyday low pricing and value. Now electronic commerce would appear to demand the opening of a new channel, more investment, new skills and possible head-on conflict with the retailer customers that they have for so long been struggling to keep on side.

For companies in this position moving to private label supply may now be the most attractive long-term solution that maintains shareholder value and has the prospect of increasing it. Work with, rather than in competition to, the retail customer, become integral and integrated into the customers' supply chain, tie future development into the customers' strategies – and hope that the customer understands its market challenges and has itself a clear view on how to deal with ES.

There are successful private label suppliers in every industry sector. Dewhirst, for example, is a clothing manufacturer which long had established relations with Marks & Spencer and prospered by building that relationship into a mutual dependence that would make it difficult (though far from impossible) for M&S to find an alternative source of reliable quality supply. Dalgety had for many years an established contract with McDonald's supplying buns and other food ingredients which had grown into an open understanding on ways of operating, profit margins and future product development. United Biscuits, the food and biscuits group, has been one of a number of companies that have developed a substantial private-label business but still managed to maintain its own product brand integrity.

Moving down the 'private label' path can certainly provide a meaningful route for dealing with the ES challenges. It forces and forges a sharing and collaborative response. But as with the 'partnership' route, it leaves the manufacturer much less room for manoeuvre if the retailer itself is outwitted and disintermediated.

3. 'Technology-led'

As we go down the list of strategic options we start moving away from retailer-based initiatives. Instead, there are alternatives which are 'pull-based'. They demand of the manufacturer the capability to stand alone in the market place and build the strongest possible consumer proposition.

Being technology-led simply assumes that it will be the uniqueness of the product's performance, its advantage in quality, functionality and reliability, that will drive success. This approach carries with it an implicit disregard for channel conflicts. It assumes that consumers will so obviously and clearly recognise the product's differentiated benefits that they will demand the product – wherever it might be available. There will be a 'pull' for the product such that the manufacturer need not 'push' it through intermediaries. It will sell itself.

Such a strategy requires the manufacturer to build its core competencies around its R&D and ensure there is a continuous pipeline of new products and new developments that can keep a product's uniqueness and advantages firmly in place. This is especially demanding as it requires substantial investment and a deep-rooted commitment to keep that long-term spending in place even when short-term earnings are under pressure.

It has become an even more challenging option in the late 1990s. This is because product performance life-cycles are generally shrinking as imitators become more successful in quickly eroding any advantages. But also in a number of industry sectors technology has reached a level of maturity where there is limited further product improvement to be had. In cellular phones, the Walkman, watches, calculators, high-fidelity equipment, household consumer products like soaps and cleaners, basic financial services such as mortgages, pensions and insurance and in many other sectors there appears to be little scope for new technical breakthroughs.

Therefore any manufacturer considering this strategy must look hard at its technical skills and their long-term potential and applicability in the marketplace. For sure, a number of companies show it can be done. For example, Merck, with its commitment 'to be the pre-eminent drug maker through the best R&D capability', Toyota with its emphasis on superior product quality and reliability, Sony with its long-standing research and development in consumer entertainment equipment, Procter & Gamble and Unilever with their extraordinary efforts to keep innovating in an otherwise tired commodity soap and cleaner sector – all these companies and others have successfully built their businesses around technically superior products.

But as these same organisations now face the challenge of electronic commerce they must look over the next ten years or more and both question and reassure themselves that this distinctly 'pull' approach can continue to work even as consumer choice and sophistication grows and as channels of distribution fragment further. Those who remain determined to be 'technology-led' may nevertheless also want to combine this approach with one of the later strategies to be discussed and also set up some form of direct electronic communication to customers in support.

4. 'Brand-Driven'

Like being technology-led, this approach takes a 'pull' rather than 'push' route. It demands the creation of a set of emotional values, awareness and recognition that are so strong that the consumer will demand and search out the product, in whichever channel it is available. The approach requires all the emphasis to be placed on to the product and its branding and again, as with being technology-led, the commitment and funding must be unwaveringly in place to sustain success.

A number of companies have already established their brand-driven credentials. They come from many different industry sectors. So we see, for example, Coca-Cola and Pepsi soft drinks, Canon Copiers, Intel inside, DuPont Lycra material and Teflon coating, Citibank banking services, in fashion clothing the likes of Donna Karan, Giorgio Armani and Liz Claiborne and in sports equipment (the latest 'battle of the brands') Nike, Reebok, Adidas, Puma and others. For all these companies, and many others like them, their goal is to continue to build this pull brand so that even as new ways of shopping emerge, the awareness and desire remain strong. Such an approach can remain indifferent to the distribution challenges of ES, assuming that consumers and intermediaries will work out ways on their own to find, distribute and purchase the product.

Of course, this 'go-it-alone' approach has the risks associated with any such strategy and no company can afford to do this without at the same time being also close observers and watchers of their marketplace and of consumer desires and behaviour. If the competitive environment begins to shift such companies must be well placed to anticipate these changes and move in tune with if not slightly ahead of consumers' evolving needs. Only in that way can the brand stay lively and the pull approach truly work. (More detailed discussions of brand-driven strategies can be found in my book *Strategy in Crisis* (1997), which provides many case examples on how to effectively establish a branding or 'emotion-based' approach.)

5. 'Information Only'

This is the first of the strategies that begins to deliberately and explicitly explore electronic commerce. It simply takes the route of providing information only to would-be purchasers about the product, its features and then directs where it can be obtained. It's the starting point for most companies looking to develop and learn more about electronic commerce. Most organisations have already moved down this non-contentious path and set up their own website. The initial applications have invariably been information-based without adding on transaction features. Digital Equipment Corporation, now part of Compaq, provides a good case study.

Eighteen months before actually setting up its web pages, Digital had begun exploring alternative ways to reach the market place and provide customers and prospects with information about its products and services. Its goal was to build some foundations to anticipate the coming convergence of the computer, telecommunications and consumer electronics industries. It had already developed a CD Rom demonstrating products and software and it was excited at the opportunities of interactive communication on line and establishing its own direct consumer links without having to go through traditional distribution channels.

Digital evaluated its options against three particular criteria: (1) customer demographics – what sort of customers did Digital typically target, and how responsive would they be to on-line access and communication? (2) product characteristics – did their products lend themselves to description and demonstration electronically? (3) cost – as this was a new marketing approach, Digital wanted to manage its initial investment costs so that it would provide a learning environment, without putting pressure on getting quick payback.

The internet appeared to Digital to meet all its early needs – a global reach, a suitable environment for its products and relatively low start-up costs. The sales and marketing department could immediately see opportunities to set out their products and show their capabilities, provide technical specifications but make it available only to those who wanted that level of detail, provide information, locations, telephone numbers of all its distributors organised geographically, list details of upcoming conferences and shows and invite customers and prospects to send in information and comment on products of interest and give their views on products' strengths and weaknesses.

As a result, as Digital developed its website so it offered e-mail to encourage this two-way flow of information and reinforced that with newsletters and also setting up user groups to continue the exchange of data and experiences. From all this Digital could learn a lot about its products, its customers and its competitive strengths and weaknesses. Digital first launched its website in October 1994. It contained among other things:

- New product announcements
- e-mail and user group facilities
- The ability to learn first hand about new software and hardware by logging on and actually 'test-driving' new systems
- Product brochures and specifications
- Interactive catalogues detailing all the products and where they could be obtained
- Links to related information to clarify new concepts
- Audio and video multi-media displays to illustrate particular product features and examples of usage
- Interactive features engaging the customer in a dialogue about product requirements or usage ideas
- Customer feedback pages.

Digital's website was accessed 4 million times by over 100,000 customers and prospects in its first two years. We shall discuss in Chapter 15 the marketing of websites and how to go about attracting customers and prospects to it. But for the moment this Digital story shows how a company can get an information only website to work very effectively as a business-building tool in its own right.

As it happens, Digital has gone on to build in transaction facilities to make it easy for customers to order and buy direct. But companies who face difficult channel conflicts with existing retail distributors could do well to consider this strategic option on its own merits. They should consider how much additional business they can generate through an excellent implementation of an 'information only' response to ES.

6. 'Forming a Club'

Consumers in Japan are getting together to buy in bulk from retailers. They are specifying the source, quality, ingredients and delivery method of certain goods and agreeing to buy a fixed quantity. According to a *Financial Times* report:

> 'as these consumer groups have become more organised so they are beginning to use the internet to shop around for the best bargains and are getting more comfortable with the idea of buying electronically.'

For the first time the internet offers a meaningful opportunity for consumers to take control for themselves of the shopping experience. Without the physical constraints of location access and hours of opening and with developing software search engines that can shop the internet to compare prices and value, consumers now more than ever have the opportunity to decide where and when and how to shop – at their convenience.

This poses a challenge to retailers, of course, but also provides a new route to market for manufacturers who can now look up these groups of consumers – these communities of like-minded souls – and build their own direct links with them.

While this development is still in its early stages there are already a few clubs forming and manufacturers have the opportunity both to sell direct to them and to encourage and facilitate their growth:

- One of the fastest growing 'communities' is *SeniorNet* – which has around 20,000 members. It's a non profit organisation whose aim is to build a community of computer-using seniors. SeniorNet maintains forums on America On-Line and on Microsoft Network, for example. They cover a range of interests such as the Christian Corner, Divorced Pals and Senior Entrepreneurs. Among other activities the community has started more than 80 SeniorNet learning centres around the US. SeniorNet is now investigating what other services it can provide for its subscriber members. These include combining the purchases made to set up direct purchasing and distribution links with hardware and software suppliers. For such suppliers, SeniorNet provides a targeted electronic sales opportunity. Because the whole operation is still immature there is an open opportunity for various manufacturers to come in as sponsors and supporters and gain a marketing and sales advantage with this growing community of like-minded souls.
- *Motley Fool* is another community of interest website. This one is targeted at people interested in personal financial investments. The groups of people drawn to this site are diverse but it provides a unique ability to connect people who share relatively narrowly defined interests. The entrepreneurs behind Motley Fool have already begun to sell books and other products related to financial investment and are establishing their own direct lines with stock brokers. For financial service providers, this consumer grouping represents a new opportunity to reach target customers, bypass traditional channels and work out how to establish a meaningful sales relationship directly.
- Procter & Gamble has a long history of building a consumer franchise in the diaper market. For many years it has directly sponsored pre- and post-natal services in certain communities and provides a 'goody-bag' of product samples to new mothers. It has also held forums of mothers and babies to discuss product usage, baby care and future

product requirements. A natural evolution for P&G in this area is to sponsor mother and baby clubs on the internet, providing the financing infrastructure, giving out information and advice but also setting up for itself direct targeted consumer purchasing groups. Such 'mother and baby' clubs have a natural community of common interest and combined with local home delivery services could provide companies like P&G with a substantial direct business.

7. 'Treat as Another Channel'

For those manufacturing companies who are exploring electronic commerce, a number have already made the decision to move beyond an 'information only' path. They are determined to explore the new routes to market and exploit additional target sales and marketing opportunities.

Most of the manufacturing ES activity to date, however, has been in the business-to-business arena. For example, Cisco Systems conducts over 50% of its sales – in 2000 c. $50 million each day – over the internet. And Cisco expects volume sales over the internet to grow substantially in the next year. Boeing, the aerospace group, has reported conducting millions of dollars of trade over the internet every day. GE, IBM and Seagate are but a few other examples of companies who have made rapid strides exploiting internet technology and building high levels of sales. The Forrester Research group predicts the value of goods and services traded business-to-business will grow dramatically and could reach over 1 trillion dollars during 2001: 'The effect on business of this new channel of distribution will be unprecedented, spawning dynamic new trading relationships and selling routes.'

This is all very encouraging at the business-to-business level but it appears to have been easier for manufacturers to move more aggressively into electronic selling in that arena. Outside of the consumer goods environment, the balance of power is typically less polarised in favour of one party, there's somewhat more flexibility to sell through different channels. Furthermore, in many business-to-business situations, product technology or branding do still provide a clear pull advantage, relationships generally with customers tend to be less antagonistic and there appears to be greater willingness to work together. Customers tend not to produce their own private-label rival manufactured products!

However, many manufacturers operating electronically and successfully business-to-business, like IBM and GE and others, also have a vibrant and sizeable consumer-selling operation. They will surely be asking themselves why can't they achieve the same direct success with *consumer* end-users. Whatever channel conflict blocks exist, they will surely take the ES and Manufacturer Tests and quickly realise they do have the capabilities to start developing the internet as a consumer sales channel as well. One good example of such manufacturer initiative in the consumer arena comes from Sony, who are slowly building up their direct selling operation.

- Sony has established its own on-line retail store and it's set up to provide a total entertainment experience as well as a sales opportunity. Its 'station' site is like an on-line urban theme park. Its opening page looks like a neon-lit city street and the neon signs point to games, chat rooms as well as music stations. It's a site that's designed to be explored. The shopping sign leads not only to music sales but to a 'Men in Black' clothing store, a T-shirts counter, videos, books, cinema tickets and inevitably its own hi-fi equipment.

   On the shopping pages every item is described in some detail. At the foot of the page is a quantity box, price and the option to add it to a shopping cart. At present, the Sony site is primarily geared to young adults and older teenagers but there are plans afoot to establish a separate station targeted at older, more affluent consumers groups.

   To date sales are not yet significant (Sony isn't actively marketing the opportunity) but in the meantime Sony is also learning hard about how to make its website attractive and shopping friendly. Once it gets that sufficiently developed it will be in a prime position to take advantage of faster easier internet access as it becomes more widely available.

For many companies like Sony, selling on line in the retail environment is still treated as exploring a new channel of business. For these manufacturing groups their caution is driven by a number of factors, but especially the desire to protect existing retail distribution business. Many will wait for new user-friendly internet access technology to fuel consumer interest and make volume sales targets more readily achievable. In the meantime, organisations like Unilever, as we have seen, have publicly declared their interest to push down this path, while other leading manufacturers like Procter & Gamble, Rubbermaid, Nestlé and Kraft are getting on exploring how to eventually take advantage of this new opportunity. Recently, Procter & Gamble started selling Hugo Boss perfumes direct to consumers off their internet site. A spokesperson for P & G said this niche product would only reinforce mainstream volume sales through existing distributors.

8. 'Set Up as a Separate Business'

There are even fewer examples of manufacturer suppliers to the retail sector who have already so grasped the ES opportunity that they have established an electronic commerce business unit, with its own funds and infrastructure to operate alongside but also potentially in competition to existing retail distribution-lines.

The best example to date comes from the financial services sector and again from one of its leading suppliers – Direct Line. As has been well-documented, the Direct Line operation has been an enormous success but it took that bold vision to set it up and give it its freedom. Most other insurers have been less ambitious and have tried to keep a tight rein on their direct activities to minimalise the cannibalisation risk. This conservatism has in fact provided an opening for greenfield new entrants, with no existing retail business to protect, to additionally enter this market and take share.

The financial services sector looks the most likely to generate more self-funded, fully resourced, stand-alone businesses selling into a consumer retail environment (see Appendix 2, p. 312). One reason is that retail distributors are typically less aggressive in this sector, allowing provider suppliers a greater sense of operating freedom and experimentation. We now wait to see who will first emerge out of the consumer goods pack, burst out of their website chrysalis and develop something more substantive in sales terms.

9. 'Band Together'

Those manufacturers determined to be among the more ambitious may consider this option. It involves groups of manufacturers with complementary product ranges banding together to provide an alternative one stop shop. Examples might include:

- **'The Coffee Shop'** – a virtual site potentially sponsored by Nestlé including a coffee and tea products shop, a Jakobs Suchard chocolate and confectionery shop, United Biscuits McVities biscuits, Coca-Cola as a soft drinks alternative, Frito Lay potato chips and snacks and Time-Warner magazines and books.
- **'The Household Products Shop'** – a virtual site featuring Procter & Gamble home cleaning products, Rubbermaid sinkware and storage products, Home Depot kitchen and bathroom accessories, Bath Bed and Beyond towels and linen, Toys R Us, and Sears for white and brown goods.

These companies could combine to establish and host websites or TV home shopping channels or even more traditional catalogue phone/fax operations. Provided they communicate effectively and build awareness and branding they could become the new 'retailers' of the twenty-first century. They could displace the physical retail distributors stuck with expensive real estate and struggling to transition themselves into the new virtual environment. These manufacturers could enter the distribution business greenfield, ally with distribution and warehousing partners to access new skills and competencies and establish their own direct consumer-sales operation. In this way, they could get out from the historic tension and difficulties of dealing with their often powerful and sophisticated retail customers, bypass those 'old-fashioned' ways of distribution and enter the competitive environment entirely shaping their *own* sales development.

10. 'Go Fully Direct'

Who's going to be the first to go the whole way, transition deliberately out of existing retail distributors and fully embrace electronic communication and selling? Will the financial services sector be the first arena where provider suppliers ultimately decide that running physical and virtual distribution networks in parallel makes no sense and go the 'full monty' after the lower-cost more profitable electronic transactions?

In retail banking services, the traditional branch banking has already been whittled away by ATMs, debit and credit cards. We already have the 'no-people' branch where the shell that was the fully staffed bank has been turned into a room full of machines. Cash can be withdrawn or paid in (acknowledgements sent by e-mail, mail or fax), foreign currency purchased and information provided on statements and balances. Only the more complex of the retail banking transactions (e.g. loans and mortgages) may still require a human interface. But even with these there are alternative electronic purchase channels available.

None of the retail banks operating today will publicly acknowledge that the physical branch service is dying, but they have all been gradually consolidating and reducing the number of branches available. A few may survive where they play an important commercial development role but stand-alone staffed branches in every town are surely on their way out. Eventually some currently physical banks will bite the bullet.

*   *   *

Figure 14.3 Manufacturers' Strategic Options Comparison

Summary

We can now draw these ten different options together and summarise the risk and benefits attached to each (Figure 14.3).

The Partnership options 'woo the retailer' and move to 'private label' naturally carry the least risk in terms of jeopardising existing retail business. In contrast the more direct strategies do confront the channel conflicts head-on, carry greater risk but also potentially greater long-term reward. Manufacturing companies that score high on their test have the flexibility to examine the marketplace and choose which path they want, how aggressive they wish to be, which risk reward profile they are comfortable with. Others, as we have discussed, will have much less room to manoeuvre (Figure 14.4).

Whichever the strategy that's chosen, business success can still certainly be achieved. In each case the winning formula will be a combination of choosing the strategy that best meets customer and market needs plus pursuing an implementation path with rigour, determination and a single-minded dedication to making that strategy work. The best strategies won't succeed, of course, without effective implementation and in contrast tasking the workforce to work hard and fast will inevitably be futile if the appropriate direction has not been set.

Figure 14.4 Strategic Choices from the Identified Ten

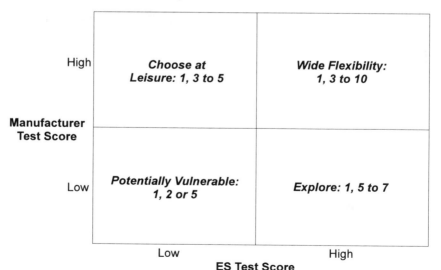

Choosing the 'right strategy' can be guided by the tests and checks we have described. Making the implementation successful can be driven by the discussion and frameworks to be shown in Chapters 15 and 16. But whatever the path, the company must continue to stay close to the market place. It's evolving fast and every organisation must stay on its toes as electronic commerce develops and matures.

15 The New Marketing Imperatives: Marketing in the Electronic Age

At least half of multinational companies surveyed are 'missing the link': they're not marketing effectively on the internet. According to a study in *The Economist*, many websites are still sorely lacking when it comes to communicating with their audiences. Companies may be on line but websites are often difficult to find and difficult to use, information is often patchy or incomplete (only 37% of the companies in the survey gave any details of where their products could be obtained), sales efforts can be half-hearted (e.g. J.C. Penney's handbag department for some time featured precisely one item, the Argos gift service sold only barometers) and on-line support and services can be surprisingly limited (only 21% offered any interactive service or further communication beyond the initial information dump).

There is still a huge gap between the marketing potential of the internet vs companies' understanding of how to exploit it. But there are a growing number of leading organisations across most retail sectors who are demonstrating that the potential *is* there and showing how it can be realised. Dell, Auto-By-Tel, Amazon, CDNow, Peapod, Tesco, Land's End, Karstadt, Citibank, Directline, NetMarket and many others, in just two or three years from inception, have built impressive electronic selling and marketing operations. They are generating new interest and excitement amongst target customers. They are improving their overall market reputation. They are starting to see significant sales as consumers increasingly get wired up and get used to transacting on line.

But the majority are still 'missing the links'. They've been in experimental mode since the initial net frenzy in 1994–5 and still have a long way to go to reach best practice levels (Figure 15.1). According to further 1998 research by Forrester, more than 50% of companies seemed confused about the role of the internet in their business, unclear what their strategy should be and with no immediate plans to graduate from trial and information to a level of greater selling sophistication. For Forrester, one of the key roadblocks preventing progress is that 'electronic commerce is still the domain of the IT function – marketing departments have not yet gotten sufficiently involved nor claimed any real ownership'. By way of illustration, Forrester calculated that budgets for developing and maintaining an effective website had risen steeply to an average $3 million a year (and sometimes up to $5 to $10 million or more). But many spend less than $250,000 and European companies especially fall short in this area.

Can every company make the necessary sales and marketing connections? Can any organisation succeed in electronic commerce? Or does the new medium pose some unique sales and marketing challenge that only a few have cracked? Is it just about applying basic principles or is it inherently more complex? What's the learning that can be taken from the best-practice examples – from the companies already out there reaping the benefits? Can that be translated into a 'how-to' framework of broad application that helps electronic laggards arrive at the best sales and marketing solution? In this chapter we first consider the specific and new marketing challenges posed by the growing electronic revolution and then detail a marketing solutions framework to provide a step-by-step guide to would-be marketers facing up to the new environment.

In developing the marketing framework, the key learning is that organisations must recognise they are indeed dealing with something different. Those companies already successful on the internet, for example, say that their own break-throughs only came once they acknowledged that the electronic marketplace does pose new and distinct marketing challenges and opportunities. It's not just a question of

Figure 15.1   Electronic Marketing Evolution

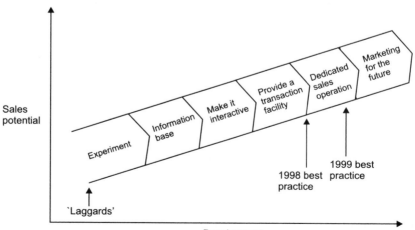

carrying on as before with an additional channel to market through. With electronic commerce, what can be done and achieved breaks rules and stretches horizons. New approaches, and thus new skills and competencies, must be developed.

The particular challenge facing marketers has a number of dimensions to it (Table 15.1). Some have already been referred to and discussed, such as the many new technologies, the number of new electronic connections and the inexorable global reach of the world-wide web. But much of the new marketing opportunity lies in knowledge capture, information management and exploitation. These 'information' areas specifically require further explanation here to fully establish the new marketing scene and context that sets up the solutions framework. The next section therefore looks at the first three of these new marketing challenges in more detail.

Table 15.1   Seven New Marketing Challenges for an Electronic Age

- More information for sellers about their customers
- More information for buyers
- New intermediaries
- New technology 'interconnectivity'
- More automation
- World-wide sourcing and access
- Greater value consciousness

Marketing challenges

More information for sellers

In the new electronic environment it will be possible to gather a lot more data on customers. This can be managed to create many new communication and marketing opportunities. For example, Amazon.com is able to track what book reviews customers look up, what categories they are interested in, what they buy, how many and how frequently and where they live. It has a richness of data which it can automatically gather about each and every person who visits its site. From a different perspective, Procter & Gamble can organise virtual focus groups where invited consumers from all over the world can meet in a 'chat room', compare notes, talk about their interests and offer detailed feedback on products. Hotel companies like Marriott and Ritz Carlton, airlines like British Airways and American already have detailed databases on people who use their services, but this can be extended to capture every inquiry, each would-be purchaser who can then be subsequently e-mailed, contacted and incentivised.

The internet and other forms of electronic connection offer considerable potential for what's called 'database marketing'. There will be better opportunities not just to build profiles of consumers but to track how trends change, look at individual needs and target potential new purchasers. What is new is that the information can be captured immediately on line and instantaneously processed. *There's a significant competitive advantage for the organisation that thinks through and works out how best to exploit the knowledge that is available.*

Financial Services companies like First Direct and USAA have been in the vanguard of the knowledge bandwagon. Another specific example comes from a relatively new company on the internet called Firefly. It proactively seeks permission from people who visit its site to gather more detailed information about them. (It's been especially keen to reassure about privacy and data confidentiality and uses Coopers & Lybrand to audit its safeguards in that area.) Firefly then builds psychographic profiles of customers and uses that to target other potential customers of a similar disposition. The knowledge it obtains is used to pinpoint carefully tailored advertising messages. Its knowledge about its customers also attracts other advertisers to its site who want to reach the same target audience. So Firefly gets a double benefit from its information capture – improving its own marketing and exploiting its niche to attract others.

Firefly is but one small illustration of how electronic connections can provide a continuous stream of personalised information. If it's captured efficiently that information can provide new insight and understanding and help the development of tailored sales and marketing initiatives.

More information for buyers

Just as sellers can learn more about their customers, so customers can get a lot more information about the products and services they're interested in. Their reach through the internet becomes global, they can sift through vast amounts of often detailed specification that might otherwise not have been easily attainable. They can look at samples. They can review extracts from movies, newspapers, books and music. They can compare prices. They can interact with others sharing a similar interest and get 'inside' feedback on what the product is like. They will be able to experience the product more vividly in three dimensions. And they will be able to do all these things at their leisure, at their own pace and when it suits them.

Buying over the internet puts the consumer firmly in control of the process. But it also makes them harder to reach and market to. They're not caught up in a retailer's catchment area compelled to shop only where they can drive to and select from only what's on the shelf. They're not limited by the manufacturer's brochure and what information they happen to glean from the salesperson. Nor are they constrained by a manufacturer's distribution and lead times. They'll be in a better position than ever before to call the shots. Bargaining power shifts firmly in their direction.

In the new electronic age, marketing must take on this new dimension. It needs to become even more of a two-way process. Creating awareness, stimulating interest but also being able to respond to that interest, deal with requests, capture passing surfers, manage interactions, develop relationships. To reach out to customers and win their business, sellers are going to have to be much more tuned-in to a dialogue that's interactive. They'll need to embrace all the marketing 'Ps' (place, product, promotion, people, price, packaging) as never before. The marketing framework set out below can be their guide.

New intermediaries

As the electronic value chain takes shape, new companies will emerge with dedicated competences in focused areas. They can provide best-practice solutions or help other organisations achieve stronger market positions.

One such opportunity may come in the information-management area. There, new intermediaries will develop who start off providing cost-efficient storage capabilities. But they may evolve into processing and integrating massive amounts of data. They may then progress to providing additional value by sorting and reporting for client companies. At every stage they could sell information or insight to others to improve their marketing databases.

Other intermediaries may appear in the logistics part of the chain. Dedicated warehousing, transportation and home delivery operators could enable companies themselves to go virtual, outsourcing most or all of their previous physical infrastructure. Especially in home delivery, there looks to be a substantial opportunity to establish a local neighbourhood network that builds strong ties with the consumer, ultimately taking responsibility for all things delivered to the home. Such an organisation could end up replacing the retailer as the company closest to the consumer. They could have the best database on consumer habits and needs and through that offer the best value-added and personalised service.

Back up the value chain, internet access providers like AOL are gradually evolving their role into powerful intermediaries and portals who can control and influence where consumers go shopping. At the start of 2000 AOL had over 20 million customers. Would-be electronic sellers are beginning to realise that they need to be present and have a high profile on AOL if they are to make sure customers can easily find them. AOL has taken on the value-added role of location manager and companies are willing to pay significant sums for prominent placement on high-traffic websites such as AOL's home page. For example both Amazon and 1-800-FLOWERS recently announced they had entered into long-term exclusive agreements with AOL. Amazon has agreed to pay $19 million and 1-800-FLOWERS $25 million plus a share of revenues. In addition, CUC International is paying AOL $50 million, again plus a share of revenues, for becoming AOL's exclusive discount shopping service.

As AOL Network's president Robert Pittman commented:

> 'We're in the land-grab period and this is the Malibu real estate . . . AOL is going to be of increasing importance to get access to home and at work users . . . we control the access to the customers in the electronic environment and sellers have to be there.'

'It's a land rush' commented the *Wall Street Journal*, 'for what many consider one of the greatest and least developed parcels of territory in cyberspace.'

The marketing solution framework

Now we understand more about the marketing challenge the 'marketing solution' can be set out. A framework of ten steps can be identified that can act as a guide for successful electronic selling and marketing. It is drawn from research and interviews with those companies like Amazon and Dell who are demonstrating current leading-edge approaches and best practices. It has a mix of basic underlying marketing principles as well as embracing the new competences required to succeed. It should be no surprise, then, to see fundamentals such as 'understand the customer' alongside relatively new ideas like 'interactivity' and 'networking'.

All ten steps must be followed through. The learning is stark: miss out one of the steps or carry it out half-heartedly and it can seriously undermine the total effectiveness of the marketing campaign. Winners

Figure 15.2   The Information and Knowledge Master

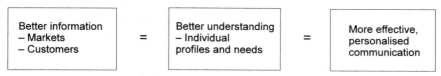

appear to be aggressively pursuing and investing in every part of the framework. But if there's one overriding theme that runs through the framework it can be captured in this way: become an information and knowledge master (Figure 15.2).

The ten steps of the framework focus on effective marketing on the internet, to pick the potentially most powerful medium. The individual steps form a total integrated process or value chain (Figure 15.3).

Figure 15.3   Marketing Solutions Framework

> *1. Set overall electronic objectives*

Research by Forrester, the *Wall Street Journal* and others continues to show that many companies are unclear about the role of their website in particular. Initially many could genuinely claim it was early days and they were researching and working out what sort of website to develop. But customers' patience with 'website under development' notices, single handbag offers or obviously incomplete home pages is fast running out. 'Best practice' examples of what a good website can do are already much in evidence. They are setting standards and expectations. Those that fall short are now especially conspicuous and are beginning to generate negative publicity for the entire business.

Companies have a choice of role on the internet and in the electronic arena generally. They can develop it either for promotion or for content or for transactions – or a combination of all three. But the choice must be deliberate.

- Promotional sites are about creating awareness and reinforcing brand image and reputation. They deliberately stop short of providing detailed information. But to be effective they need to signpost where that information can be obtained. They also deliberately stop short of providing transaction facilities but to be worthwhile they have to set out where the product or service can be purchased.

  A number of consumer goods' companies like L'Oréal, Nabisco and Kraft featured sites of this type where the key role and emphasis is brand reinforcement and image-building.
- Content sites that are successful are designed to inform, and entertain, with material specifically designed to work well in an internet environment. Levi's and Sony are two examples of companies who've gone beyond the promotional. They are attempting to attract an audience in their own right with games, features, news and chat rooms. Such sites usually take six months or more to develop and often contain 2,000 pages or more of content. They are demanding in terms of resources, requiring a dedicated team of often 10–20 people to update information content on a daily basis and continue to keep the site alive and fresh. There are usually interactive elements with their sites in the form of e-mail or message centres.

  These sites can be exciting places to visit but a number of companies anticipate that their 'content' role is only a stepping stone till they become fully-fledged transaction bases offering the full range of goods and services.
- Transaction sites may also contain plenty of content but their principal objective is to sell product. Forrester estimates that such sites can require staff of 30+ people to operate and maintain. They will have clear sales targets and no doubt in these early days of the internet will be expected to generate incremental revenues over and above the base business.

Making a choice of internet role is critical. It determines the reasons why a company is setting up electronically, what it is trying to achieve. Is it simply another advertising medium or is it a sales channel with specific targets? Is the goal here to entertain or provide a full sales and service operation in its own right? Making clear decisions in this arena will drive investment and resourcing, identify new skills that need to be developed, establish network partners to provide the total internet package and the communications that must be made to customers. The choice itself of internet role is unlikely to be at the providers' unfettered discretion. Taking the ES Test will provide clear guidelines on consumer interest levels in the medium generally and in purchasing in particular. More detailed research will show whether customers are interested in the whole product range or in some parts only and more precisely what type of promotion, content and transaction facilities they require.

> ## 2. Understand each customer

For companies that are already market and customer-driven, this step in the process is straightforward and plays to core skills and understanding. Such companies will have been among the first to take the ES Test, they will have further developed their customer segmentation beyond the six basic categories laid out in that test (see Figure 5.8), they will have their own tailored and targeted insights attempting to understand each and every customer.

Database marketing and the information-rich environment of the electronic age allows this level of detailed understanding to be distilled and processed and still be available in convenient intelligible form even though the customer base may number millions of individuals. Examples from the insurance industry have provided early illustrations of what can be achieved. USAA has such a sophisticated database and such a developed call-centre environment that when people call in the telephone operatives have on their screen details that allow an intensely personalised call: 'when we last spoke I see you bought life assurance, are you satisfied with that still? I see it was your wife's birthday last week, how are your two children, you may be interested in our new family health care service that we have just set up . . .'

Fred Meyer, the regional grocery chain, provides an intelligent approach to understanding the customer in an electronic age:

'We understand that in the grocery industry the internet must play a role in our future, we know that a significant number of our customers expect this and we are experimenting with it at various levels. One area where we've learnt there is particular interest in internet shopping is among our customers in Alaska. Most of the Alaskan shoppers travel hundreds of miles, some of them live days away and many can only come in the spring and summer. So we started offering a service over the internet that enables them to do their shopping. We take the orders into one of our seven stores in the region where they pick the items but then we have to get them out to the customer and normally that means by bush pilot. Now the cost of doing that will make most say just forget it. But we are looking at supplies that normally last from three to six months. We are experimenting with this in the Alaskan market, adding on various complementary products and services and seeing just how much business this can amount to.'

Understanding the customer is a basic principle for doing business. There is no substitute for the Triple I model (Figure 5.6) and approach. The internet environment makes this market immersion, intuition and innovation process all the more challenging but equally more rewarding for it can provide the more personal information detail that enables the individual customer to be targeted even more precisely with what they want.

> *3. Design your presence*

Research among internet surfers and customers throws up some satisfied shoppers but many frustrations: 'can't find my way around, too much information, not enough information, too many distractions on the page, too many steps between access and ordering' (16 clicks is not uncommon versus a target benchmark of 3!). Sites are often poorly laid out and suffer too from trying to cater for different types of consumers – some only who want information, others who want to play one of the games, still others who want to look through a range of products to choose what to buy and some who know precisely what they want and just want to go straight to the order page. No matter who they are, what their interests, consumers still typically have to go through a standard page sequence and they have to put up with the same level of often superficial language whether they're a teenage surfer or a corporate finance director.

Looking at best-practice sites today such as Dixons (the UK electricals retailer), Auto-By-Tel, Karstadt's 'My World', AT&T, World Net and Dell, these sites are laid out and designed according to some simple rules that research can identify:

- the purpose of them is clear – if they're intended to sell product then they provide clear order–pay sequences
- there is an overall site map for navigation

- it's targeted at distinct types of consumers, e.g. the teenage surfer is immediately directed to a different site via a click-on icon allowing the would-be shopper to get on with the transaction
- information and news is dated so the customer knows how current it is
- once a satisfactory process is established, stick with it and try to resist constantly changing it, evolve it within certain parameters
- provide click-on access to complementary products and services.

4. Entertain!

An internet site can provide a wealth of experiences. There is the unique opportunity to build images, video and text and do so in a creative way that captures imagination and interest. Beside the simple convenience that can be provided by electronic shopping there are many other reasons consumers can be persuaded to visit the site or spend more time there associating with the brand and the products and naturally building a closer affinity to them.

Successful sites do more than just provide content or transaction facilities. They involve and entertain. They engage consumers in a way that teaches them more about the product/service and why it is better than competition. They provide this learning in a fun and subtle fashion and by providing different incentives encourage repeat visits – to play and, if appropriate, with the option to buy, always just an icon-click away.

Procter & Gamble has a site for its Tide Laundry brand. Apart from some basic information, P&G invites browsers to play the Tide 'Stain Detective' game: 'If you spill red wine on your favourite cotton shirt you can ask the Tide detective's help. He will help you find an answer that is fast and proven.' American Airlines holds a daily airline seat auction that invites consumers to bid for spare seats in up-coming flights and wait to see if they've won. General Mills has a created a top children's site called You Rule School that's chock-full of games, education materials, news and features on top bands and new movies. Gap has a 'try-on' sequence that shows how different outfits can look and a 'mix and match' section that shows which accessories could complement the preferred choice of clothiers. Gap is working hard with software houses to get 3-D displays that could significantly enhance these 'try-on' experiences.

Other organisations ranging from Bristol Myers and General Motors through to start-ups like Kidsoft have begun to appreciate the entertainment opportunity, and in doing so are setting standards for others. It's this experience factor that differentiates the internet even more starkly from most current shopping environments. It's the added draw that brings in new users as well as sustains the interest of existing and frequent customers. When appropriately designed, it's reinforcing of the total product proposition and is a key ingredient for making internet sales incremental to the total business base.

> ## 5. Make it interactive

There's been a lot of hype about interactivity and how the internet creates a unique environment for it. But it must be said that any effective marketing campaign – whether it's on the internet or through more 'prosaic' media such as print or TV – should always contain some interactive element. Successful sellers will always be trying to engage their customers, get down to individual requirements, have some conversation with them, answer questions and move the prospective buyer towards a purchase decision.

Certainly the internet provides more opportunity to do that and to accomplish it in a more sophisticated way. It can provide something close to a genuine dialogue in real time between two parties, 'listening' to customers' queries and providing an immediate response. The particular attraction for consumers is they can manage the pace of this interaction. They can get what information they want when they want it. They can make several visits to the site without feeling under pressure to buy. They can take their time making their minds up. It's an attractive interaction for sellers, too, because as they're indulging in the consumer's questioning so they can be learning and capturing data about the type of person they are dealing with, what are their points of interest, what their hot buttons and how they can best be responded to. A sophisticated internet interaction can be as powerful as fielding your best salesperson, listening, learning and adapting the 'sell' to meet the customer's needs.

One example of this is a US law firm based in California that used to send out an annual and rather weighty booklet called *Intellectual Law*. Subsequent research showed it mostly got sent for filing in clients' libraries or gathered dust on shelves. The lawyers saw an opportunity to use the electronic medium to change the whole communication context and get their clients interacting with the material. It was first established as a CD-Rom and then subsequently put on the internet itself. It was designed to be a marketing rather than simply an information-giving tool and prospective clients were asked to take a quiz – an entertaining ten-question test to identify what gaps if any there were in their knowledge in this field. There was an interactive e-mail facility and a daily schedule set out when individual legal experts would be available to field particular questions. It was set up so that some basic issues could get resolved in that way and it was possible for potential customers to dig deep into the subject. The basic interactive service was free. The CD-Rom version was installed in kiosks and displayed in the lobby area of the law firm's offices. The firm says this electronic service has definitely enhanced its reputation as a leader in its field. It has new clients who say it was this innovative service that brought them into the firm's net.

> ## 6. Advertise your presence

Companies are beginning to learn about the power of advertising on the world-wide web. In 2000, advertising spending is forecast to hit $10 billion by the year-end – that's a near threefold increase vs the previous year and it's expected to carry on growing at very fast rates. 'Net-advertising', according to Andrew Grove, CEO of Intel, 'is becoming a big deal' and many companies are ramping up their web advertising plans:

- Bristol Myers Squibb teamed up with software-maker Intuit Inc to launch an on-line advertising campaign for Excedrin one of its over the counter (OTC) medicines. For 30 days Bristol Myers ran ads on financial websites offering free samples to net surfers who clicked on the ad and typed in their name and address. Just during that trial Bristol Myers added 30,000 new names to its customer list and that was three times the company's best estimates. What's more, the cost of obtaining those names was substantially less than other traditional marketing methods. The ad agency that produced the campaign commented: 'We've turned a packaged goods company into QVC.'
- IBM announced that for 2000 it would continue to place ads on others' websites increasing its advertising spend on the web significantly. Microsoft has said its spend will top $50 million.
- E*Trade Group Inc. has been an early success on the net. This financial services company specialises in on-line stockbroking and has established an integrated advertising campaign using print, TV and

the web itself. E*Trade started off spending c. 5% of its media budget on the web but now expects that to rise to 15–20%. Its early campaigns on Yahoo!'s finance site brought thousands of new customer leads in just the first few days. As the company's CEO has said: 'we can't imagine growing our business without this, a media strategy without the internet would be suicidal'.

- Toyota had 7 million web surfers visit Toyota.com in its first web advertising campaign in 1997. More interactions than on its 800 number. Toyota has now signed up Saatchi to produce a new net advertising program integrated with its print and TV campaigns. Toyota found that as a result of its advertising c. 170,000 people typed in their names and addresses and over 7,000 went on to buy cars – a remarkable near 5% conversion rate.

Advertising interest was originally dominated by the computer companies. But there's been an explosion of interest from makers of everything from Toyota cars through to Kellogg's Corn Pops. Excite Inc. a leading web search company, has seen its proportion of non-tech advertisers rise from 38% to 59%. General Motors, American Express, Walt Disney and Procter & Gamble have all become relatively significant spenders and for these companies and others it's becoming part of their mainstream advertising planning, like TV or print.

A recent innovation is known as the 'interstitial' (soon no doubt to find a more colloquial label). This is a full screen that pops up either in the lag time between requesting a web page and its appearance on screen or between segments of information. For example, one site featuring the quiz show 'You Don't know Jack' has attracted such major advertisers as Seven Up, Hugo Boss and 20th Century Fox who reach out to the site's 150,000 players each month showing 'interstitial' ads of up to 15 seconds including previews of forthcoming movies. The cost is less than $20,000 which is a fraction of what companies normally pay to reach such customised target consumer segments.

And internet audiences are fast becoming sizeable enough to provide significant contact and communication to a number of target sectors (Table 15.2). This makes cost per thousand (CPM) comparisons with traditional media begin to look favourable. Versus direct marketing costs, estimates suggest that web advertising CPM on a well targeted site could be as low as one-fifth. Versus a mass TV audience the internet still is more costly as it hasn't yet achieved that mass penetration but the differential is reducing all the time as more and more households get wired up and connected.

Table 15.2 Internet Penetration of Specific Consumer Segments

Target group	% of total segment size using the Internet in past 30 days
Students and young earners (18–24)	20
Young women (25–34) earning more than $20,000	21
Young men (25–34) earning more than $40,000	26
Men (35–44) earning more than $75,000	43

Source: Simmons database, McKinsey analysis.

WPP, one of the world's largest ad and marketing services agencies, has found that the vast majority of their clients are now turning to them asking how they can use the internet as an ad vehicle. Clients include a large number of the world's top 100 advertisers and so the significance of their awakening interest cannot be underestimated.

> *7. Network the net*

Location, Location, Location: if consumers don't know about the site or cannot find it then their custom is lost. Just as this is the fundamental rule for all physical retailing so it just as critically translates into the internet environment. If anything, it becomes an even more fundamental challenge because there's no neighbourhood presence or catchment area that automatically brings a seller to a customer's attention. It is a virtual world and companies are going to have to work harder to brand, build and draw attention to themselves.

One route being especially developed is to locate ads on others' sites where there is some related or complementary product or service being described. The intent is to scatter a series of signposts and billboards across the information highways to direct traffic to your rest stop:

- **Banner ads** are usually small rectangular graphics that sit like roadside bill boards typically at the top of a web page. They're usually static, though new technologies are looking to make them more animated.
- **Button ads** are small squarish ads that are placed at the bottom of a web page, often only referring to a brand name. Clicking on the button takes consumers directly to that brand's website – for example, Netscape have their button ad on most web pages and a click on it takes users instantly to the Netscape website to download the Navigator browser software.

- **Sponsorship or co-branded ads** attempt to get information seekers on one product to associate that with another. So Toys Я Us sponsors a toy guide on the Third Age senior citizens' website, showing the older generation the toys their grandchildren are likely to be asking for.
- **Keyword ads** feature primarily on web search engine sites such as Yahoo! So Miller Brewing has 'bought' the word 'beer' on Yahoo! and every time someone conducts a search using that term, an ad for 'Miller Genuine Draft Beer' will appear.

Companies will also have to make much greater efforts to integrate their marketing across the different media available. They will need to determine the role of each medium they choose to advertise or sell through and work out how each can complement the other. There are a range of choices now available, of course, ranging from traditional physical communication via direct mail, retail outlet or salespersons through to the electronic media of 800 numbers, direct phone lines, direct PC links, fax and the internet. Should a company run both 800 number call centres and internet sites for example? Should each connection contain details of the other? Does the internet address appear on all letter heading, packaging and other advertising? Or should there be a segmentation of channels and communications directing target consumers to a more limited selection of communication options right for them?

The 'networking the net' challenge has been put most succinctly by Doug Cormany, president of the IBM systems' users' group and VP at retailer Fred Meyer:

> 'we all know how important adjacencies are in terms of store layout and department connections in a physical store. The same thing can be applied to electronic retailing. And it's even more powerful because we have the opportunity for hot links, not only to complementary retailers but to manufacturers as well. We need to think about merchandising this electronic business in the same way we think about merchandising the physical store today.'

8. Deliver the promise

After all the hype and excitement of entertainment and banner ads and networking the site, it's clearly going to be important that the product or service does get delivered on time and in full and to the satisfaction of the consumer. Otherwise, no matter how attractive the site, if the logistics don't fulfil their side of the bargain then the customer won't come back and word-of-mouth recommendation will not spread in the way it was hoped.

As was discussed in Chapter 7, home delivery logistics is likely to be a new competency and skill for many companies. As they learn and get up the experience curve they're likely to make any number of mistakes. Only a few companies happen to have these logistics already established and in place and this is likely to drive substantial competitive advantage in the short term, at least till others catch up.

One such example is Sears Home Services. This division of Sears US turned over some $4.5 billion of revenue in 1999 but expects to triple in size very quickly as demand for home services generally grows. Importantly, it has the network in place. Its principal business has been home repairs and maintenance and has an established workforce of some 15,000 operatives who have been professionally trained and who Sears claim have an average 15 years' experience. They visit millions of America's homes every year, reckoning they cover some 20% of all households. With a sophisticated communications network already in place, isn't Sears a significant step ahead of most other retailers and manufacturers in being able to deliver to the consumer? They may be sitting on a goldmine of an operation – which could become a home-services/home delivery powerhouse in the emerging electronic age.

> *9. Manage loyalty*

In this increasingly competitive and complex world it's not enough to think about customers in the context of a one-off transaction. A business cannot afford to lose customers at all, nor can it just serve them once and not care less whether they come back. From the moment contact is made, companies need to be thinking about a relationship, a connection that can last a lifetime. The art of keeping customers is akin to a marriage, the cost of losing them now the equivalent of a divorce.

The challenge is made even tougher in a virtual world where freedom to choose is so much greater, where the consumer can access every available supplier across the globe and on each purchase occasion readily compare prices and other features and make a most informed value decision. It's easy for customers to be promiscuous and they often perceive no disadvantages or costs to them in switching suppliers. Indeed the research shows that on average most companies will experience defection rates of 10–30% a year.

Can this customer instinct to check out different suppliers be in any way contained? Can companies do anything material to develop relationships with customers that can be lasting and satisfying on both sides? The answer lies in developing a better understanding about what drives customer loyalty and what incentives and levels of performance need to be delivered to keep the customer totally satisfied.

There is no question about the value of doing this. Numerous studies show that retaining a customer pays back many times. Reichheld and Sasser, for example, in their research showed that a 5% increase in loyalty could lead to a 25% increase in profitability. Among other things, expensive 'acquisition costs' for each new customer can be avoided and the studies also show that customers who keep coming back typically spend increasing amounts with the same supplier.

But achieving these loyalty gains is hard. It requires an extraordinary level of effort, motivation and commitment throughout the company that gets each and every employee determined to make a personal contribution to the loyalty effect. Companies like Xerox, Ritz Carlton Hotels and others have won Baldridge quality awards for their high levels of customer satisfaction and for the quality of product and service made available right the way through from the first contact with the customer to the last.

Providing incentives or specific loyalty-based schemes has become popular in recent years as a way of topping up individual service activities and providing additional incentives to keep people coming back. The best known schemes, of course, are the air miles programmes developed by airlines and these have been copied by hotels, credit cards and more recently supermarkets. Sainsbury, for example, launched its Reward Loyalty scheme in 1996 and within a few months had 7 million cardholders. That's one-third of all UK households signed up with a specific bonus and incentive plan to keep visiting and spending more. Another illustration comes from the Dutch food retailer Edah which has established a smart card interactive kiosk operation in all its stores designed to build loyalty. Shoppers can apply for smart cards with personal details about themselves and their shopping preferences on them. They insert their card at the kiosks in the store. They are greeted by name and immediately referred to special offers targeted at them and based on what they have purchased previously. Take-up of the smart card system has been high and the touch-screen system also has novelty quick games and questions which generate target coupons. Edah reckon this loyalty scheme has by itself contributed to a c. 5% growth in like-for-like sales.

The flexibility and sophistication of the internet can help companies set new standards in loyalty-building and in 'relationship marketing'. They can achieve a depth and breadth in the information they gather that gives greater insights into what are customers' needs not just for this one transaction but on a longer-term basis. Customers do appear responsive to specific loyalty building programmes and at relatively little cost it is possible to dramatically improve retention rates – with all the profit upsides that brings. For marketers keen to take on the new electronic age and find new forms to build the business this will become an increasingly critical area to innovate and master.

10. Measure

Marketers want to be able to measure the effectiveness of what they do and how they spend their money. TV advertising, for example, has developed sophisticated measures that record among other things how many people saw an ad, at what time, what type of demographic profile those people represent, what their typical weekly shopping basket contains and what are their preferences. The challenge now is to translate a degree of that measuring sophistication into internet marketing activity.

Already a number of measures have been identified:

- **Cost per thousand**: a standard measure to compare advertising costs of reaching target consumers
- **Cost per click**: a new way of evaluating advertising based on the internet surfer clicking on response to a displayed ad
- **Click through**: measures how often a viewer will respond to an ad by clicking on it
- **Cost per head**: measures only those people who respond to an ad with personalised information such as an e-mail address or other details about themselves enabling the company to follow-up
- **Number of hits**: measures the number of files retrieved; accessing one single page containing hyperlinks to, say, ten other files would count as ten hits
- **Number of visits**: an approximate estimate of the number of individual surfers to visit a site; it is usually a derived number dividing the number of hits by a factor representing the average number of links per page.

Advertisers are becoming increasingly concerned at their ability to report on how well their marketing investments on the net are doing, how they compare with alternative media and whether they are paying back. In a seminal speech by Bob Wehling, a Procter & Gamble Vice President, there was a call for the advertising industry to get its act together:

'we need to establish clear, broadly-accepted standards for measuring cost effectiveness. We have no doubt the web can be a highly cost effective marketing medium but to become truly valuable it must demonstrate it is highly efficient. We need accurate and reliable measure to gauge that efficiency. The measurement systems today are nowhere near accurate and reliable enough.'

One consequence of this is that P&G has so far adopted a conservative approach to web advertising and has insisted that it will pay for ads only when someone clicks on them. As a marketing heavyweight, P&G typically sets standards that others eventually follow. But without alternative measures, P&G is in practice forcing service providers and search engines to share the risks of this new medium. As Yahoo!'s CEO Tim Koogle commented: 'it's like someone saying you're going to deliver the ads and you're going to have a vested interest in increasing the performance of them'.

The latest initiative in this arena has seen accounting giants Ernst & Young, Coopers & Lybrand and Price Waterhouse setting up specialist units to audit claims made by websites about their audiences and the numbers of visitors and hits a site says it gets. For example, from the beginning of 1998 Microsoft started sending to all its advertisers quarterly reports of all its websites audited by Coopers & Lybrand.

As Percy Barnevik, CEO of ASEA Brown Boveri has commented: 'only things that are measured actually get done or improved upon'. Without recognised and reliable measurement systems marketers will struggle to convince their Finance department colleagues to invest more and truly test out and stretch the potential of internet selling and communication. The new medium is still in its infancy. It took the TV Broadcasting industry and associated companies fifteen years or more to put reliable measuring mechanisms in place. With the internet and the general explosion of interest and revenues, the demand and need for an adequate measurement environment will undoubtedly ensure that some effective framework is put in place much sooner.

*   *   *

Let's leave the final words on this marketing challenge to Bob Wehling, the Procter & Gamble VP quoted earlier:

'We're moving down the information highway at warp speed. Our destination is the future, the future of marketing, actually a future where smart marketers will be surfing across the internet into the homes of billions of consumers in hundreds of countries, at the speed of light. We'll be driving by the virtual storefronts of other companies who are also participating in and creating this future. Pay attention because we're all going to have to get wired into this . . . The key marketing challenge is to tap the *full* potential of these exciting new electronic media especially the internet. How do we make it a global opportunity for advertising and a rich source of entertainment, information and community for consumers . . . what's the add-on sales potential? What's important is to remember it's not just about piping a 30-second ad over the internet or converting printed materials into electronic form. It's going to require a fundamentally different approach to succeed.'

16 Setting the Strategy and Mobilising the Organisation

In a recent study 78% of senior executives felt that electronic commerce would significantly change their organisations over the next ten years. They anticipated there would need to be radically different structures and to be effective they would have to develop new competences and skills and manage an inevitable cultural upheaval. Similar findings came through in a detailed study by *The Economist* involving more than 400 business leaders across 34 countries. Two out of three interviewed said that their organisation in 2010 would be very different from today and that there would need to be a keen emphasis on flexibility and faster response. Forrester Research, who have been closely monitoring the progress of electronic commerce, believe the new strategies required will cause 'massive disruption and will challenge many corporations' basic operating model'.

There seems to be growing recognition of the impact that e-commerce will have – not just in the marketplace with customers – but on the way the whole company gets structured. It's a business challenge that's going to be so significant that it cannot be left to one function to sort out. It's not just a matter of some new software for the IT department or more funds for Marketing. It's becoming an organisation-wide phenomenon requiring an organisation-wide response. It's potentially sizeable enough in revenue terms that large parts of existing physical distribution structures may either no longer be required or may need to change radically. And it comes on top of a competitive environment that's already fast-changing, becoming more global, consolidating, deregulating and demanding, with customers searching aggressively for greater innovation, more comprehensive service solutions and better value.

What are the most specific organisation threats and changes, what structural, skill and systems issues will managers have to deal with? Will the whole organisation truly be affected or can any restructuring be contained to one or two areas? And once the impact on a company has been identified, what will be the keys to the most effective response, what process or actions will help the business transition efficiently to the new operating models and ways of building business? What role should strategy-making play in determining how best to move forward? How can senior managers make sure their whole workforce is engaged and mobilised to drive the new changes and structures through?

To address these questions we should first understand what are the specific organisation impacts that companies will have to deal with. We can then review what are the key success factors in strategy-setting that can help shape and determine the type of structural responses required and then how to engineer the most effective people-empowered implementation.

Organisation impacts of electronic commerce

Reviewing company experiences of electronic commerce and work done especially by Don Tapscott, President of the New Paradigm Learning Corporation, seven issues commonly get cited in research and interviews:

- Digitisation is removing the need for human interface
- Virtualisation renders physical location and proximity irrelevant
- Networking enables everything to be outsourced or done through alliances
- Knowledge capture or 'information flow co-ordination' needs to become a central, driving core competence
- Disintermediation requires new supply lines
- Convergence demands a new relationship between Marketing and Information Technology
- Organisation agility in terms of adaptability to change and fast response becomes the necessary platform on which to build success.

Digitisation

Information in any form – pictures, graphs, video and audio – can now of course be digitised and compressed and transmitted fast to any link anywhere in the world. Most parts of a business transaction can be reduced to bits. Exchanges are fast, often instantaneous and error-free. Once equipment has been installed, software customised and debugged, business can take place automatically. There's no need for any human interface. Let the machines communicate! They save time. They save money. They cut out human imperfection. They remove personal prejudice or embarrassment that might have got in the way of a sale. EDI (electronic data interchange) has already been established for some years and a number of companies, like GE, like the major retail chains, now insist their suppliers link with them in this way. Tendering for business, orders, invoices, queries, delivery notes, messages can all be handled electronically and automatically. Once the contract is established, re-ordering can take place with little or no human intervention.

Apocalyptic stores of factories run by robots, offices without paper run by computers have long featured in dramatic visions of our future world. But the sheer speed and capability now of computers makes a people-less, paper-less environment ever closer and more achievable for those who choose to advance down that path. What's emerging, however, is that business generally may have no choice about taking this digital and electronic route. Commerce is moving that way. Competitive pressures, the inexorable demands of stakeholders for growth and added-value, may well force the pace and direction of change for many corporations. If one company doesn't do it, it might get beaten by another taking advantage of the electronic world. Preparing for that is tough. Getting there will involve ever-more wrenching change. But building an effective and powerful IT environment will be the vital platform to provide the flexibility and capability to manage any such transition.

If electronics replaces people then what role can individuals still play in the value chain? That will be one of the major challenges for corporations moving through the next two decades. Dell's response is to see this as a major opportunity to get their employees out there with customers on site assisting in their customer's operation with expertise, know-how and general customer care. Might the new world of electronic commerce act as a general catalyst to move the organisation's focus and the majority of its people at last away from internal administration and instead more generally out into the market place, finding new ways to add-value with the customer base?

Virtualisation

This is an inevitable consequence of digitisation. Physical space and distance become irrelevant. The virtual corporation will become the norm. Teams of people will come together, discuss and resolve issues and make plans without ever physically coming face to face. Shopping, chat, information exchange, education and play can all take place in a virtual arena.

Why, then, build more administrative office space, why not invest instead in better computer training and equipment for employees? As has already been pointed out, why build more shops when one option at least is to conduct all business electronically? Why keep printing paper when information can be stored and retrieved in paperless form? Why keep printing money when the future lies in plastic smart cards?

In *The Economist* study referred to earlier 42% of executives believed that their companies would evolve to a more or less virtual state by 2010. It conjures up a future scenario which is both intimidating but exciting. Changes along these lines appear inevitable, but no doubt the pace of change will vary by industry sector. It also looks likely that US corporations will confront these issues first and be in the vanguard of working out how best to deal with them. Future winners, no matter what country they are born in, must take a proactive view and get their organisations to understand these changed dynamics. They will need to take a very different view of their asset base. (See further in Chapter 11 on how intangible assets may gradually replace fixed assets.)

Networking

As part of the move toward virtualisation, one response many corporations are already considering and testing out is to build value networks. As discussed in Chapter 7, this is a grouping together of different suppliers, partners and outsourced operations to bring together the best skills and integrate them into a cohesive proposition to customers in the market place. It's a recognition that trying to do it all in one corporation may just be too impossible a challenge in the competitive arena. Better to focus on core competencies and value network the rest with others who are best at what they do. The challenge then lies in the integration management of scattered core skills and stages of the value chain. No easy task, but beginning to be made much more achievable by the onrush and sophistication of electronic communication.

First Virtual Corporation, a US producer of desktop multi-media, sees its world moving fast in this direction. 'We focus on only two core competencies', says founder Ralph Ungermann, 'fast and continuous innovation and building powerful partnerships . . . everything else is deliberately outsourced to "best of breed" suppliers . . . we depend on these partnerships and we'd die if we couldn't make them successful'. Hewlett Packard's Vice President, David Logan, makes a similar comment: 'one of our primary core competences is to manage alliances . . . it will become more important in the future'. In further research conducted by *The Economist*, in all 22% of executives interviewed felt that through this decade they would increasingly find themselves working 'as part of a large network of companies'.

The corporation of the future is likely to look more like an organic enterprise rather than uniform and rigid throughout. It will leverage this new organisation form to have more flexibility. Partners can be dismissed if they fail to deliver. If the market grows, new partners can be added. If customer needs change new competences can be easily and quickly incorporated into the value-delivery system. Even supposedly 'core competencies' will be made to justify their retention inside the corporation. 'Every thing we do is up for grabs' is part of a new approach to organisation structures being adopted by some like NYNEX Cable Comms and British Airways. BA's John Patterson foresees a scenario where there is no longer any certainty about which core competencies are retained: 'if we are to stay successful in the twenty-first century we have to make sure we can organise with the best possible combination of talents and abilities'.

Knowledge capture

Knowledge, as Drucker has pointed out and as described in Chapter 11, becomes the driving core competence in twenty-first-century commerce, replacing land, labour and capital. Its prominence is due wholly to advances in IT which have made the capture and distillation of data into knowledge more immediate and accessible and achievable at reasonable cost and affordable investment.

Moving to a state where the right information is available with the right people at the right level of insight at the right time is now a major challenge for business generally. Only a few such as Fedex, UPS and USAA can claim to have got most of the way there already and reaping the benefits. One best-practice leader in this field is Chaparral Company, a US mini mill, that produces steel. It has achieved extraordinary levels of productivity by becoming 'a learning laboratory dedicated to knowledge creation, collection and control'. It describes its central purpose as 'tapping knowledge and translating that into enterprise-wide success'. Another leader has been pharmaceutical group Hoffman-LaRoche. One of its managing directors, in workshops through 1997, found there was great scope to speed up time-to-market for new products through knowledge management techniques. By mapping out what information was held where, identifying who were the key providers at the centre of informal networks, making selected other data available to key people in the chain and removing roadblocks slowing down data transmission, astonishingly up to two-thirds of the time it had taken could be saved on certain products.

Knowledge management will create value and the key organisation learning is to eliminate 'knowledge silos' where information is held by some and only selectively released on request. Logging and recording *all* the available information is an important step to realise the potential and this needs to get at both explicit data as well as the 'tacit knowledge' that's in people's heads. Powerful new software tools and 'neural networks' can help make rapid sense of masses of data, but organisation structures will likely also need to change to facilitate knowledge capture. At Unilever, for example, there is a move to reduce hierarchies and numbers of reporting levels to make it easier for ideas to flow up and down the organisation quickly. Most corporations now acknowledge that there is significant potential in improving their knowledge-capture competencies and that all parts of the organisation will need to be enlisted to make the essential and continuing contribution to the central knowledge pool.

Disintermediation

The potential impact of disintermediation on organisation structures and ways of doing business is immense. It displaces the intermediary, cuts out the broker, agent, distributor and retailer from the supply chain. It will force a search for a new identity, a revised role in the marketplace and a significant shift in the value-added the intermediary aims to bring. It will also challenge manufacturers and suppliers to build their own direct supply lines to customers. Can they effectively forward integrate in this way, can they master new competencies in customer management and home delivery? It further demands new skills and systems to make direct electronic selling and communication effective and satisfying. Does a company have the in-built flexibility and agility to learn these new approaches and respond quickly enough?

The competitive environment will give no respite and those seeing the disintermediation phenomenon coming to their market place will need to take a total view of how it affects their organisation. Honest appraisal may well confirm that for some companies the new competencies required to take advantage of the situation are just a step too far to take on their own. This is where 'value networks' (see Figure 6.2) can become part of the solution path, putting together the select group of partners, allies and outsourced operations that can still enable an effective response to be made.

The growing sophistication in information management and communication technologies will continue to encourage and facilitate direct exchange between sellers and buyers. As skills and systems develop and mature so disintermediation threats and opportunities will become more widespread. Managing that effectively, as suggested in many places in this book, will become a key factor for business success through this decade.

Convergence

There is much discussion about the coming together of the computer, content and communication industries (see Chapter 11), but internally, within the organisation, perhaps one of the key dynamics is the relationship and interface between two particular departments. Historically, IT and Marketing have been disconnected – one immersed in technical know-how and systems maintenance, the other with a mostly outward-only orientation towards markets and customers. That's been acceptable up to a point but communication and collaboration between the two departments has been limited. Different perspectives and even different cultural orientations have kept the two in silos. There's been little 'convergence'.

The new world of electronic commerce demands a much more integrated approach. IT is no longer just an enabler, it becomes a primary route to market. It can't stay in a back office concerning itself with systems maintenance or arcane developments. It has to come out directly into the market place. It has to meet up with Marketing. In similar fashion, marketers must become technically literate. They cannot just concentrate on being creative and developing innovative advertising campaigns. They have to come to terms with the electronic information age and learn how to be innovative in that environment too.

Such a coming together may not be easy. Marketers have typically eschewed technical literacy, IT departments have often had little time for what they perceive as something ephemeral and insubstantial and sometimes hard to see the immediate payback. But electronic commerce will force this organisation issue to be resolved. Joint action teams, secondments and learning from each other will be critical if an organisation is to effectively respond.

Organisation agility

To quote again from the *Economist* survey, 85% of companies in the research cited 'flexible organisational structure' as a key factor and challenge for the next decade. Larger organisations appear to see this as especially important, recognising their current struggles to respond quickly to new marketplace issues. As Professors Bartlett and Ghoshal have pointed out: 'the traditional multi-division matrix organisation such as General Motors looks out of place, a new structural paradigm is called for'.

At the heart of the twenty-first-century corporation the research and evidence is highlighting the requirement for 'agility'. There's a need for companies to develop an institutional capacity to effectively and speedily manage an environment of constant change. A new mindscape is required, involving how individual employees see their role in the organisation, the relationships they have with others and their alignment and commitment to the targets and strategies that are set. Agility has been described by advocates CSC as establishing the inner entrepreneur, the aptitude and energy and capability to respond quickly, an unleashing of the human spirit for enterprise to meet the challenges ahead.

In order to create this environment new approaches to organising the company and its workforce are appearing. There's an emphasis on focusing down on a few core business areas, divesting or demerging activities which might distract or don't naturally fit a parent's core competencies. There's increasing emphasis on delegation or more fashionably empowerment, pushing out responsibilities and accountabilities and encouraging local decision-making. There's a recognition of the flexibility that small teams can provide where there are limited hierarchies and reporting levels, easy communication and a clearer shared mission and purpose.

Sheer scale and size of organisation appear increasingly irrelevant in this new age and if anything a handicap rather than a disadvantage. 'There is a growing sense', as pointed out in a recent *Financial Times* article, 'that big companies do not have what it takes to compete in the twenty-first century, they struggle to develop the flexibility, rapid response, and openness to innovation that's required, they no longer attract the best people'. And as Professor Michael Porter, once a proponent of scale as a source of advantage, has recently acknowledged: 'the big company of today is not being defeated by another big company, but by small companies. As information flows very rapidly, as companies compete globally, scale is no longer a competitive advantage.'

Companies, therefore, that are rushing into multi-billion-dollar mega mergers should take heed. Economies of scale may be illusory and there may be a hidden cost to that scale that can seriously handicap the corporation's ability to respond to new market challenges. Driving to a state of 'organisation agility' may be the only means to deal with rapid change on an effective and sustainable basis.

Strategic Response

In order to deal with these various organisation challenges, the very first step is to develop a long-term game plan and strategy for electronic commerce. Given the various options available, ranging from embracing the new electronic age through to bucking the trend and defending vigorously the status quo, which route forward is the company to take? What will maximise shareholder value? What future targets should the company set in its chosen markets with its major customers? What dream or vision can most propel the company forward? What stretching reality is achievable and what's it going to take to get there?

Earlier chapters described two key tests for the electronic age – the ES Test and the Manufacturer's Test. These give guidance as to the options, they help understand how specific marketplaces are evolving and how many customers will be looking for what degree of change. They also help establish how capable the company is to deal with the upcoming challenges and whether it has the strength to resist and pioneer or must go with the flow.

But these test inputs need to be brought together. There needs to be a developed and cohesive understanding of what it all means. Stakes need to be put in the ground, horizons extended, targets set, funds and resources allocated and the commitment instilled. Competitors must be assessed, customers' reasons for buying from one rather than another evaluated, opportunities for differentiation reviewed and sources of competitive advantage determined (Figure 16.1).

There can be no avoiding the need to set a clear strategy, conduct the market analysis and appraisal and get to grips with the electronic future. As a number of studies have pointed out, only in this way can a company hope to achieve the growth it's looking for. In a *Sunday Times/* Coopers & Lybrand review of what factors enabled companies to keep growing and sustaining their success the key that emerged was 'a strong focus on clear strategy-making'. In another study by the British Quality of Management association, the attribute that most distinguished Britain's leading companies was their strategic thinking and the way the leadership of the company harnessed that to drive their business. And in a *Fortune* magazine assessment of 'Most Admired US corporations', developing the vision to take constructive risks in the

Figure 16.1   Key Elements of Effective Strategy-Making

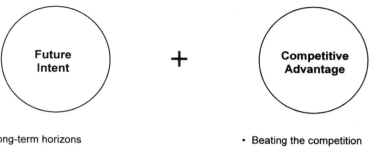

- Long-term horizons
- Future goals and targets
- Funds and resources

- Beating the competition
- How to get there ahead of rivals

marketplace emerged as a hallmark setting the most admired apart from their peers and rivals.

Despite the compelling evidence, those companies that do develop effective, driving strategies are surprisingly a minority. Most in practice pay lip-service to strategy, putting out plans which are often no more than extrapolations of twelve months' budgets. Few truly invest the necessary time and resource to rigorously review where the company is headed, what the opportunities are five, ten years out, what knowledge gaps there are in understanding what core competitors' future strategies and intentions are, what customers are really going to want in the future, which product lines are making money and adding shareholder value and which unlikely ever to contribute.

The research described in my book *Strategy in Crisis* shows that many organisations are caught in a vicious circle (Figure 16.2) where strategy-making is a lost art. It's often low on agendas, displaced by short-term financial performance goals, or pressing operational issues like Y2K (year 2000 systems compatibility). It's often replaced by an internal orientation toward process change or restructuring. The basic strategy skills get submerged, corporate planning becomes de-emphasised and there's no voice at senior executive committee or board level counter-balancing these alternative agenda items and urging the longer-term perspective. Without the appropriate strategic framework there's the risk of knee-jerk reaction to events or market changes, actions taken in a vacuum and the organisation appearing rudder-less, vulnerable to the storm-tossed seas instead of sailing a purposeful course.

Figure 16.2   Strategy-Making – Caught in a Vicious Circle

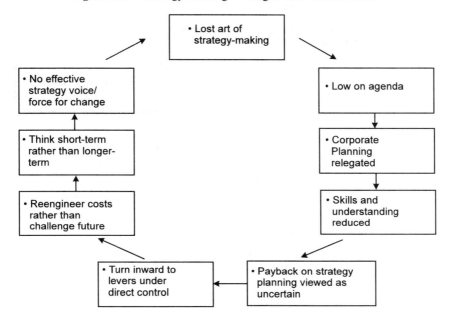

Companies that are visionary, that do embrace strategy – *they* set out to make sense of their environment. They've discovered strategy's power and potential. They've arrived at a balance between all the short-term agenda items and the longer-term health of the corporation. They know they can't do without it. As the Chairman of UPS has pointed out:

> 'nowadays we are making ever bigger bets in our investments in new technology so we can't afford to back one direction and then find out five years later it was wrong . . . putting time and effort into strategy-making is vital . . . strategy is our most important management issue and opportunity.'

Putting strategy first and developing it rigorously unquestionably helps a company understand its markets thoroughly, evaluate its options and determine the most appropriate and leveraged course of action. In extensive research by Collins and Porras (Figure 16.3), companies that did this out-performed both their rivals and the general stock market many times over. They demonstrated that this is a key test for would-be shareholders. If the company is to add sustainable value it must show it has the capability and skills to think and plan strategically and set its long-term game plan.

Figure 16.3   It is Companies That Do Plan their Way Through
Which Emerge as Winners

Source: Collins and Porras.

People-empowered implementation

As companies begin to get their minds around their e-strategy, so they
will get a much better perspective on what it's going to take to achieve
their new ambitions. The organisation changes required will inevitably be
considerable as the impacts caused by electronic commerce are so
widespread. Each of the issues described at the beginning of this chapter,
from Digitisation and Virtualisation through Disintermediation and
Convergence will create their own distinct challenges and opportunities.
Each needs to be separately thought through and the appropriate
structural, system and skill response determined. It's a daunting task. So
much change, encompassing so much of what the organisation does. Few
parts of the operation can be left untouched. The amount of time, effort
and application to see things through and make the changes will likely
appropriate significant resource, funds and energy.

Strategy-making can help with navigating the path through this. It can
establish priorities, mark out what's important, highlight the key success
factors (e.g. the main source(s) of competitive advantage) and keep things
focused. But the people in the organisation are still going to have a lot to
deal with, they are still going to be expected to go the extra mile, take on
new challenges and treat them as part of the everyday job.

The key is to engender a collective effort, mobilising employees, suppliers, value partners and others behind the new strategy so that the whole is capable of achieving significantly more than its individual parts. There are ways in which senior management teams can engage the organisation so that the workforce are excited about the future, rather than daunted by it, energised to go the extra mile rather than enervated by the prospect. A supportive working environment can be set up which encourages open communication, sharing of ideas and problems, promotes co-operation, rewards hard work and harnesses the total energy and effort. We can describe the holistic approach required as the Sharing Plan (Figure 16.4).

The goal here is to develop that powerful sense of ownership and personal responsibility among the workforce. The opportunity is to create that passion and excitement that is often seen around successful founding entrepreneurs or around the more driven and inspired organisations such as Wal-Mart, The Limited, Nike and Microsoft. It's about generating a genuine enthusiasm for the job that finds Home Depot associates saying: 'by giving 100% to my customers, I'm helping to write the success story of this rapidly expanding industry'.

Figure 16.4   The Sharing Plan

Sharing the strategy

Charles Handy in his book *Age of Unreason* explored the attributes of successful companies. His analysis, corroborated by others, is that any strategy that's set must be 'involving'. It must be developed into a vision 'that gives point to the work of others'. Business leaders have a responsibility to communicate something to their employees that is a compelling and believable vision of where they want the company to go and what role and contributions the workforce has in getting the company there.

As Anita Roddick of Body Shop puts it so succinctly:

'You have to find ways to grab people's imagination. Most businesses focus all the time on profits, profits, profits. I think that is deeply boring. You want people to feel they are doing something important.'

There's a requirement to translate the strategy into something that even the most junior employee finds exciting and engaging. So Toyota's formal strategy may be based on product excellence but in its communication to the workforce it's put in the context of 'Beat Mercedes'. Avis may have determined its strategy around service leadership, but it was communicated in a way that rallied the workforce: 'we may be No. 2 but we try harder'. McDonald's may focus on superb service but it landed on the expression QVSC (Quality Value Service Cleanliness) as a simple mnemonic that its employees could remember, be measured against and deliver on.

The strategy provides the platform to set the direction. If the strategy-setting is rigorous enough it should provide plenty of opportunity to be translated into motivating goals and in a language and context employees can readily buy into and accept. It must 'touch the spot', be informal and honest, come from the heart as well as the head. 'If people are to put out the extraordinary effort we now require to realise corporate targets then they must be able to identify with them and share in the ideas and goals they represent' (Jack Welch of GE).

Sharing the values

If it's the employees who can make the difference, then why treat them as second-class citizens? Why have separate management canteens (a peculiarly European phenomenon), reserved car-parking spaces, separate floors in the building, restrictions on information flow? These things are symbols of divide-and-rule and they cut people off from listening, interacting, sharing and communicating with the rest of the company. They are just the kind of needless barriers that get in the way of effectively sharing the values and the strategy that can unite the organisation.

How much better to have more open-plan offices or a 'no-closed-doors' policy, as at Nike. At Solectron, a contract manufacturer that has won the Malcolm Baldridge Award, neither the chairman nor the CEO has a private office. At Asda, the UK supermarket chain, when Archie Norman was CEO, he abolished chauffeur-driven-cars – except one. He kept it, not for the senior officers of the company, but for 'the employee of the week'. Each week the employee, whoever they were, who came up with the best idea for the company to improve things, was awarded the car for the week, with the chauffeur, to take them about wherever they needed to go.

This was a simple but highly symbolic act which quickly entered company mythology and helped change the way people felt about their employers. They appreciated the sharing, the 'we're all in this together', the removal of barriers. Not surprisingly it helped, with other things, to create a tremendous sense of shared purpose and mission.

Sharing the information

Why not openly share detailed financial and other information throughout the company? If the feeling is that employees cannot be trusted with that information then that is surely a sign that there is no common purpose and effective shared values and beliefs. Jack Welch at GE has a policy of open communication and explanation as to how the company is doing, what it's doing well and what it's doing badly. At Lincoln Electric, 'information is shared with all employees regarding the financial and market position of the company'. At Advanced Micro Devices every employee has been specifically trained to use the company's IT network to access information about all aspects of the company's performance.

Open information-sharing makes employees naturally feel more involved and more responsible for the company's performance. How much better to hear it from your department manager and be able to discuss and think through what its implications are than read about it with the rest of the world when the third-quarter results are published in the press. An openness and readiness to share and trust employees with the information has to be a major reinforcement to the strategy and values platform just described.

Sharing the skills

People cannot be expected to make the difference unless of course they have all the skills required to do the job. And as the competitive environment becomes more complex and demanding, so there is a growing imperative to continue to improve the skill base and give employees from all parts of the organisation a chance to continue to learn and gain in experience and capability.

There is a constant battle in most companies today between, typically, the human resources function who are the usual sponsors of better training, vs the company's financial engineers who are concerned with reducing costs wherever an activity or investment is discretionary. It's part of the ongoing short-term vs long-term debate which continues to pressurise companies into sacrificing the long-term for the sake of the short-term earnings.

However, what research has shown – conclusively – is that companies that do treat training as a priority and invest heavily in it reap benefits and dividends often far more quickly than they expect. Rather than complain about not having enough good people and not having the right skills in the company to meet the new global market challenge, advocates of increased training would argue that people do have the innate core competencies and if only they are given requisite training it will unleash a new set of energies and abilities.

Some companies have grasped this particular nettle with vigour and investment. McDonald's, for example, has established its 'hamburger university' which rigorously trains all its employees and recognises their achievements in QVSC. Toyota will deliberately take people out of the manufacturing plant and put them in the salesforce for a period to experience first-hand what it takes to achieve total customer satisfaction, understanding how important it is for them to get things right. And there is the Raychem college of further education which was the particular initiative of founder Paul Cook and which offers a substantial programme of courses open to all employees, not just related to business and management but to help improve more generally 'people's capacity for personal growth'.

These companies and others like Procter & Gamble, Gillette, Publix Supermarkets and Eddie Bauer, featured in the book *The 100 Best Companies to Work for in America*, have committed to their workforce in this way. They have seen the benefits that can come through from a more highly skilled and thereby more motivated workforce. It does take investment but it is certainly one of the keys in helping and getting people ready to put out the extraordinary commitment that's now required.

Sharing the benefits

There are a number of best-practice examples:

- The John Lewis Partnership is the largest employee-owned firm in the world. *All* profits are distributed as a bonus to all employees. Sales have grown consistently and have achieved a compound rate of over 12%. It has performed better than all its major rivals. The partnership continues to perform outstandingly well today.
- Among the top-performing stocks in the USA many like Southwest Airlines, Wal-Mart, Intel, Microsoft, Nordstrom and Compaq appear on the 'Employee Ownership List' (a listing of 1,000 companies where employees own > 4% of the stock).
- 91% of listed Japanese companies have employee stock ownership plans in which > 50% of the workforce are eligible and participate.
- Levi Strauss announced in 1996 that it would pay each of its 37,000 employees one year's salary as a bonus to hail the new millennium. News of the millennium bonus sparked wild celebrations at Levi Strauss, according to press reports, and predictable gloom at rivals!

  'It's about sharing our success with our employees . . . we all want a company that our people are proud of and committed to, where all employees have an opportunity to contribute, learn, grow and advance . . . we want our people to feel respected, treated fairly, listened to and involved. Above all we want satisfaction from accomplishments and friendships, balanced personal and professional lives and have fun in our endeavours.'

*　　*　　*

This chapter has been all about coming to terms with the new era of electronic commerce. It indicates some possible paths and solutions that may help companies move forward. It sets out a framework for strategy-making that discourages anything less than a thorough and rigorous approach. It provides a tool kit for getting the workforce involved and mobilised behind a future game plan and ready to go the extra mile to deliver it.

The organisation impacts are going to be wide-ranging and only a dedicated and committed approach can ensure they are effectively dealt with. Of a necessity new structures will be required, new customer management skills will need to be learnt, new knowledge capture systems developed. The whole will take time, resource and considerable application. But success in any field never comes easily. Getting the workforce to make the difference means battling with the wills and egos of individuals, managing their natural concerns and uncertainties and some wavering of confidence as to whether a team truly has the capability and skills for the battles ahead.

What's critical is to acknowledge the magnitude of the change management challenge. It is difficult, it does require a specific task force to handle it. It will need to be led consistently and proactively by the senior people in the company. What's also important is to acknowledge the success stories among those companies who are succeeding. There's great advantage in learning from what they have done and recognising the effort they take in sharing and involving and communicating. Harnessing the energies of the whole organisation will be pivotal. It can provide the platform to inspire a common purpose that drives relentlessly toward lasting e-success.

17 The Next Wave in Electronic Shopping

In recent times e-commerce has centred around the internet and the PC. But are we about to see a new era in e-comm development? Is there going to be a new wave of technology and communication that will take us even further into an electronic world?

Hot on everyone's lips now is interactive digital television. It could bypass the PC completely. It doesn't need internet technology. It can broadcast directly onto the TV into everyone's home. It can use satellite, cable, enhanced telephone wires or standard terrestrial broadcasting through the TV aerial. Potentially it reaches out to the 90% + of households who have TV sets, often several. It is accessible to all those who have computer phobias. It is user-friendly – we all know how to use a remote control – and connection is low-cost.

Could TV replace the PC for home shopping? Will digital TV broadcasts take over from internet shopping sites? Will Amazon and CDNow need to evolve to a TV-interactive format? Or can the technologies and media sit side-by-side, complementing and reinforcing rather than cannibalising and confusing? Will this television revolution

Figure 17.1 The Continuing Revolution in e-commerce

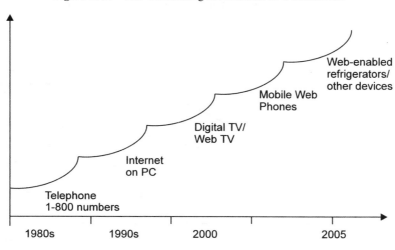

finally make the whole population 'e-comm literate'? And as we accelerate into the virtual world do these developments finally spell the end for traditional bricks 'n' mortar shopping? (see Figure 17.1).

What we do know for sure is that many large corporations are investing heavily in TV interactive shopping channels. And the UK, as it happens, is emerging as a pioneer in this digital TV arena. The world is watching how this UK test bed will develop. Rupert Murdoch's News International is heavily committed through BSkyB, its satellite company, and BiB, its interactive venture. Other companies involved include NTL, where Microsoft has a stake and now together with Cable & Wireless, Carlton Television and also Dixons, a UK leading internet service provider (ISP), rivalling AOL, and a major consumer electricals distributor in its own right. Attracted to this TV opportunity are also some of the world's leading advertisers such as Procter & Gamble, Ford and Coca-Cola. These companies are already experimenting with this medium and wondering whether it might be an easier, more naturally evolutionary, way for them to sell direct.

With both UK and USA governments committed to a digital television environment – the UK is talking about switching off analog signals by 2010 at the latest (see Figure 17.2) – we can be certain that digital TV will quickly become omnipresent. The decoder box, too, will be built into the next wave of TV sets – no need for extra kit and boxes cluttering the room – so we will all have digital TV in our homes, whether it is ordered up or not. And it is just going to be so easy to press the button on the

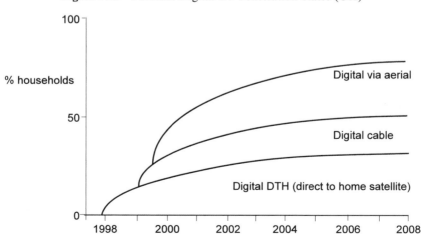

Figure 17.2 Forecast Digital TV Penetration Rates (UK)

simply revised remote control and find ourselves in an interactive environment. Ordering will be just a click away – no need to get up and walk into the den or study, switch on the PC, dial up the website and find the product. Digital TV takes us straight there while still sitting in the comfort of our armchair.

But how exactly are these new developments going to shape up? Can we predict which of the new technologies will be the winner?

This new chapter considers the views of four leading experts and commentators to help answer these questions. Curtis Kopf from Amazon is perhaps closest to what on-line consumers are looking for and so understands well which of the communication options might have the biggest impact. Mike Nevin from Dixons was one of the first people in the UK to see the potential of e-commerce and has seen how his company's Freeserve internet access has taken UK consumers by storm. Bruce Lynn heads up Microsoft's Web TV initiative. He is a believer in the TV but how does he see it fitting in with the internet on the PC? And, finally, James Ackerman and Julian Eccles are leading the BiB TV home-shopping launch. They are committed TV men, as we might expect, but what does their map of the future look like?

Let them tell it in their own words.

Mike Nevin, Dixons

As one of the early participants in the e-commerce revolution, what is your general view about the future of digital TV home shopping?

As I see it, the internet is primarily a one-on-one experience. But TV always has been the mass medium. I can see home shopping over the TV as being the next stage in the e-commerce revolution. It is potentially greater than the internet and could result in the most phenomenal growth. It is immediately into everyone's home and of course there are often multiple sets. It more naturally involves sound and vision and movement.

Can you bring us up to speed with what's going on in this arena?

There are three major participants. The leader is BiB with its home interactive service 'Open'. Then there is Telewest with its service available through cable. Finally there's NTL who are investing very heavily in this arena.

And how does it work from the consumer's perspective?

There is an adapted TV remote control. One press of the button, like a Teletext connection, will take you to the home shopping channel broadcasts. Menu options will appear on screen and consumers can select, for example, more advertising information or list of distributors or order and shop. The interaction takes place through the telephone line (or cable) back up to the open legacy systems of the supplier. Extra interactive services are available for a higher monthly subscription.

Are there going to be any factors which in your view might limit the take-up rate by consumers?

Bandwidth is still going to be an issue. For advertisers, one of their main costs will be the amount of bandwidth they buy. And for example if they purchase 1.4 megabytes then a 30 second video takes up at least half of that so it will limit how much 'typical TV' will be used in the broadcast (though of course bandwidth technology is itself improving all the time).

Another factor will simply be that if the interaction takes place on the family's main TV then one member of the family isn't going to be allowed to monopolize the TV set for hours for example while they go to the home shopping channel to get the latest pair of Nike trainers being advertised. So the whole interactive process will have to move from information to ordering quite quickly.

What do you see as the main advantages?

I think there will be four main advantages with the digital TV format. First there will be this simple click through from conventional TV into the interactive format. That is going to open people's eyes and really accelerate consumer interest in home shopping. Second, the content is being organized so it can be as quickly updated or changed as an internet page – no need to reshoot long infomercials. Third, there is likely to be an e-mail facility between subscribers though I understand that is not immediately available. And finally, of course, it is going to be a major means of Brand reinforcement and representation of how a particular company is committed to being at the leading edge in reaching its customers. If a company is not there it is going to be perceived as behind the times and out of date.

Do you see this medium replacing the PC internet environment for consumer electronic shopping?

No, I would expect the two to be complementary, reaching different consumers. As the chart illustrates (Table 17.1) each will have its own set of characteristics and so its own appeal.

Table 17.1   PC vs TV Comparison

	PC + Internet	TV + Home shopping broadcast
● Information	✔✔✔	✔
● Comparison	✔✔✔	—
● Interaction	✔✔	✔
● TV channels	✔	✔✔✔
● Ease of use	✔	✔✔
● Local context	✔	✔
● Movement/imagery in communication	✔✔	✔✔✔
● Secure/safe	✔	✔✔

Do you expect this more pervasive electronic environment to be the death-knell for physical store distribution?

I can just never see the demise of the physical store. Going out to shop is still a fundamental part of our life and a main form of social interaction. Most products have a touch–feel element to them that people want to see and explore physically before deciding which to buy. So I would say that the 'bricks 'n' mortar' stores will remain a cornerstone of the retail shopping experience.

But does this mean that existing retailers used to selling only through their shops are now going to have become expert at also selling things electronically?

Yes, I would say the core competence through this decade is for retailers – as well as suppliers for that matter – to become 'multi-channel operators'. They are going to need to develop a comfort and capability for selling through shops, over the web, through the TV and probably also through mobile phones. It will be a multi-layered environment and no company will be able to ignore these other channels of communication and distribution. At Dixons we see it as our duty to our customers to enable them to purchase whenever and wherever they want.

How do you see Web TV (Microsoft's internet on the TV initiative) fitting into this environment?

I think it will play more of a role as the technologies converge. Currently the consumer has to buy a separate decoder box to get these digital TV broadcasts (though there are promotional offers where they are being given away for free). In the next few years all TVs will have this decoder built-in. What's more it is also going to be possible to include internet access into the TV as well, either through Web TV or through cable or satellite. So the consumer will be able to access the whole electronic shopping scene through their TV if they wish.

Sounds like the TV is going to play an ever bigger role in people's lives?

Yes, my vision is that just as years ago people had their hi-fi centre or their audio centre, so in years to come people will have their 'information centre' in their home. Imagine a large flat screen on the wall, the facility to switch effortlessly between web and TV technologies, camera-mounted devices so there can be personal video screen connections with friends, family and suppliers – music broadcasting will be naturally included. It will be the entertainment, information and communications centre for the home.

How quickly do you see this vision being reached?

The answer is quicker than we think. The rate of take-up of new technologies is now extraordinary. It took the fax machine over 20 years to reach critical mass. The VCR took over 10 years and the mobile phone about 8 or 9. The internet has taken just 5. So I have no doubt the future 'information centre' is only a few years away.

James Ackerman of Open (British Interactive Broadcasting, BiB)

Can you start by describing what Open is about?

Its goal is to bring the experiences of e-commerce to the mass market. How do you do that? You use the television. How do you make it attractive? You make it an easy-to-use, comfortable, secure and involving experience.

The service launched in the UK in September/October 1999, under the Brand name 'Open', how successful has it been?

Yes the UK was the first in the world to launch with a full national marketing campaign. In the time since we announced the launch date we've had tremendous interest. We have signed up a number of the UK's leading brand names such as WH Smith, Woolworths, Argos, Little-woods, Iceland, Somerfield, Dixons as well as HSBC Midland Bank and Abbey National. We have also got other organizations lined up like Manchester United, The Press Association, Yellow Pages, ticketing firm First Call and E*Trade. We expect up to 60 or 70 companies to be broadcasting interactively with us.

How big is Open going to be in your opinion?

At the launch date we had 1 million UK households (c. 5% of all households) as subscribers to the Digital TV service and that should deliver about 2 million adults. We are looking at this consumer base growing fast to around 5 million households in the next few years and 10 million by c. 2008 – that's about one-third of the UK population.

How are you marketing and promoting the service?

BSkyB for example has been giving away the set-top boxes for free. That's had a tremendous response. It's forced competitors to match the offer. It's all creating a lot of market noise and awareness. At the launch, our own $25 million marketing campaign had a big impact.

What exactly are you offering consumers?

There are four main elements. There's shopping and banking, of course but there's also an Entertainment Service and an e-mail option via the internet.

Why are you so convinced that the TV will work as a mass shopping medium?

There's a number of reasons. Of course consumers are already familiar with using the remote control to navigate their way round the TV. In the UK there's also the Teletext information channel and again most people seem very comfortable using the menu options to select certain pages of text, find information, search for holiday details, etc. And people have also become comfortable using the TV together with the telephone to order up items advertised.

Unusually the UK appears to be the world's pioneer in using digital TV for home shopping, why is that?

Again there are a few reasons. The main one is that the UK government has committed to switch off analog broadcasting and has said it will mandate a switch-off date. As a result there's not going to be a choice. UK consumers will get digital TV. Another point worth bearing in mind is that there is a very undeveloped Pay TV environment in the UK and many TV broadcasters will be looking for opportunities to promote this service and build it around a digital TV platform.

In contrast then, is the USA behind the curve in this one?

Well the situation is a bit different in the USA. First of all PC and internet penetration is already much more widespread than in the UK. Then the US Government has been more cautious in its approach to digital TV and has not made any commitment to switch off analog. Finally the US does already have, of course, a well-entrenched analog pay TV market (around 80% penetration) which has been built over the years at high cost so there's no additional revenue benefit to encourage consumers to switch to digital.

Do you think nevertheless that home shopping on TV will develop in the USA?

I'm sure it will. It's already there to some degree with the likes of QVC. All the major content and communication companies are now very aware of the UK initiative and I know they're watching our progress very closely.

Your research is telling you that this is what consumers want?

Absolutely, it's beginning to dawn on companies that digital TV will be the future of e-commerce. Commercial organisations have a choice. Do they want to be where their customers are? Many consumers will not be on the internet. In our research, even when the internet is on the PC somewhere in the house, people on average still spend ten times more time watching the TV. To be successful companies need to be everywhere their consumers are. It's the concept of 'ubiquity' which I know companies like Dixons and Amazon also talk about. Here at Open our mission is dedicated to meeting consumers *where they are!*

How do you see interactive TV sitting alongside the internet?

E-commerce will grow on the internet as well as the TV. I think we'll find some products and services doing better in one environment rather than the other. Take grocery shopping as an example. Do you want to go up to Dad's study to switch on the PC and do the regular weekly food shopping? Or would the typical shopper rather do it more comfortably via the television? The internet is more of a big information encyclopaedia and it's likely to have more appeal where the shopper needs more opportunity to search, get informed and compare products and prices. (See Figure 17.3)

Figure 17.3   Which Products/Services Sell Best on TV vs the Internet on PC?*

*This figure is intended as illustrative only.

Can you summarize the benefits of your service versus the internet?

Our broadcast service is fully encrypted, there's no hacking possibilities, consumers use PIN passwords in a secure intranet environment. Because there's no internet browser there's no risk of the kids in the family accessing any of the pornography currently so pervasive on the web. And, of course, right now our broadcasts have a rich mix of sound and video to make for a much more lively experience.

What would you say to companies who are considering where to invest in e-commerce and weighing up television versus the internet?

I'd say you must do both. But you can't just sit on the website. You have to be as proactive as possible, get to where your consumers are, build an effective e-commerce platform. And it's important to emphasize that it's not a totally separate investment stream. Yes, our front end is a proprietary standard but our back-end systems are http compatible.

Finally, do you think all this e-commerce activity will lead to the end of the physical retail store?

I'm sure existing established retailers can continue to be successful. But they do have to respond to this changing environment. Look how quickly e-commerce is developing. Just one year ago in the UK there were no households with digital TV, now a year later there are one million. During that time, we've moved from no retailers interested to many of the leaders busily signing up. If the existing companies don't respond to this e-commerce challenge then of course they're going to lose out.

Curtis Kopf, Amazon.com

First of all, how do you see the development of e-commerce generally?

Let me give you some basic stats. There's now nearly 200 million people connected on line. That's up from practically zero just 5 years ago. Our forecast is that this number will more than double over the next few years. We reckon on 320 million by 2002. As internet connections spread we find the demographics of the users change as well so it is quickly now reaching the mainstream of the population.

Do you see internet reach and penetration hitting some kind of platform, however, after say 2002?

Well Jeff Bezos has been quoted as saying this is just Day 1 of the internet. In fact more recently Jeff has said this is just 1.00am of Day 1. And I think we all feel it's just started and there's a long way for it to go.

With no doubt Amazon leading the charge?

Certainly we're continuing to grow very fast. As an example, Quarter 1 2000 revenues were over 200% up on the previous year. What's more as a corporation we've expanded our activities to sell more than just books. We have established ourselves as market leaders in video and music and have added toys and electronics to our offering. We've also invested in new sites like Drugstore.com and Pets.com. The strategy is to have a website where people can find and buy anything they want on line.

What is your view on the impact of Digital TV home-shopping?

Rather than focus on any one medium I'd prefer to talk about the concept of 'ubiquity'. We need to be where our consumers want us.

At the end of the day, one of the keys that will influence the shape of the future e-commerce scene will be how well each initiative is marketed and fulfilled. Look at the old Betamax vs VHS video format wars. Many commentators believed Betamax to be superior but in that instance it was the VHS suppliers who did the best marketing job with the consumer.

You talk about marketing and also fulfilment as being the key to success. Can you describe what Amazon are doing to ensure they get these areas absolutely right?

We believe our future success is going to be based on providing a great customer experience. Our key success factors revolve around selection (we have a list of over 1.5 million books), easy comparison of titles, convenience and price. But the main emphasis is on the on-line customer service revolution.

Supporting this customer proposition is making sure we have got the right people in our workforce. This is vital. They have got to be completely committed to what we call achieving 'customer ecstasy'. We have got countless stories of employees going the extra mile. For example one of our people recently drove himself to a customer's house to make sure they got the book in time for a birthday party. It is this sort of spirit that we want to build.

You have certainly got a success model that many others would like to copy but I also have to ask you this question – is Amazon ever going to make a profit?

Look, we're investing here for the long term. We think it would be short-sighted to focus on short-term profitability at the expense of building the business. Our success is going to be based on our building a growing customer base and providing great service to these customers. We are getting up to 20 million customers in 2000 and high levels of repeat purchase. We have got 260,000 Associates – that's an enormous on-line community of other websites who have signed up to our Associates Program and get a commission on all the sales they generate to us through their own web pages. This is a business that's going to be around and there's so much growth and potential – remember we are still at Day 1 – that it would just be inappropriate to start predicting now what future profits will be.

Bruce Lynn, Microsoft Web TV

What's been Microsoft's experience to date with Web TV

More than a million Americans now use Web TV to access the internet from their televisions. Specifically, in 2000, 2.5 million people use Web TV, with about 900k paid subscribers averaging 2.2 users per subscription. Web TV Network has a subscriber growth rate of over 200%. In short Web TV has gone from 200,000 in 1997 to about close to 1 million subscribers in just a couple of years.

How did Microsoft and Web TV get involved?

Microsoft acquired the company in 1997. Since then Web TV has been able to extend its technology with new products and capabilities mostly focused on enhanced television experience. While Web TV started as a way to access internet on your television, since the acquisition the focus of the development has been more on TV-centric enhancements such as electronic program guides, interactive programs and digital VCR. In these innovations, the internet link is an essential component that enables and complements these other capabilities rather than standing out for its own sake.

Do you find consumers preferring Web TV to accessing the web over the PC?

In some cases people prefer Web TV, in some cases they prefer the PC and in many cases they prefer both. Going forward we feel that there will be clear roles for both enhanced television and the PC and they will co-exist not just beside each other, but also alongside a growing array of access devices that will all be web-enabled such as AutoPCs, handhelds, mobile phones, telephones, etc.

What does the research say?

Our research shows people who are intimidated by the perceived and real complexities of a PC find Web TV much more approachable and less daunting both for its design and its usage through a very familiar appliance. Other people require much more functionality and access to applications that, at this point, only the PC can offer. In many cases, the preference is context-dependent. If they are working in their study and need some information for a report, the PC is a natural and convenient choice. If they are relaxing in their lounge and want to check out a sports score or weather report, Web TV is more preferable. The PC won't replace the TV in the home. They will increasingly use the same underlying technology, but they will remain two separate appliances which are used for different purposes.

What would you say are Web TV's main advantages?

First of all one needs to distinguish between Web TV Networks, which is the complete service that runs in North America and Japan, and the Web TV platform, called Microsoft TVPAK, which essentially makes the technology underneath the Web TV service available to network operators for their own offerings in their markets and for their customers.

Web TV has been engineered based on actual user experience, over 300 million hours of connect time over 3 years to be precise. Lots of people wax eloquent when hypothesizing about the future of interactive TV, but Web TV bases its product requirements on real customer feedback, broadcaster input and service tracking. Many of Web TV's most significant innovations are not flashy or even visible, but developed in response to a critical need identified in the process of running the service firsthand. This lends the TVPAK technology platform advantages in terms of flexibility and cost effectiveness of deployment.

Can you tell us a bit about how Web TV works?

Architecturally, one of Web TV's most obvious innovations is the integration of significant local storage in the form of a hard drive in the set-top box. This dramatically extends the type and extent of applications that you can deliver through the box as well as the degree to which you can enhance the user experience. For example, it enables a whole class of digital recording functionality like 'TV Pause' which allows you to stop a normal TV program and later resume watching it. But, it also simplifies the delivery of the service and allows the operator greater flexibility in implementing various services. For example, even with limited bandwidth, operators can offer up media including video by downloading the material to the hard drive in off-peak times.

Finally, as its name implies, Web TV is focused on the exploitation of internet standards such as HTML. The entire product and supporting technology are all web-centric. We feel strongly that the web will be the focal point for innovation and market development for interactivity. Not 'web surfing' necessarily, which is what many people often associate with the web, but rather the broader array of enabling technologies and connected content.

As Microsoft looks to develop Web TV further, can you say what is the vision and thinking behind it all?

The Web TV vision is very much a part of Microsoft's larger vision of a 'Web Lifestyle'. More and more consumers are beginning to live a 'Web Lifestyle,' a fact made evident by changes in last holiday's shopping patterns, URLs appearing on every television commercial and internet companies encroaching on traditional market-holders' turf. Emerging technologies such as broadband internet, next-generation PCs, intelligent appliances and smart objects, all connected by networks in the home, will do even more to change the way consumers find and do business with most corporations.

How is the marketing going to work?

That will vary by market and by partner. In the US, Canada and Japan, we will continue to offer a Web TV Networks service run by the Web TV subsidiary. This is a strong business for us, but more importantly by having hands-on experience, we achieve an important advantage in understanding the product requirements and developing the best platform to enable enhanced television. In other markets around the world, we will license the technology to Network Operators who want to build and deploy a similar service. These may be Cable operators, Telcos, Satellite companies and even ISPs using Microsoft TVPAK. TVPAK was created by combining Web TV technologies with Microsoft technologies such as Windows CE on the client, and with Windows 2000 Server and BackOffice on the server.

How do you see Web TV complementing internet access through the PC?

The more appropriate question is really the other way around: how does the internet complement the television versus the PC? In some, its contribution is similar. For example, both the TV and the PC can be valid devices for surfing the Web and reading e-mail. However, for more focused interactivity we feel that the PC will remain the primary focus for this type of activity. Still, checking out a website related to a movie about to show, sending fan mail to a favourite character, surfing in the comfort of one's lounge, getting more information on shows or advertised products, or group exploration of a family holiday planning are all popular reasons among our Web TV subscribers for exploiting the internet from the television. The internet really starts to complement the TV in unique ways when you start looking at interactive programming where web-based content is tightly and seemly linked with the program content and the user can control it. In these cases, the internet makes it all possible, but typically the user doesn't even know they are on the internet, just that they are doing something really fun or useful with their TV.

One argument against the potential of Web TV is that the TV is a passive medium and will never get used interactively, do you agree?

TV is indeed mostly a passive medium, but while people may be couch potatoes, they're not comatose. If you think about how the TV is already used today, you see numerous examples of interactivity already. QVC has proven to be a successful home-shopping format. Call-in voting has proven popular with shows like Stars in Their Eyes. In the UK, Teletext has a very high usage. Even simple channel surfing is a crude form of interactivity and users attempting to assert greater control over their viewing experience. Furthermore, people are already choosing to carry out more and more of their daily chores in their leisure hours, for example, the success of 24-hour telephone banking, home shopping. Web TV opens up the option to make these tasks much easier and comfortable to accomplish in a home setting. It adds a new dimension to the TV that makes it (not the viewer) work harder.

Does Web TV require a separate set-top box and is there a danger we're going to just be overwhelmed with different set-top boxes for different applications?

Recently we launched software technology in kit form to OEMs and Network Operators to enable them to incorporate Web TV capability in their own devices and offerings. This platform approach eliminates the complex, costly and unsightly prospect of stacks of set-top boxes because people don't have to necessarily buy a separate Web TV TV set, just a box that does include Web TV technology.

What would you say then to a corporation that manufactures or retails, say, consumer goods – should they invest in their website and the internet right now, or alternatively into digital TV content? Should they do both or should they do nothing and wait and see?

Companies should absolutely not wait to start investing in the new medium of interactive television, but they should adopt an approach which minimizes costs and risks given the many unknowns. From Microsoft's perspective, the primary way to achieve this is to focus on working with universal standards that have established themselves and in the world of interactivity the standard above all is quite clearly HTML. If companies use HTML as the basis for their interactive developments, then they can certainly exploit those investments immediately on the web itself but they can also leverage them in the interactive TV world.

Where does that leave the main UK digital TV provider, Open, who have chosen a different technology platform?

Using proprietary technology not based on internet standards could leave BiB isolated and make it much harder for their partners to work with the medium. Potentially, BiB could overcome this by incorporating technology in future boxes which does provide the internet protocol support.

Finally, as you look to the future, obviously Web TV is more advanced in the USA, how do you see that developing?

The Web TV momentum is gathering strongly and we will continue to push it along through partnerships with industry-leading operators and through technical innovations like digital VCR. With the availability of the software platform, Microsoft TVPAK, we can expect to see Web TV capability in a variety of different offerings from the existing Web TV Networks' service (one of Microsoft TVPAK's biggest 'customers'), other MSOs (multimedia service operators) as well as new types of offerings like integrated digital televisions.

*   *   *

The Battle for the Digital Consumer – a Case Study

One prediction that can be made with real certainty is that all forecasts, whether total market expenditure or individual household spend, will be incorrect! However, all forecasters agree that within the next few years there will be substantial changes in consumer retail behaviour and significant shifts in expenditure to online e-commerce.

The digital telecommunication and broadcast companies are currently among the leaders driving this change. They have identified the opportunity to create interactive service platforms alongside their telephony and broadcast services. In the UK, BSkyB has launched its interactive services company, Open. . ., on the Digital satellite platform. Telewest, CWC and NTL have launched interactive platforms on digital cable. OnDigital has launched a limited interactive platform on digital terrestrial. Freeserve, AOL and BT Openworld are the largest of a growing number of interactive platforms created on the internet. Video Networks, YesTV, and Future TV represent the new ADSL-based interactive platforms using the BT digital network. Vodafone, Cellnet, Orange, one2one, Virgin and Carphone Warehouse are all developing significant interactive platforms for WAP and third generation mobile telephony consumers.

Walled gardens

All these companies are looking to leverage maximum value from the massive investment they have made in their digital networks and e-commerce presents one of the largest new potential revenue streams. They are driving the e-commerce market by creating large interactive platforms, which they will promote to their TV and telephony customers. BSkyB, Telewest, NTL and CWC have created "walled gardens". These are enclosed interactive platforms containing interactive content provided by companies and organisations that have agreed commercial terms in order to have their service included. The "walled gardens" do not allow access to the internet. The ISPs such as Freeserve, mobile telephony

291

companies such as Orange, and the digital terrestrial broadcaster, OnDigital, do provide direct access to the internet. However, they have also created additional interactive platforms, which contain 'preferred' content partners who have paid to be included and are presented to the customer in a privileged position onscreen.

The commercial terms agreed by the content providers and paid to the interactive platforms include a combination of fixed fees and commission based on a percentage of the gross revenue generated by the customers subscribing to the company. The commissions vary according to the products sold and typically range between 5 and 10%.

Technology issues – digital satellite and terrestrial

The digital TV market being pioneered in the UK is complex and highly competitive with the five major operators offering a wide range of digital television packages, e-mail and interactive services across three digital systems. This is already causing confusion in the consumer market. However, the consumer confusion is minimal in comparison to the complex technological and commercial issues facing retailers who wish to become content partners on the interactive platforms. Each digital platform has significant advantages and disadvantages that impact on the decision as to which platform or platforms potential content providers should agree commercial terms with. BSkyB has first-mover advantage and will have achieved phenomenal success by recruiting 5 million digital satellite TV subscriber households by December 2000. All BSkyB digital customers are required to have their digital satellite receiver connected to their telephone line for a minimum of 12 months in order to qualify for equipment free of charge. The digital satellite interactive services platform Open. . . will access approximately 25% of the UK population by the end of 2000 and reach is forecast to increase to 33% by December 2001. This audience comes with a price should a retailer wish to become a content provider on this interactive platform. A commercial agreement with Open. . . for a large retail site could cost a content provider several million pounds in fixed fees for a 3 to 5-year term. In addition to the high fixed entry fees, a commission is charged against the gross value of each purchase made via the BSkyB and Open. . . customer.

The digital satellite platform has a number of technical challenges, which could limit the appeal of the medium to the consumer. BSkyB and Open. . . are constrained by the expensive and relatively limited bandwidth available for the broadcast of TV channels and the interactive services into the digital satellite home. The content provider is constrained as to how the service is presented onscreen. The Open. . . service typically takes 10 to 20 seconds to download onto the customers' digital satellite receiver and on average takes 30 to 60 seconds to dial up to go on line to the requested content providers' service. The digital satellite receiver has a 56k modem that suffers from the normal delays of low-speed modems. These time delays can cause a negative response from the consumer. Open. . . has the added complication of a propriety operating system called OpenTV that runs the interactive services on the digital satellite receiver. Content providers are required to re-author their content in OpenTV, which can be expensive. Retailers have recently been restricted to presenting up to 200 products on the standard retail Open. . . platform, which is a challenge for retailers who stock thousands of product lines. Open. . . is now launching the extended retail platform as well, which will allow more than 200 product lines in the near future. However, as Open. . . is restricted to a limited number of content providers due to cost of bandwidth, their strategy to date has been to recruit only a small group prepared to pay significant fees, to gain access to the large digital satellite audience.

OnDigital has second-mover advantage and should reach 2 million UK households by December 2001. The OnDigital digital terrestrial receiver also has a 56k modem, which has similar dial-up problems to the digital satellite receiver. In addition, the majority of OnDigital receivers are not connected to customer telephone lines, as customers are able to obtain the equipment free of charge from retailers, with self installation and no obligation to connect on line. The OnDigital interactive services platform has severely restricted bandwidth, limited technical capabilities and slow dial-up. These technical constraints provide those customers who are connected on line with a connection to the internet and an e-mail service. However, the internet websites were designed for a PC resolution and presentation with expected viewing from a distance of 12 inches. Reading internet websites on TV from a distance of 12 feet can be extremely difficult with small text, graphics and pictures. Also it can take several minutes for a full screen picture to be downloaded via the internet.

The big opportunity – digital broadband

The real opportunity for retailers to become on-line content providers and provide an exciting and compelling e-commerce customer experience is with broadband technology. This will initially be provided by the cable operators' digital fibre optic cable and secondly, by the ADSL network provided by BT and utilised by the ADSL broadcasters.

Digital cable has a number of significant technical advantages over digital satellite and terrestrial. The digital broadband cable operators Telewest, NTL and CWC have significant bandwidth allowing the broadcast of 100s of TV channels and interactive services. The digital cable receiver has a high speed 512k modem that also has a permanent on-line connection without dial-up, resulting in instant access to the interactive service platform. The digital cable interactive services platforms of Telewest and CWC are designed as 'walled gardens' where retailers wishing to become content providers pay a relatively low fixed fee and commissions against customer expenditure. NTL have a similar 'walled garden', however, one with a 'back gate' which allows the viewer to access the internet. Some cable executives believe the term 'walled garden' is too restrictive and prefer the term 'fenced prairie'!

The digital cable interactive services platforms will provide a wide range of services from 100s of market leader retailers. The digital cable interactive platforms of Telewest and CWC use the Liberate operating system and NTL uses PowerTV, both of which are HTML and Javascript based. Content providers simply re-purpose their existing internet websites with the Liberate and PowerTV authoring tools, adapting existing Web page template designs for TV presentation. The HTML content remains unaltered on the content provider's server. This is a relatively simple process and can be completed on average between 4 to 8 weeks at minimal cost. Most Web design agencies are able to re-author in Liberate and PowerTV. The templates are re-authored for a viewing experience of 12 feet on a TV and the size of typeface, colours and graphics are designed to give the viewer a real televisual experience. The design guidelines provided by the cable companies recommend content providers to use the maximum amount of pictures and moving video in order make the presentation as appealing as possible.

Once the digital cable viewer has accessed the interactive service using the remote control, the desired content provider is accessed with a further two or more clicks of the remote control. The final click on the relevant content providers' icon on-screen will give the viewer almost instant access on line to the re-purposed content. There is no dial-up and subsequent dial-up delay as the connection is permanently on. This is described as a 'point-to-point service' where the cable operator simply provides the viewer with a direct connection to the content provider without interfering in the process. The content provider is responsible for the customer experience and service from here on, including stock control, rotation and pricing, merchant acquiring, order processing and fulfilment, and post-purchase customer service, including all customer queries. The high bandwidth capability of cable allows content providers to broadcast video within the content in addition to text, graphics and still pictures.

The major disadvantage of the digital cable networks is the current lack of reach of digital subscribers, with estimates of 1.2m UK households by December 2000 in comparison to the estimated BSkyB digital universe with 5 million households by 2000. The ADSL network and ADSL interactive service platform companies are following a similar route by creating a walled garden and e-mail with access to the internet. However, they are 12 months behind the cable operators.

Battle lines drawn

The major players in the broadcasting and telecommunications industry are driving the volume of UK digital subscribers with on-line connections to walled gardens and/or the internet, with a forecast penetration of UK homes in excess of 75% within 5 years. The majority of UK retailers, banks, financial services, travel operators, information providers, publishers, broadcasters, entertainment providers and education organisations are developing on-line strategies which include a presence on the interactive platforms. The big questions are whether the consumers will use the services as forecast and what will be the key drivers that motivate the consumer transactions.

The next section describes the Telewest interactive TV strategy by way of case study and how the company believes the e-commerce opportunity can be maximised on broadband digital cable. It is written by Telewest executive Chris Townsend.*

Telewest – a case study

Telewest Communications and Flextech merged in May 2000 to form a UK top 30 company valued in excess of £10 billion. Telewest is the second largest cable operator in the UK with 4.7 million homes passed within its cable franchises, totalling approximately 40% of UK cable homes. Telewest has 1.7 million TV, telephony and internet customers.

---

*Chris Townsend is the Director of Interactive Services at Telewest Communications, one of the UK's leading cable companies. Telewest launched their Active Digital TV platform in 2000 with many leading brands providing on-line shopping, banking, information and entertainment. Chris regularly lectures at industry seminars, Oxford University and London Business School.

Figure CS.1   Telewest Content Providers

Money	News and Directories	Shopping	Learning	Holidays and Travel	Games	Entertainment and Sport
1st Quote	Bloomberg	Argos	Dorling Kindersley	Air Miles	Gameplay.com	Blue Square
Abbey National	CNN	Domino's Pizza		Air Tours	Gameswire.com	Carlton Online
Bristol & West plc	Exchange & Mart	First Quench		Avis Europe	Two Way TV	Cartoon Network
Cahoot	Fish4	Iceland		British Airways	UR wired!	EMAP Online
Cheltenham & Gloucester	Loot.com	Interflora		Cosmos		First Call
Eagle Star	Scoot	Lastorders.com		First Choice		Ladbrokes
GE Financial Insurance	Teletext	Littlewoods Leisure		Future Travel		Nickelodeon
Globalnetfinancial.com	Yell.com	QVC		(Instant Holidays)		Scene One
Newcastle Building Society		Shop!		Hertz		Sportingbet.com
Northern Rock		Somerfield 24-7		Landmark Travel		The Way Ahead Group
Norwich Union		The Gadget Shop		Channel		Turner Classic Movies
Screentrade		Tie Rack		Lastminute.com		William Hill
TD Warehouse		Toyzone		Lunn Poly		Yourscreen.com
Yorkshire Building Society		WHSmith		Online Travel		
		Woolworths		Red Balloon		
				Telme Global Travel (phonelink plc)		
				Thomas Cook		
				Thomson Holidays		
				Travel Choice		
				TV Travel Shop		
				Utravel		

Telewest Walled Garden Content Providers May 2000

Source: Telewest.

It launched the Active Digital TV platform in October 1999. The company has invested in excess of £4 billion in building a 3,000 km fibre optic broadband cable network linking the Telewest franchise areas which include Bristol, Birmingham, Liverpool, Sheffield, Bradford, Newcastle, Edinburgh, Aberdeen, north London, west London, south west and south London.

Telewest launched its walled garden interactive digital TV platform (see Figure CS.1) on 27th March 2000 with 60 content provider brands. The interactive services are made available to all Telewest Active Digital customers. By July 2000, the number of content provider brands on the interactive platform increased to 120. The company is aiming to achieve 150 by December 2000 and 300 content brands by December 2001.

Consumer research has consistently demonstrated that customers want choice of content delivered by trusted, market leader companies. The main concerns that consumers have using interactive services for purchasing goods and services are related to the security of transacting on line and the reliability of companies to deliver goods ordered. The Telewest strategy is to provide the best choice in trusted market leader high street and on-line brands. Although the walled garden cannot provide the complete choice of the internet, it can deliver to the customer a range of brands that account for 75% or more market share within key consumer on-line market sectors, such as travel or finance. The Telewest walled garden includes shopping, travel, financial services, entertainment, sport, information, learning, games and e-mail. The famous UK brands on the platform include WH Smith, Woolworths, Thomas Cook, Abbey National, Cartoon Network, Ladbrokes, Teletext, Bloomberg, Dorling Kindersley and Gameplay.

The service is positioned as a 'total utility' for all members of the family, to use every day as part of the daily routine, 'to make life easier and the TV more entertaining'. The range of brands and services is designed to accommodate the requirements of the majority of demo-graphic and social sectors of the UK population (see Figure CS.1. p. 296). Each of the content providers will have re-purposed their website for the Telewest walled garden, to ensure all content is presented as a television experience that can be navigated intuitively using the remote control. The on-screen navigation and design must appeal to all consumers regardless of technical ability, from technophiles to technophobes.

The overall mission of the Telewest walled garden, is to deliver the best of the internet to the mass market on the television screen. It is delivered in an easy-to-use format, to an audience who may not have had access to the internet previously or who may have had access but not have used the

Figure CS.2   Telewest UK Coverage

Source: Telewest.

internet for e-commerce. The content providers will provide access to the latest and most competitively priced products and services. Content on-screen will be changed frequently and promoted constantly using TV advertising, banner-bars and video within the content provider sites.

The additional benefit of digital TV is the ability to cross promote the interactive services with interactive advertisements during the advertising breaks on the broadcast channels. The interactive ads have the ability to take the viewer directly to the interactive site within the walled garden or 'book mark' the site for future access. The average UK adult watches approximately 24 hours of television per week in a satellite or cable household. This viewing time offers significant potential for cross promotion of the interactive services.

Maximising broadband technology

Launching the Telewest walled garden with best of breed brands presented on-screen in vertical market sectors is the first phase of the content strategy. The second phase will be to launch a series of 'value added' services, overlaid across the vertical market sector content, in order to provide additional value for the customer. The objective is to ensure the customer is maximising the benefits of the services provided, resulting in higher frequency of use, expenditure and increased customer loyalty. These services could include personalisation of content, search engines, auctions, community bidding and an infomediary service.

Personalisation will allow the customer to choose their favourite content provider sites and position them on their personalised section of the walled garden. The search engine will be an easy to use search function that operates in a similar way to internet search engines. It will however, only search across the content providers included within the walled garden. Auction services will be delivered by content providers. These will include an auction facility within normal retail offerings and by specialist auction content providers whose total proposition is based on the auctioning of goods and services.

Retailers and specialist companies will also provide community bidding. Customers are invited to state their interest in purchasing a product, setting a maximum price at which they will buy, and the final selling price is reduced as more customers commit their interest in the purchase. Community bidding is perceived by the price conscious customer as a method of extracting the best deal from the retailer and is forecast to grow significantly.

The infomediary application is a service that can reverse the buying process, where the retailer effectively bids for the customer's purchase request. The customer simply enters the product or service required and the maximum price they are prepared to pay. The infomediary sends this information to the relevant content providers who have the opportunity to bid for the sale at their most competitive price. This type of service may not suit all customers and not all the content providers will respond to their request. A number of e-commerce forecasters are predicting the on-line infomediary market to generate a significant percentge of e-commerce revenue within the next decade.

Telewest will continue researching content that will appeal to the digital TV audience and alternative methods of presenting the walled garden content on-screen. This could involve packaging content into defined lifestyle groups or activities. For example, a 'Kids' category could include games, learning, sport and entertainment content customised for children. This 'Kids' category could be further segmented by age band and gender.

Alternative payment methods are under evaluation such as on-line micro payments. The digital cable receiver has a second card slot for electronic payment cards such as Mondex. The Mondex system allows cash to be downloaded on line onto the Mondex card and used as electronic cash for the purchase of products and services from on-line retailers. The electronic cash payment will be particularly relevant for customers without debit or credit cards, and also for small one-off payments, such as pay-per-view content or pay-per-use interactive services like gaming.

Technological innovation

The key competitor benefits for digital cable are the permanent on-line connection, speed of access to content and significant bandwidth. The Telewest interactive strategy will focus equally on technological innovation in order to achieve the position of market leader in UK interactive services. Probably the most significant technical innovation that Telewest will develop is video on demand (VOD). Digital cable has the capability of delivering true video on demand, which allows the viewer to access video content instantly, at any time. Video on demand movies for example, will provide instant access to films at the viewer's preferred start time and not according to a pre-planned programme schedule. Video on demand will also be included within the content presented by the content providers in the walled garden. This will allow customers to choose and view videos of the products and services they require prior to committing to purchase. The travel operators, for example, will include videos of resorts, hotels, facilities and tourist attractions available on demand for customers to view before booking the holiday. It is anticipated that VOD will significantly increase the buy rate of travel e-commerce. VOD is particularly relevant for the catalogue companies such as Argos and Marks & Spencer who can bring their service to life with live demonstrations of products on video.

In addition to Digital cable, Telewest will launch a UK national ADSL service as soon as BT rolls-out its network. Telewest is currently working with BT as an ADSL partner testing VOD. The new BT network will allow Telewest to operate outside of the cable franchise footprint and offer a national broadband service. The company will become a national brand for the first time in its ten-year history. The ADSL broadband service, in time, will include the TV channels, VOD and the walled garden interactive services. Telewest is also investing in a mobile telephony service in partnership with a major mobile telephony provider. A re-purposed version of the walled garden content will be available on the WAP and 3rd generation mobile handsets for Telewest customers on the move.

Appendix 1:
The Retailer Dilemma –
Can Shops Still be Profitable?

Retailers generally have been under increasing pressure in recent times. In many sectors, margins and sales densities seem to have peaked and retailers have been forced to look elsewhere for continued growth. Now electronic commerce is rushing toward them the need for continued change is even more important. Yet just when they need to be at their most flexible and adaptable they find themselves hamstrung and hesitant. Their commitment to their physical space is so ingrained, it's so woven into the fabric of what they are and what they do that they're finding it extraordinarily difficult to stand back and consider all their strategic options openly and evenly. Their temptation is to make the real estate continue to work for them. But as we've seen that may be achievable on some products and services with some consumers, but it won't work in many other situations.

This retailer dilemma is considerable. Invest in space or embrace the new electronic age? It's a clash between the need to change and the vested interest and commitment to physical real estate. It's making many hesitant and encouraging others to still bury their heads in the sand and hope that electronic commerce will never develop and mature. Such a policy is doomed and it's clear retailers must confront this 'clash of interests' and learn how to move through it. They've long had a history of adapting to survive and grow and the next few years will present one of their biggest challenges yet. Just how significant is this real estate commitment? To what extent are retailers tied to the land? What other pressures are they facing? Will they be forced to experiment and innovate or can they comfortably carry on as they are?

In some ways this retailer dilemma is similar to the predicament in which IBM found itself in the early 1980s. IBM was committed to mainframes and saw this as the future of the computer age but it was soon confronted by new technologies that were making small-unit PCs increasingly powerful. Stick with mainframes or embrace the PC? Try to do both? Mainframes at the time so dominated IBM culture and future

303

planning, it was so fundamental a part of what they did that the organisation just found it very hard to think objectively about PCs and react effectively to the early signs in the market of a shift in customer interest toward them.

Even though IBM records show the company was probably the inventors of the PC they of course stuck with what they thought they knew best. Their marketing of the PC was half-hearted and peripheral. They hoped it would go away. In the meantime other unencumbered players like Apple came along and cleaned up.

Fifteen to twenty years later and the successful PC manufacturers are now facing their own distribution dilemma. While Compaq continues to sell principally through retailers and its own salesforce, Dell is growing at an enormous rate taking market share by dealing direct with the purchaser. Dell bypasses the traditional channels and is aggressively taking advantage of the electronic media. Should Compaq, Hewlett Packard and others follow? Do they too abandon traditional ways of operating and rush into the new way of doing business? Do they have the objectivity to see the nascent shifts in consumer habits of buying what is increasingly becoming a commodity? Or are they so ingrained in 'their way of doing business' that they'll continue as they are while Dell and a pack of smaller rivals come in and clean up?

Will retailers take these history lessons on board? Will they recognise they are about to face the same major channel and technology threats? Will they confront the shifts in consumer shopping interests and habits? Will they evolve or will they, too, be finally caught out by new entrants with no historic baggage and infrastructure? Certainly retailers show no signs of slowing down their commitment to their physical real estate and they continue to behave as if that traditional way of doing business will endure forever.

Typical retailer reactions to these challenges could be summarised by this selection of quotes:

- 'Well, yes, it might happen but right now it is off our planning horizons.'
- 'Shops have been around for 2000 years, we're not going to be replaced.' [Dinosaurs probably said the same thing!]
- 'We're not worried, it's just an additional channel and it will all be incremental business anyway.'

That retailers are locked into their real estate is evident from the amount of money they have invested and continue to invest in land and buildings.

Balance sheets of US retailers show some $250 billion of fixed investment in land and buildings. The UK equivalent figure is nearly $50 billion. And that excludes banking, other retail financial services, restaurants and fast-food outlets.

The amount of physical space retailers are committed to also continues to grow. For example, between 1987 and 1996 the number of supermarket outlets operated by supermarket chain Sainsbury in the UK grew from 54 to 227. This involved more than trebling the sales space from c. 7 mn to more than 25 million square feet. Taking a US example, the number of domestic stores owned by Wal-Mart has grown from 980 to nearly 2,000 over the same period with sales space again more than trebling this time from 58 million square feet to more than 180 million square feet.

There is little sign that this rate of investment is likely to slow down, with all major retail chains continuing to make announcements of their plans to grow their space and to do so fast:

- In its 1997 annual report Wal-Mart listed total planned capital expenditures for 1998 alone of $3 billion, targeting 50 new Wal-Mart stores, 100 supercentres, 5 to 10 new SAM's clubs – and all that just in the USA aside from continued space expansion overseas.
- In November 1997, Marks & Spencer announced a major new space expansion involving $3.5 billion over three years opening more space both domestically in the UK and overseas adding some two million more square feet to take its total retail space to 10.5 million square feet.
- Thornton's, the UK chocolate manufacturers and retailers, proudly revealed the following space expansion programme through till 2001 more than doubling square footage from 1997 levels (Table A.1).

Table A1.1   Four-Year Stores Plan for Thorntons, 1998–2001

	1998	1999	2000	2001
New openings	52	57	56	42
New square footage	31,000	33,000	30,000	21,000

Home Depot opened its 500th store in 1996 and has boldly announced plans to reach 1,300 by year 2001. It has grown square footage at a rate exceeding 20% each year through the mid-1990s (Figure A1.1) and plans to continue at that rate, even though in 1997 actual sales per square foot grew at only 3%. The company says there is still plenty of room to grow.

Figure A1.1 Home Depot Space Expansion, 1992–8

Source: *Annual Report*.

- In the UK alone, some six major new out-of-town shopping centres were scheduled to open between 1997 and 2000 providing an additional 5 million square feet of retail selling space (Table A1.2). In fact latest predictions by Verdict are for some 28 million new square feet of space between 1998 and 2003 in the UK.

Table A1.2 UK Major New Shopping Centres, 1997–9

Centre	Opening	Sales area (000 sq ft)	Anchor tenants
White Rose	March 1997	650	Sainsbury, Debenhams
Cribbs Causeway	March 1998	725	John Lewis, Marks & Spencer
Trafford Park	Winter 1998	1000	Selfridges, Debenhams
Braehead Park	Winter 1998	696	Marks & Spencer, Sainsbury
Bluewater Park	April 1999	1454	John Lewis, Marks & Spencer
White City	Winter 1999	620	Not finalised

Source: Corporate Intelligence on Retailing.

A trawl through the *Financial Times* almost any month of the year provides a stark illustration of the pace at which retail chains are continuing to add space. For example, in one month Boots were announcing plans to open 30 new stores in the Netherlands with each store three to four times larger than its existing average store. Carrefour, the French retailer, was talking up its plans to double the number of its stores to 500 world-wide over the following five years. Eroski in Spain said it planned to open 30 new hypermarkets and 80 new supermarkets by the year 2000. Liedl & Schwartz, the German discount grocery chain, committed to open 30 more units in Germany and Scandinavia over the following twelve months. And these were just the more significant of the store space announcements in that month!

Retailers seem incapable just now of jumping off this new space bandwagon. They seem reluctant to pause to take stock of electronic commerce, how it will impact and whether they should be modifying their plans. What makes their current headlong rush even more challengeable is the long-term commitments they have to make to the space they buy. To get the payback on the massive investments in land and buildings retailers often have to set 20–25-year time horizons. Leases are invariably taken for that duration – sometimes with upward-only rent reviews! – and depreciation schedules usually assume life expectancies from 10 to up to 45 years! The size of the investments in land, buildings, fixtures and fittings can easily top $20 million and is sometimes considerably more than that involving further investment in infrastructure, road networks to ease access and compensations to the local community for disruption and disturbance.

The size of these commitments has always represented a significant gamble but through the 1980s, especially as consumer spending and confidence soared, they seemed a relatively safe move. There did seem to be plenty of demand for these new large stores, many areas had yet to be penetrated, there seemed to be opportunities for further improving margins and sales per square foot. It was as close as business is ever going to get to a one-way move. But since the early 1990s' recession, the competitive environment has toughened considerably and now with electronic commerce coming along this historic way for retailers to build their business no longer appears as secure or as financially attractive.

Going forward the situation for retailers is exacerbated by the growing pressures on their business. These make facing up to the electronic shopping resolution even more challenging but equally all the more important to see if it can provide new sources of real growth and advantage. Current pressures include:

- Margins are already wafer thin
- Sales densities appear to have plateaued
- There is saturation now in the number of shops
- The major supply-chain efficiencies have largely been captured
- For supermarkets specifically, there is a growing shift from eating in to eating out.

Margins are wafer thin

US and European retailers get by now on net profit margins of just 2–3%. Wal-Mart's net margins, for example, in 1998 were just 3% and with its recent acquisition of the Wertkauf supermarket chain in Germany it is entering a market where average profit margins are only 0.7%, dragged down in recent years by aggressive price discounting by the likes of Aldi. Only in the UK do retailers continue to post higher margins of around 4 or 5% but these, as we shall see, look to have peaked.

As Bill Gates recently put it when addressing a retail conference in the US: 'I'm in a 20–30% margin business, you're in a 1% margin business. Not too many of us are trying to figure out how to get into 1% margin businesses.'

Sales densities appear to have plateaued

US retail sales per square foot between 1985 and 1997 grew in real terms at only 0.4% and since the boom of 1987 have actually stayed flat to marginally declining (Figure A1.2).

The UK has seen a very similar pattern with real sales per square foot declining by 3.9% between 1990 and 1996. While absolute sales did continue to grow overall across this period, it was offset by significantly faster growth in the amount of selling space leading to inevitable cannibalisation and dilution of sales per square foot effectiveness. This sales decline is compounded by pricing pressures such that prices are static to falling in retail sectors like food, despite a 2–3% rise in overall inflation each year.

Figure A1.2   US Retail Sales

Saturation in the number of shops

In the home improvement sector in the USA, analysts estimate that the country can successfully support about 2,000 'big-box' stores. Yet at current rates of growth, Home Depot and Lowe's – the two leaders in the field – will by themselves have that number of stores by the year 2001. By that time every market with a population of 50,000 people or more will have *at least* two big-box stores each! In similar fashion, Marks & Spencer in the UK is continuing to add retail space but it has already saturated most of the country. Every urban centre or catchment area with a population of more than 100,000 has its own M&S store. There were only six relatively small areas without. Yet as M&S continues to add space can it expect it all to be incremental, isn't there likely to be some dilution creeping in?

Most retail commentators acknowledge much of western Europe and the USA is already potentially saturated with shops and that can only lead to reductions in effective sales per square foot and continued pressure on margins:

- 'As the big superstores near saturation of the major urban areas they are being forced to move in on smaller communities, pushing out the "mom and pops" but also finding it harder to maintain sales and margin levels.'

  (*Oxford University Institute of Retail Management*)

- 'There is too much floorspace sharing too little spending. But retailers are not shedding space but opening yet more of it.'

  (*Verdict retail report*)

- 'We are overshopped. Do we need a world-beating food industry or a world-beating spending industry? We don't need more supermarkets.'

  (*Archie Norman, as Chairman of Asda*)

The major supply-chain efficiencies have largely been captured

When the early 1990s' recession began, retailers redoubled their efforts to improve the efficiency of their operations. They worked across the whole supply chain involving suppliers in cost-reduction programmes and partnerships to improve transportation, warehousing and logistics. They also looked at their store operations and improved staff scheduling and productivity. They invested heavily in total in new systems like EPOS that gave them better information to manage stock levels and availability and generate the maximum utilisation and leverage of shelf space.

The work was intense during the 1990s and the innovation was considerable. But most of the major chains have now put much of these supply-chain efficiencies in place. They've put in EPOS, established EDI links with suppliers, outsourced where they can, fine-tuned the way the stores operate, developed private label and that too has reached saturation levels in many chains (in Sainsbury it accounts for c. 50% of all sales). Much of the cost reduction benefits have now been achieved.

At the gross margin level things look to have plateaued at around the 25%–30% mark. Sales per employee, like sales per sq. foot, have flattened out. While there are no doubt further initiatives in the pipeline in many retail organisations, it looks like the big wins have already been taken and what's left is a series of smaller incremental adjustments which by definition will have less impact on profitability.

For supermarkets specifically, there's been a change in eating habits

The pressures just described are affecting all retail groups but food supermarkets are facing an additional threat. That is the shift in consumer spending habits. As general levels of affluence or disposable income have risen and as 'time poverty' makes life-styles more and more difficult so consumers are looking to spend on eating out rather than eating in. They are switching their spending away from the supermarket to restaurants and other catering outlets (Table A1.3).

As *Business Week* highlighted in its survey of the prospects for different industry sectors: 'for the past 25 years the traditional supermarket has

Table A1.3   Trends in Consumer Spending, 1975–97

	(% of total)					
	1975	**1980**	**1985**	**1990**	**1995**	**1997**
Food	18.8	17.1	14.1	12.0	10.7	10.1
Drink and tobacco	11.6	10.7	10.4	8.6	8.3	8.0
Catering	5.3	5.8	5.7	8.6	8.7	9.0
Entertainment	9.1	9.2	9.0	9.7	10.3	10.9

Source: UK National Accounts.

been sliding toward oblivion. Once responsible for almost two-thirds of food sales its share in recent years has fallen to only just above 50%.'

*   *   *

Robert Tillman, the head of Lowe's, provides us with a succinct summary of the challenges ahead for the retail industry:

> 'the competitive landscape in our industry is changing, it is inevitable and unavoidable. For many it will probably mean failure. I believe retail saturation combined with growth coming in e-commerce represents the biggest challenge facing our industry today. How do we grow shareholder value when we can no longer grow what we are doing and what is growing is something we are unfamiliar with?'

Tillman has argued strongly that there is an urgent need for retailers to really get close to their changing consumer needs and adapt their proposition accordingly. 'Stay current with the wave of technological change,' he argues 'or get swept away by it . . . planning and positioning for tomorrow must relentlessly assess and challenge today's status quo.'

Retailers must come to grips with the need for the change and not let their vested interests in space and physical real estate get in the way. They must try to shake off the historic baggage and look objectively at their future and what it will take to stay in tune with their customers. If they don't they could lose out big time like IBM did. If they do get themselves free from their physical shackles then they can start to play an active and leading part in setting the shape of consumer shopping in the future.

Appendix 2: Retail Banking Case Study

Bill Gates has described retail bank branches as 'dinosaurs of the digital age'. A report by the London Centre for Financial Innovation has commented that 'the growth in electronic technology could lead to many of today's cherished banking institutions being replaced . . . in their stead may be a new generation of electronic service providers and screen-based markets'. Former Citicorp chairman John Reed has warned that in this decade retail banks may become nothing more than 'lines of code in a big computer network'.

As the electronic infrastructure builds, the role of the bank branch is under increasing threat. Consumers and providers can deal directly with each other. Telephones, faxes, e-mail and the internet all make it easy to carry out transactions from home or office. What possible value-added can the branch continue to provide? As we rush into this new century we're beginning to see the traditional distribution system for retail financial services becoming obsolete. It's suffering from 'creeping disintermediation'.

Of course, this is not just a retail banking phenomenon. Financial services generally seem vulnerable. One reason is the intangible, 'virtual' nature of a financial transaction. Taking the ES Test, product characteristics have a high 'intellect' score – it's a rational rather than emotional or physically involving purchase. Consumer familiarity and comfort with basic transactions like withdrawing and depositing cash is high and there are typically well-developed brand values offering reassurance and reliability. Combine this with the latest consumer demand for convenience and a readiness to experiment and retail banking begins to score very high on 'ES potential'.

In fact disintermediation in banking is not some new trend in response to the internet. It started back in the early 1980s when technology first presented new opportunities in customer service. There was a boom in the use of Automatic Teller Machines (ATMs) and the plastic card that went with them. People enjoyed having their personal password or PIN and the flexibility to withdraw cash when they wanted to, especially since at the time bank branches often opened only Monday–Friday 10 till 3.

312

Alongside the widespread use of ATMs, there have been other developments in electronic technology which have further brought into question the future role of the branch. Telephone banking has grown to substantial levels, especially in the USA where some 40% of households now conduct some or all of their banking in that way. PC banking is now being increasingly made available with software for example allowing users to log on with nominated financial services providers to pay bills, move money between accounts, buy basic insurance and reconcile balance and cash statements. Payments generally are now available through both credit as well as debit cards eliminating the need for paper cheques and expensive cheque clearing systems with transfers now able to be carried out automatically.

As consumers become comfortable banking electronically so the disintermediation threat will grow. Indeed Gavin Shreeve, the Director General of the Chartered Institute of Bankers, commented in a recent speech that: 'there is no longer a need for bricks and mortar to sell and deliver financial services.' Retail banks are faced therefore with either becoming 'the next dinosaurs' or responding proactively to the new challenges. The response doesn't necessarily involve abandoning all the real estate and rushing onto the internet. But it does involve among other things taking the ES Test and identifying what a bank's own target consumers are actually looking for. To what extent do they still want face-to-face interactions, are they content to do *all* banking electronically, how many are determinedly after the convenience of telephone/PC banking?

Certainly one response is to reappraise the number of branches. If target consumer demand *is* shifting electronically then adopting a transition policy of closing branches as and when appropriate would be advisable. Not only does this make the necessary strategic shift but there are obvious cost saving benefits as well. To date, however, there's been only limited action by banks in this direction (Figure A2.1). Sometimes there are national or political considerations which get in the way of a bank's restructuring, on other occasions banks fear public opinion which can create bad publicity when a local town branch closes threatening the commercial life of the community. Another excuse for inaction is fearing the loss of market share by being the first to cut and seeing the resulting business shift to other banks who've kept their branches open. But market share need not be lost if the closures were part of a deliberate strategy to retain and transition customers from physical to virtual banking with the investment, promotion and incentives required to make that transition as comfortable and desirable as possible.

Figure A2.1   Growth and Decline in Branch Networks

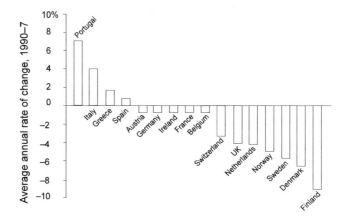

Source: Datamonitor European Banking Database.

In the meantime consumers aren't waiting for banks to make their minds up and sort out their market strategies. ABC1 consumers especially have been moving away from traditional branch banking (Figure A2.2). They are the consumer category typically with the most time-pressured life-styles but also with the greater PC literacy and comfort in dealing remotely. They have shown the least bank loyalty, appearing ready to switch their business to other providers who can deliver the more convenient electronic services.

For banks who do transition from a branch to an electronic connection, the cost savings look considerable. A study by Booz Allen found that the expense ratio of costs to income for an internet bank is 15–20%. This compares with traditional branch banking figures of 50 to 60% expense ratios. Figure A2.3 shows how this translates into substantially lower unit transaction costs for an electronic transaction. Put another way, the average cost for a bank of maintaining a customer's account in a branch network is nearly three times what a 'virtual' banking account would cost (Figure A2.4).

If banks do decide to grasp the 'electronic nettle', there are a number of options:

1. *PC private dial-up services* – proprietary software is distributed to customers which is then installed on the home or office PC. Access to the bank is effected by a modem link. As the link is a private

Figure A2.2   US Retail Banks' 'Wallet Share': Consumers with Income > $75k p.a., 1990–8

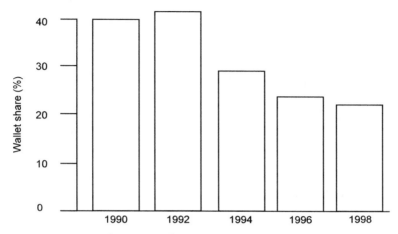

Source: *Computer Weekly*, Centre for Financial Innovation.

Figure A2.3   Retail Banking Unit Transaction Costs

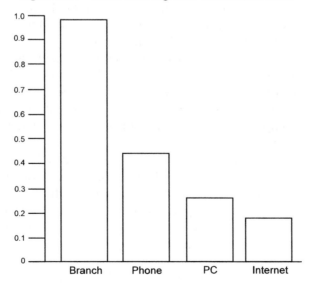

Source: *Business Week*, Forrester.

Figure A2.4 Retail Banking: Cost of Maintaining a Current Account

Branch $118/account

(Pie chart segments: IT, Branch personnel, Non-branch Delivery, Overhead, Occupancy)

Telephone $43/account

(Pie chart segments: Occupancy, Network, IT, Non-branch Delivery)

Source: US Banking Administration.

dedicated line it offers the customer a greater sense of security and privacy. It is typically a speedier connection than access through some third party providing the interface with the on-line service. This route has been the preferred option of most retail banks to date, so in the UK, NatWest, Midland, Barclays, Citibank, Bank of Scotland and Nationwide have all trialled this approach.

2. *Managed networks* – here a bank makes use of a network operated by another party. An example is Lloyds TSB's on-line bank which makes use of the CompuServe internet service network. Another example comes from the USA where a consortium of fifteen banks have linked up with IBM to provide their services on line via the IBM global network.

3. *Internet* – a bank establishes its own dedicated website and invites customers to access it and conduct transactions through it. Only a few banks such as Royal Bank of Scotland, HSBC and Barclays in the UK have trialled this approach aggressively as consumers are still cautious about security on the net (though as we saw in Chapter 12 these concerns are largely misplaced).

4. *TV-based services* – the arrival of digital TV services will probably see a rapid increase in the provision of banking services to the home or small office. Bank-account information can be delivered direct onto the TV screen via a dedicated bank TV broadcast. Interaction with the bank can be via the telephone line. Again, issues of privacy and security will need to be managed to reassure prospective customers.

5. *Interactive kiosks* – as retail supermarkets look to reinforce their own consumer-value proposition by extending the 'one-stop' range of services, so they are increasingly interested in providing basic banking services. These could be provided through a kiosk or private booth utilising touch-screen technology and enabling customers to carry out transactions and interface with a bank call centre for advice.

These options are not mutually exclusive. Banks can viably establish an electronic strategy which embraces some or all of these routes to market. Indeed a rigorous customer segmentation analysis may well show sufficient but distinct customer interest in each of these options, depending on levels of comfort with an electronic environment: TV services for the 'habit die-hards', PC private links for the computer-literate, managed networks for the more promiscuous consumer who might surf the net but still be directed or channelled back to a target site. It's a question of developing the understanding and response to what target consumers need.

Some banks have already determined that a significant part of their future does lie with electronic consumers. Wells Fargo and Citibank, for example, have been particularly innovative in establishing direct customer connections. In the UK, HongKong & Shanghai's First Direct Bank decided to go after 'dissatisfied, progressive and affluent customers' and within four years had acquired over half a million customers and achieved a cost-to-income ratio some twenty percentage points below its branch average. Also in the UK, Northern Rock has been actively encouraging customers to carry out transactions by phone while consolidating the branch network – some twenty-five branches closed in one year alone. In Germany, the Bayerische Hypotheken und Wechselsbank has had success with its 'direct banking' venture. Among other things, to attract customers to switch from branch to direct telephone or PC banking, a 50% discount on bank charges was offered. At a more dedicated virtual level the USA has seen the establishment of a growing number of banks to operate on the internet. First Virtual and Security First for example are solely internet-based financial service providers.

How far and how quickly is electronic banking going to replace traditional branch banking? An analogy can be drawn from the world of personal insurance which especially in the UK has already experienced dramatic disintermediation – even before the advent of the internet. Direct Line, the direct telephone-based insurer, has demonstrated how easy it can be to get consumers to switch in large numbers away from traditional branch, brokers or agent distribution. Its rise has encouraged

Figure A2.5   Personal Insurance Distribution, 1990–2005

Source: ABI; Datamonitor; Mintel; CSC Kalchas.

many competitors to offer the same route to market and their total
market activity is forecast to move 50% of the market direct by 2005
(Figure A2.5). The respected trade journal *Financial Adviser* predicts that:

> 'in the future being able to give the best advice and the most
> advantageous products to clients may well depend on an adviser's
> ability to deal direct and trade electronically in some form . . . the
> growth already seen in direct transactions is just the tip of the iceberg
> and providers will be well-advised to start putting their plans in place
> now.'

*   *   *

Retail banking and insurance may well represent a microcosm of what
will happen across the total retail environment. They may well be the 'tip
of the iceberg' for the challenges and changes that will face all retail
chains in the years to come. Certainly the financial services industry
appears to be in the forefront. No doubt it will provide both some painful
lessons but also indicative success models for dealing with the electronic
revolution. Some pioneers already see branch networks as redundant,
others believe they will have a role to play but in a different form.
Whatever the eventual outcome, success can come only from confronting
the challenge in the manner of a Citibank, a Direct Line or a First Direct
and determining a clear strategic response.

List of Figures, Tables and Plates

Figures

319

Tables

Plates

Sainsbury's self-service
Shopping in the electronic age
Iceland's home delivery service
Ordering your Tesco shopping on the internet
Direct Line – insurance over the phone
Lakeside Shopping Centre and Retail Park
Web TV
AsiaOne Commerce
Karstadt's My-World
Dixon's website
Abbey National website
The Information Skyway
Ordering from Dell over the internet
On-line banking via Quicken at Citibank
www.eassist.com
www.liveperson.com
sothebys.com
www.netgem.com
www.nextcard.com
Sun microsystems

Index